"I DARE!"
KIRAN BEDI

Revised and Updated Edition

a biography

The book was first published in 1995. After that there have been 12 reprints and the book has been a bestseller till date. It has been translated into six languages and was voted as the 'biography of the decade' by *India Today*. Since the last publication, Kiran's career has soared and she moved up in rank and got various postings, equally challenging and productive.

All this happened in the last five years. The book needed to incorporate the happenings — most of all her 'spiritual journey' on which she embarked not only for the prisoners or the trainees in the Police Training Institutes over which she presides, but also for herself.

In an exclusive opinion poll conducted by *The Week* in September, 2000, Kiran Bedi ranked fifth amongst the ten Most Admired Indians in a galaxy of personalities that included, among others, A.B. Vajpayee, Lata Mangeshkar and Sachin Tendulkar. *I Dare* is an insight into Kiran Bedi; Who she is and what makes her such an admired person in India.

"I DARE!" KIRAN BEDI

a biography

Revised Edition

PARMESH DANGWAL

Photographs
AJAY GOYAL

 **UBSPD**

UBS Publishers' Distributors Pvt. Ltd.
New Delhi • Bangalore • Chennai
Kolkata • Patna • Kanpur

UBS Publishers' Distributors Pvt. Ltd.

5 Ansari Road, New Delhi-110 002
Phones: 3273601, 3266646 • Cable: ALLBOOKS
Fax: 3276593, 3274261
E-mail: ubspd@ubspd.com • Website: www.gobookshopping.com

10 First Main Road, Gandhi Nagar, Bangalore-560 009
Phones: 2253903, 2263901, 2263902 • Cable: ALLBOOKS
Fax: 2263904 • E-mail: ubspdbng@bgl.vsnl.net.in

60 Nelson Manickam Road, Aminjikarai, Chennai-600 029
Phones: 3746222, 3746351, 3746352 • Cable: UBSIPUB • Fax: 3746287
E-mail: ubspdche@eth.net

8/1-B Chowringhee Lane, Kolkata-700 016
Phones: 2529473, 2522910, 2521821 • Cable: UBSIPUBS
Fax: 2523027 • E-mail: ubspdcal@cal.vsnl.net.in

5 A Rajendra Nagar, Patna-800 016
Phones: 672856, 673973, 686170 • Cable: UBSPUB • Fax: 686169
E-mail: ubspdpat1@sancharnet.in

80 Noronha Road, Cantonment, Kanpur-208 004
Phones: 369124, 362665, 357488 • Fax: 315122
E-mail: ubsknp@sancharnet.in

Distributors for Western India:
M/s Preface Books
Unit No. 223 (2nd floor), Cama Industrial Estate,
Sun Mill Compound, Lower Parel (W), Mumbai-400 013
Phone: 022-4988054 • Telefax: 022-4988048 • E-mail: Preface@vsnl.com

© Copyright: Kiran Bedi, Parmesh Dangwal and Ajay Goyal

First Published	1995	Twelfth Reprint	2000
First Reprint	1995	**Revised Edition**	**2001**
Sixth Reprint	1997	First Reprint	2001
Seventh Reprint	1998	Second Reprint	2001
Eighth Reprint	1998	Third Reprint	2001
Ninth Reprint	1999	Fourth Reprint	2002
Tenth Reprint	1999	Eleventh Reprint	2000
Eleventh Reprint	2000	Fifth Reprint	2002
		Sixth Reprint	2002

Royalty proceeds of this book are dedicated to the India Vision Foundation, a registered charity organisation providing education to children of prisoners in India.

Cover and all colour photographs: **Ajay Goyal**
Cover Design: Shamli Nimbalkar

Printed at Nutech Photolithographers, Delhi

To
The innumerable individuals
whom an insensitive system
strangled and suffocated

Parmesh Dangwal teaches English at the DAV (Postgraduate) College, Dehra Dun, UP. A postgraduate in English from the University of Allahabad, he earlier taught at the University of Delhi. Besides teaching, he is actively associated with a voluntary organisation in Dehra Dun that takes initiatives in human rights, people's entitlements, women's empowerment and enviromental issues.

Ajay Goyal is a professional photographer who contributes to various magazines and books in India and abroad. Besides, he runs his own studios at Rajpur Road, Dehura Dun. He attributes his photographic skills to his father, P.C. Goyal, who is a renowned photographer himself. Ajay 'treks with his camera' mainly in the north-west Himalayas, and is constantly on the lookout for adventure.

Contents

Why This Edition ?

After receipt of the Ramon Magsaysay Award in Government Service, also considered the Asian Nobel Prize, Kiran Bedi became nationally and internationally recognized. Her work as the first woman in the Indian Police Service, and as the Inspector General of Tihar Prisons Delhi, got international attention. She is also the first and perhaps the only woman in the world to have governed a prison with a population of over 9,700 prisoners. Her work in the field of crime prevention, forging partnerships in policing and prison transformation was absolutely innovative in the field of restorative justice. She stood out as a woman in uniform making the difference wherever she went. This Book, 'I Dare' was published in 1995 and went into eleven editions with translations into six other languages. It was voted as the biography of the decade by the leading weekly *India Today*.

Kiran Bedi's life and career since 1995 also soared. She moved up in rank, got various postings, equally challenging, with their share of controversies. She travelled widely, at times on international invitations and at others due to her academic work after she was awarded the Jawahar Lal Nehru Fellowship. Her book 'Its Always Possible', released in September 1998 was introduced and released in various cities of USA, UK, Europe, Australia, Asia and within India. The book is at present being translated in Italian to be a course book in the University of Milan. It already has Australian and Bangladesh editions.

She was invited to UN conferences thrice. She received many more international and national awards and invitations. Kiran Bedi interacts internationally through her website *www.kiranbedi.com* launched by His Holiness the Dalai Lama.

In an exclusive poll conducted by *The Week* in September, 2000, Kiran ranked fifth amongst the ten *Most Admired Indians* in a galaxy of personalities that included AB Vajpayee, Lata Mangeshkar, Amitabh Bachchan and others. This is what Gautam Kaul, Kiran's guru in the police force, has to say about her:

She wishes a day had a 25th hour, for it is filled with her commitments. She has solutions to all sorts of problems and people are keen to hear her even on matters which she has not specialised in.... But you take a risk if you are are sparring with her, as Tim Sebastian of the BBC did some months ago and lost face for himself in India...

When it was decided to 'fix' Kiran by posting her as chief supervisor at the Tihar Jail in New Delhi, the officials committed a big blunder. She emerged out of that confinement with a Magsaysay in hand.

All this in the last five years. 'I Dare' needed to incorporate the happenings. But most of all Kiran's spiritual journey — which she embarked on not only for the prisoners or her police trainees, but for herself.

September 2000 **—Parmesh Dangwal**

1

The Early Years

Raj Path, New Delhi, the road leading to the palatial and stately Rashtrapati Bhavan, was dressed in its resplendent best. It always is on the occasion of the Republic Day parade on 26 January, each year. The year 1973 was no different in that respect. What did make it different was that the march-past by the prize-winning contingent of the Delhi Police was being led by a *woman officer* for the first time. So impressive was the performance that the Prime Minister, Mrs Indira Gandhi, immediately pointed the lady officer out to her aides and extended an invitation for breakfast with her the very next day! The officer was none other than Kiran Bedi, who at that time was an IPS officer, in her first posting as subdivisional police officer, at Chanakyapuri, New Delhi.

As a matter of fact, Kiran had learnt at the eleventh hour that she was not going to lead the parade. She rushed to see the late P.R. Rajagopal, then IG, Delhi Police, and questioned him.

"Sir, I'm told I'm not leading the parade?"

"Look Kiran, it's a 15-km march. And you'll have to do it with that heavy sword in hand. Can you?"

"After all the training I've undergone, Sir, am I expected to answer that question yet?" she asked, amazed.

And lead the parade she did.

A few years later, on 5 November 1979, the same Raj Path staged an awe-inspiring drama. Hundreds of Akali Sikhs in flowing kurtas, with cross-belts holding empty scabbards and swords in hand, marched menacingly towards Rashtrapati Bhavan. As they neared their destination their aggression correspondingly mounted and with blood-curdling war cries they broke into a run. The Akali Sikhs were protesting against the Sant Samagam (a religious congregation) held earlier by the Nirankari Sikhs, and were fired with religious zeal. Kiran Bedi, leading a squad of the Delhi Police to keep the demonstrators in tow, screamed at the onrushing Akalis to desist. Instead, they attacked the police party. While Bedi's men beat a hasty retreat, she herself charged at the mob with just a helmet on her head and a baton in her hand. Despite the blows rained upon her, and in an exemplary show of courage, she attacked relentlessly till the demonstrators were cowed down by her sheer guts and determination. She was soon joined by her squad and the situation was brought under control.

For this act of hers, over and above the call of duty, Kiran Bedi was awarded the Police Medal for Gallantry on 10 October 1980.

Kiran fondly remembers how her then Police Commissioner, J.N. Chaturvedi, would always encourage her to take initiatives. She attributes this award of hers to his leadership and the training she received from Gautam Kaul, one of the most admired police officers of the country.

Exactly fourteen years from that date she became the only police officer in the world to receive a *peace* award – Magsaysay – the most prestigious of its kind in Asia, at Manila in the Philippines.

The bestowing of such an award represented, to say the least, a rare combination of extremes. And yet, on closer scrutiny, one realises that all that she was doing was what she perceived as her duty, which throughout her career she has executed to the best of her abilities. In 1986 the Bharatiya Janata Party (BJP), a pronouncedly pro-Hindu party, led by Madan Lal Khurana (who later became the Chief Minister of Delhi), and other leaders, such as Kedar Nath Sahni, insisted on gathering at the Red Fort grounds and leading a massive procession into the nearby Muslim-dominated areas of the city. As District Commissioner of Police (DCP), North, she refused to give them permission. She was quite convinced that despite what anyone may claim, this procession would result in high-voltage communal tension and the police would then be hard put to restore order. She was adamant and so were the BJP members. They sat on a three-week *dharna* with just a one-point charter of demands – dismiss Kiran Bedi.

Seven years later when Kiran became the Inspector-General (Prisons), Madan Lal Khurana visited Tihar Jail as the Chief Minister of Delhi. He commended her on the tremendous work she had done there and also recounted the days of his *dharna*. Over the public address system he declared that she had done her duty then, and was doing her duty now. Quite a turnabout, but then, quite common for politicians!

She has exhibited rare flashes of overconfidence though, and these are the times when she has slipped up. But then, she also has this tenacious ability to fight her way out of trouble when she sees defeat writ large on the wall.

During the National Tennis Final at Chandigarh, Kiran was playing Nirupama Mankad(Vasant) and had lost the first set 3-6. Kanwar Mahendra Singh Bedi and the former Asian champion, Lakshmi Mahadevan, were the radio commentators. Kanwar Mahendra asked Lakshmi whether she thought it was 'curtains' for Kiran. Lakshmi remembered a match she had played against Kiran in Assam. Kiran had lost the first set at 0-6, and was trailing 0-5 in the second. From there she had come out with a vengeance and had won 0-6, 7-5, 6-0. So, asserted Lakshmi, she would not count her out. Kiran eventually beat Nirupama 3-6, 6-3, 6-1.

Lakshmi was referring to the East India Championships played in Gauhati (now Guwahati) in January 1976. Kiran's daughter, Saina had been born in September 1975 and she was still toning herself up physically. She could not get into her own tennis gear and instead wore her husband Brij's shorts and T-shirt for the match. It was almost as if she had been out-of-sorts with herself for letting the woman in her act as an impediment to business at hand. She seemed to have a point to prove and splendidly did she do it.

"To me what is important in life is not being just a police officer but the fact that I am in a position where I can reasonably provide for myself my mental and physical food. It is this position that enables me to evaluate issues and decide for myself and subsequently enjoy or suffer the consequences without apportioning blame. I have sought for and got the position where I can now give and share always and do not have to ask, seek or wait to get. It is this basic drive to achieve that I would call the foundation of the being. In my case I have pondered over this quite often and tried to discover the conscious and unconscious manner that it was nurtured in me," says Kiran Bedi while fondly showing some letters that she has received from girls and boys from across the country who hold her as their role model.

She definitely possesses a compelling streak of independence and the dogged determination to achieve her objectives, *as a woman*, despite the male-dominated history of her family (and also much of Indian society).

Kiran was born into a predominantly patriarchal joint family with paternal roots in Peshawar (now in Pakistan) but which later settled in Amritsar. Her great-great-grandfather, Lala Hargobind, a veritable Pathan, came to Amritsar from Peshawar. He set up a carpet-manufacturing unit and a utensil factory here and prospered. He started off with Rs. 50,000 and, during his lifetime itself, increased his assets twentyfold. He left behind enough property and wealth to enable the succeeding Peshawarias to not only expand their business but also prosper. Her great grandfather, Lala Chajjumal, was a simple and god-fearing man, but her grandfather, Lala Muni Lal, was something else again. At the age of twelve he dropped out of school and took private tuitions in English for about four years. He related more to his grandfather and borrowed Rs. 50,000 from the latter to set up business in the early years of the twentieth century. He opened his offices above his father's wholesale cloth shop and corresponded with manufacturers in England in the English that he had learned so assiduously. Very soon he began importing the finest muslin cloth, the famous '926 *mulmul*', from Manchester and grey and white Italian flannel from Bradford. He also purchased a dry, unused pond and constructed a *dharamsala* (rest house for pilgrims) over it that he dedicated to his religiously inclined father. Today, there are Peshawaria *dharamsalas* in Hardwar, Vrindavan and Amritsar, run by a family trust of the Peshawarias.

Lala Muni Lal was a self-made man, no doubt, but he was a headstrong patriarch to boot. He exercised his rights over his family and its properties like a true autocratic *Karta*. He was fond of a good life and spent considerable amounts of money on himself but held the purse strings tight for the rest of the large joint family to whom he gave only a pittance of an allowance for working in the family business. He was only the third man in Amritsar to own a car.

Kiran's father, Parkash Lal, is the third of a family of four sons and three daughters, namely, sister Banarso (whose grand-daughter, Kanchan Choudhary, became the second woman IPS officer), Manohar, sister Pushpa, sister Mohinder, Manmohan and Narender. Parkash Lal was, and still is, a very keen tennis player and Dr. D.R.Puri (father of the famous sports commentator Dr. Narottam Puri), who was the principal of the Amritsar College, had offered him admission and a scholarship for his Bachelor of Arts on the basis of the promise he showed as a tennis player. Parkash's father, however, stopped him from joining and insisted that he help in the factory. Parkash's elder brother, Manohar, had done his Bachelor of Commerce and would have been the right person to go there, but he did not get along very well with their father and, therefore, the more dutiful and obedient younger son was made to give up college.

Parkash was a sensitive young man who was disturbed by the way women had to play a subservient role in society and had virtually no rights or privileges. He thus decided not to marry as, in a joint family structure like his, his wife's lot would be no better than that of the other women in the household. His widowed aunt (his father's sister) also stayed with them and his father always acceded to her wishes in the manner of a kind brother helping an unfortunate sister. She had talked to, and arranged with, a well-known and respectable family of Amritsar for the hand of their daughter for Parkash. When he refused to budge from his stand of not getting married, she gave up eating food altogether. He was, therefore, compelled to accede to her wishes.

At the age of 20, Parkash Lal married Janak, daughter of Lala Bishan Dass Arora, who belonged to a religious and wealthy family of Amritsar which provided regular charity lunches to the poor and the needy. At the very tender age of fourteen, Janak, who later changed her name to Prem Lata, had the remarkable distinction of having completed her matriculation with Ratan, Bhushan and Prabhakar degrees in Hindi. Her early marriage prevented her from pursuing her studies any further.

Shashi, the eldest of the Peshawaria sisters, was born on 31 December 1945. Parkash felt as if all his beliefs about women were now to be put to the test and he decided then and there that he would try to make his daughter all that he wished women to be. At the age of three, Shashi had learnt the English alphabet and could count fluently up to a hundred. When she was five years old he admitted her to the Sacred Heart Convent, run by an order of missionary nuns from Belgium. When Lala Muni Lal, Parkash Lal's father, learnt that his grand-daughter had been admitted to a Christian school, and that too, without his permission, he was furious. Parkash told his father that the latter had the right to interfere in the case of his own son, but certainly not in that of his son's daughter. For this impudence, and for being headstrong in not listening to his father, Parkash Lal was cut off from all allowances.

Knowing that he did not even have a graduate degree to his name, Parkash Lal was wondering what to do when his father-in-law offered him a substantial amount of money to start his own business. He opened a drapery store and soon had a flourishing business going. The 1948 war with Pakistan, however, put an end to this venture.

A year later, on the 9th day of June 1949, Prem Lata gave birth to another daughter who was named Kiran (ray).

Kiran maintains that it was the genetic strain of academics and sports that she inherited from her parents. The exigencies imposed by their respective families and early marriage into a traditional home had curtailed the ambitions of both her parents. Their starved passions found their way genetically into the daughters. The parents had set high standards for themselves and, with these standards as the foundation, they instilled in their daughters the thirst and quest for excellence in the field of sports and education.

The Peshawaria sisters studied at the aforementioned Sacred Heart Convent at Amritsar. The school was located about 16 kilometres from their home and so a considerable amount of time was spent in travelling to and from school. This meant waking up very early and also spending extra money on transport. Mrs. Peshawaria would be up at four in the morning to attend to the first chore of the day, which was to ensure that the milkman milked the cow in her presence to avoid any adulteration. After an early breakfast the sisters would jog or walk around 5 kilometres to reach the bus stand. At that time, the fare, at concessional rates for children under fourteen, was seven paise per child each way. To save this amount they would sometimes seek a lift from their more affluent friends who were driven to school in tongas. Saving this money meant earning money for their parents. Whatever was saved was always handed over to their mother. Sometimes there were some awkward moments when explanations had to be given for the delay in payment of fees. "Shashi would do the explaining, as she was the eldest and in the seventh class. I must have been in the first or the second and therefore was adequately covered by her explanation. But even today I can recollect the storm it would create in me whenever such moments occurred," Kiran recalls. After all, it was not as if they were poor; it was only that the family's finances were controlled by a close-fisted, autocratic and insensitive grandfather. It was thus very early in life that Kiran developed this streak of determination when she promised herself that she would make sure that every paise invested on her by her parents would be optimally utilised and accounted for. It was almost with a vengeance that she flung herself into whatever activity the school provided. She was into tennis, NCC (National Cadet Corps), use of the library, debates, declamations, dramas, athletics and more. She was determined that not a single moment that had been bought by her parents' money would go unrewarded.

When Kiran reached Class IX she took her first major decision in life, on her own. She had completed Class VIII and was having problems with getting the right combination of subjects for the ninth class. She was not overly partial to mathematics but wanted to take up science. That, however, was not possible at the Sacred Heart Convent. She was instead offered a subject course called 'household', where she would be taught how to budget home expenses, how to maintain and run a house and other skills that would help her in becoming a good and efficient housewife. That was enough to scare the living daylights out of the tomboyish Kiran and to set her free to abandon the school she so dearly loved in order to move over to any other institution which would keep her away from 'household' and mother-in-law concepts. She explored possibilities outside her school and came to know that a private institution called Cambridge College would offer her science with Hindi and would prepare her for the Class X board examinations. She was excited about the prospect of this 'double promotion' that was being offered to her and decided she would go for it. Her father was not in town to advise her and her mother readily agreed, saying that if she thought that was good for her then that is what she should do. So, while her peers in school cleared their ninth class, Kiran cleared her matriculation. She worked for and got her 'double promotion' to the envy of all her friends. It is a different matter that if she had managed to get only one mark less in Hindi she would have been back with them! Nevertheless, she had taken the first major decision of her life and it had come out right.

2

Breaking Stereotypes

Kiran joined the Government College for Women at Amritsar after her matriculation. The political science course and the NCC (National Cadet Corps) were the two features that influenced her the most. The other subjects that interested her were philosophy and history. But it was political science that she actually wanted to master. Theories of state administration and powers and functions of governance fired her imagination. She believed that this was the subject which taught her to become a participatory citizen and also develop feelings of nationalism in her.

The NCC gave her the first taste of 'khaki'. She adored and respected her uniform and took great pains to keep it immaculately clean, starched and ironed. With such pride and determination in the Corps, it was not surprising that she soon became the platoon commander and was subsequently chosen to lead the annual day parade. She did not know then where her destiny would lead her, but this much was clear that she was proud to be the citizen of a country she loved and wanted to serve it as an active participant and a loyal soldier.

Even during her college days there was always a sense of urgency about her. She was almost always on the run. Classroom, to tennis court, to the library, with never a moment wasted. Only very rarely would she give herself the luxury of spending a few minutes with friends over a *samosa* and a soft drink. All the girls knew that Kiran was not interested in gossip or inane chit-chat and never bothered her with such trivialities either.

Her mother recollects how Kiran possessed this tremendous urge to utilise time to derive maximum benefit. If she had even a half-hour of unaccounted time on her hands, she would either get down to painting or grab a racket and rush off to the tennis court to play and, if she couldn't find anyone, she would bang away against the wall by herself.

After her theory periods in college she rode back home on her bicycle, spent a few minutes with her mother, slipped into her NCC uniform and rode back to college. Kiran has always been tremendously fond of her mother and in those days she was willing to do the extra mileage on her cycle, about 12 kilometres, just to see her for some time during midday. She could easily have taken her NCC kit to college and changed there itself, but then that would have deprived her of these precious moments. The sisters had but one cycle between them and so it meant carrying her sister Reeta also on the pillion. College life was marked by a hectic period of hard work, discipline, and regular studies. She was determined that one day she would do what was not expected from Indian women. What that was going to be was not very clear, but that did not deter her from preparing herself.

The environment in which Kiran was brought up gave her insights into the then generally accepted stereotypes of gender, which came naturally to her and were in no way orchestrated or engineered. The stereotypes were as follows: men for the outdoors, authority and sports and women for the household, tears and scoldings; men for higher education and women for primary education only; women as a burden and men as perpetrators of the lineage; women for sacrifice and men for adventure; men as providers and policy-makers and women as acquirers of gold and jewellery. She did not have to go to school or college to learn these facts because they were evident in her own home, the joint family of the Peshawarias. Her grandfather was the typical autocrat whose authority was final and her grandmother the typical collector of gold ornaments and other jewellery. And this state of affairs was comfortably accepted by the younger generation Peshawarias. The only exception to the rule were Kiran's parents. They had four daughters and no son, and were determined to help and assist them in developing into adults who would make their own mark in life. Her grandfather and uncles, however, showed great concern for what they considered to be a 'burden'. As a matter of fact, her grandfather would suggest to his sons that since

Parkash had four 'liabilities' he should be adequately compensated for by giving him a larger portion of the properties as and when they would be divided. In other words, he was ensuring that sufficient dowry was available so that his grand-daughters could get decent husbands.

Kiran's parents, however, never looked upon their daughters this way. They provided their offspring with opportunities of education, sports and various other activities so that they could lead their lives as they wanted to. They were never looked upon as girls for whom husbands had to be found, but always as children who would grow up and carve out their careers for themselves. Her father would often explain to them how Prime Minister Jawaharlal Nehru always urged women to come forward and how he envisaged the role of women in the future of India.

3

The Game of Her Life

During her academic years, Kiran was also seriously and vigorously pursuing tennis. Along with her sister Reeta she had won for the Punjab University the interuniversity women's team title. Later, she bagged the national title and eventually the Asian title. One thing very clear to her was that the world has no time for losers. The strategies that one always adopted to be a winner in tennis were the strategies that had to be used in life too. Nothing came easily and every move had to be planned and worked for. The going was invariably tough and needed a lot of hard work and a definite determination to get what one wanted. The tennis courts symbolised for Kiran both negative and positive features, such as the qualities of discrimination, misuse of power, sycophancy as also the undiluted admiration for the champion.

The girls had to fight for their rights with respect to not just travel allowances but even the choice of courts. Many a time, during important matches like the semi-finals and the finals, the girls were relegated to the side courts. They had to struggle tenaciously for their right to play on the main courts as befitted the status of the match. Once, during the National Tennis Championships in Calcutta, the finals were considerably delayed because the girls, namely, Nirupama Vasant, Susan Dass, Udaya Kumar, Kiran and others, demanded their right to play on a prominent court. The organisers did ultimately relent and the girls' protest for their rightful place under the sun was upheld. Kiran learnt her lessons well, and one of them was that one had to assert oneself for even that which was one's due. Otherwise one tended to be ignored. Those who have no influential backing have to stay alive to their surroundings and make an impression as and when required.

During the interuniversity championships at Bangalore, Kiran and her sister Reeta took on the local pair of Udaya Kumar and Chandrika in the finals. Kiran won her singles match against Chandrika, but Reeta lost to Udaya Kumar to make the score one all. It was getting late in the day and Reeta, who had a little problem with visibility, insisted that they would play their doubles match the next day. Despite this, the match was awarded to the Bangalore pair by default. Quite unfazed, the sisters won both the reverse singles the next day to give Punjab the interuniversity title.

The Asian Lawn Tennis Championships of 1972 were held in Poona (now Pune). Kiran faced Udaya Kumar in the semifinals. Kiran had won the first set 6-3, and was leading 5-3 in the second set, when the very vociferous crowd led by an antagonistic coach named Akhtar Ali rattled her and she went down 5-7. During the third set the crowd was on its feet and Kiran further slid to 1-3, 15-30. She looked at her father, who glared at her as much as to say that she had no right to give up, and with a determined shake of her head she got down to business once again. Kiran eventually won 6-3, 5-7, 6-3. In the finals she outplayed Susan Dass, her regular rival and compatriot, and went on to become the Asian champion.

Akhtar Ali was responsible for training most of the top women players those days and had wanted Kiran to join his camp. However, Kiran preferred to pursue the game under the guidance of her father and her coach Raghubar Dayal. Consequently, Akhtar had a point to prove against Kiran, which, unfortunately for him, he never could. But Akhtar, all along, admired Kiran for the stamina and determination she possessed.

However, despite her grit and tenacity, Kiran succumbs to gamesmanship. She is always willing to accept your side of the story till you yourself prove it wrong. She herself would rather take things at face value. For instance, in the Northern India tennis championships of 1972 she was playing a six-foot-two Australian in the finals. Kiran led 6-3, 3-1. At rest periods during changeovers the Australian would wrinkle up her face and let Kiran see her tears and Kiran got round to trying to buck her up. Her father, sensing what was going on, went to Kiran and scolded her. Immediately the Australian complained to the umpire that Kiran was being coached. Kiran lost the match 6-3, 3-6,

4-6. She was ashamed of herself that evening and had a hearty cry.

The very next week she was pitted against the same opponent in the Punjab State championships at Chandigarh. This time she did not speak a word to her opponent and just let her racket do the talking. Kiran beat her 6-0, 6-0. She lost her gold chain while playing that match but that certainly was of no consequence at this sweet moment of revenge.

Kiran became the national junior champion at the age of sixteen, seven years after she was initiated into tennis by her father. She was a dark and scrawny kid who would tie her hair in tight plaits, or a pony tail, to keep it from blocking her vision. It bothered her to have her hair shampooed every day and to tie and braid it. So one day she just ran across to the barber's and made him chop it off to the style she sports to date: what she was told was called the 'boy cut'.

She played her first tournament outside Amritsar at the age of fourteen. This was the national championship for the year 1964-65, held at the Delhi Gymkhana courts. Om Prakash, the son of the gardener at the courts she played in at Amritsar, accompanied her on her maiden venture. (Om later became a tennis coach and did considerably well for himself.) At the Delhi Gymkhana courts, dressed in a starched and spotlessly white frock made of *khadi* she took on one Ms Wills, who had the experience of playing at Wimbledon to awe one and all, in her very first match. With the repertoire of a good forehand and weak backhand, Kiran lost the match at 0-6, 1-6. But she was thrilled, nevertheless, to have taken a game off a Wimbledon player. Two years hence she became the national junior champion.

She travelled the length and breadth of the country in pursuit of her game, invariably in the then existent third-class compartments, at times even perched on her luggage outside the toilet of the coach. There was no prize money worth mentioning in Indian tennis those days and the gender bias being fairly predominant, she had to assert herself time and again and fight for the paltry amounts of travel fare and the like. These amounts, of course, would promptly be returned to her mother. However, from 1968 onwards, when she achieved her national ranking, she was given the benefit of travelling by first class and Rs. 30 as daily allowance. She travelled a lot those days, alone or in groups, staying in dormitories in the beginning and then graduating to single rooms in hotels. She was the contemporary of Vijay and Anand Amritraj, Gaurav Misra, Ramanathan Krishnan, Jaideep Mukherjee and Premjit Lal. She played on the same courts that Illie Nastase, Ian Tiriac and Fred Stolle did on their regular visits to India.

All the time spent by Kiran on the courts and in travelling did not, however, deter her from her studies. Tennis was there certainly but not as the top priority. She knew that it was a time-bound pursuit and always had her eyes set on joining government service.

Kiran played competitive tennis from the age of thirteen to thirty, when she was well into service. She was India's number two during her police training at Mount Abu when she read in the newspapers that the Indian women's team had been announced which was to tour Sri Lanka to play in the Fonseca Trophy, an Indo-Sri Lanka women's tournament. She did not figure in the team. This got her really incensed and she rushed off letters of protest to the authorities, who explained to her that they had imagined that as she was now in the services she would not be willing to participate. So, while the other members of the team, Nirupama Vasant-Mankad, Susan Dass and Udaya Kumar practised with trainers and coaches under the auspices of the Lawn Tennis Association of India, Kiran practised with the then Director of the National Police Academy, S.J. Gokhale, her fellow probationer, Sanjiv Tripathi and others, or all by herself against a wall specially constructed for her. Kiran eventually went to Sri Lanka as a member of the team. She won her matches and the Indian team as a whole put up a brilliant performance to come back with the trophy.

Kiran believes that her attitude to, and strategies for, life have been developed from her tennis. The game taught her many things that she would not otherwise have learnt from any book. Academics and sports could both be pursued together provided one had the single-minded determination to succeed in both fields. But then one had also to be prepared to miss out on some other recreations. Such recreations could come in their own time, later in life, but during the period of struggle and foundation-laying they had to be assiduously avoided. The rewards she knew would be adequate compensation in themselves.

Tennis taught her the value of hard work and perseverance and how important it is to be both mentally and physically strong. She would resort to autosuggestion often and would think of nothing but victory. She ran miles every day to keep herself fit and divided her time judiciously between studies and intensive sports practice. The self-confidence she has always exuded is the reward of her self-training. She also attributes her qualities of fair play, team work, concentration, indefatigability, endurance, tenacity and, most of all, that ability to stretch out that extra bit under conditions of stress and exhaustion to her years on the tennis courts.

Kiran recalls how she was exposed to a considerable amount of gender and class bias those days. Men were always paid more than the women and even then the women had to assert themselves to obtain what was legitimately due to them. Players from metropolitan cities were considered 'more equal' than those belonging, for instance, to Amritsar which was disparagingly considered to be an urban village. A particular case reveals the extent of the prejudice against women. Kiran used to call the secretary of the Punjab Tennis Association, Shamsher Singh, her 'uncle'. This 'uncle' would often make her wait hours outside his office when she went to collect her railway concession forms, but she was thankful that he had been considerate enough to have at least a washed out wooden bench there. It was this endless waiting that made her promise herself that if ever she were in a position to give someone something she would never ever make that person wait.

In 1966, when she was the national junior champion, there was a tradition that the junior champion represented the country at Wimbledon. But it was this very same 'uncle' who cancelled her trip for his own vested interests.

If one were to go by the statements players make against their respective associations even these days, it seems that politics is still very much a priority over sports with most of them. Such a state of affairs is, indeed, deplorable because the 'games' played by the selectors and organisers could jeopardise a player's entire career.

Another vital lesson she learned from her tennis was the ability to not let the feeling of what others would say override her own interests. For a girl more concerned with working hard at the targets she had set for herself rather than adding frills, she would often even attend weddings and functions in her sports outfit. To go home and change would have meant sacrificing precious time from her tennis and she certainly seemed to have her priorities cut out for herself. Her achievements even at that very young age had made her feel confident that she did not have to feel less than anyone because she knew that she had achieved much more than they had. Her family had become a recognised tennis family that had brought laurels to the state of Punjab. Kiran had won for Punjab the state title, the zonal title, the national title and finally the Asian title. Along with her sister Reeta she won the interuniversity title thrice. The youngest of the Peshawaria sisters, Anu, later became the national champion for three years running and played not only the university, state and the Asian championships, but also at Universiad and Wimbledon. Anu's son Aditya is now on his way to be a champion. He has already won many tournaments in the USA where Anu is now a practising attorney. On the other hand, Kiran's tennis partner and younger sister Reeta has made her mark in the field of special education by authoring innumerable books. She is a most sought-after speaker in the field of mental disabilities. It seems that tennis in the family has made champions out of the girls.

4

A Wedding without Bells

It was at the Amritsar tennis courts that Kiran met Brij Bedi. The chemistry bond between them was very strong and they soon decided to make their relationship permanent. Kiran and Brij 'tied the proverbial knot' in one of the most simple ceremonies that Amritsar had witnessed. On 9 March 1972, a very small group comprising their parents and a few friends went to the Shiva temple at 2 a.m. and there they garlanded each other. That was it. Kiran and Brij were married. Three days later, at the reception, Kiran wore a sari for the first time in her life. She has donned this attire on only few other occasions. During one of her early postings as an IPS officer in Delhi, her then IG, Bhawani Mal, suggested to her that she should don the sari as a working dress. Her answer was pretty characteristic: "Sir if there is one thing which can put me off the service, it is to be compelled to wear a sari!"

What does she have against the sari? Nothing, she would say. It's a graceful garment and makes women look very feminine. And, would she not want to look feminine? "Let's put it this way," she would say. "I haven't got used to it at all, and dress, in my view, is a personal choice and reflection of an attitude."

To meet her is to realise what gender equality is all about. In her designations as DCP(North) and DCP(West) in Delhi she went out on numerous night raids. M.B. Kaushal (a former Police Commissioner of Delhi), whom she considers to be one of the very caring officers, would always try to dissuade her from making these night rounds. She, on her part, insisted. But she does not consider this to be gender discrimination and insists that it was merely a protective feeling dictating his suggestions. Somehow, somewhere, despite the overtures of boldness and the cut-and-dry professionalism, there emerges a girl who somehow got lost in the woods.

The very morning after her wedding Kiran went over to her parents' house quite early to take her usual glass of milk from her mother's hand and then drive younger sister Anu to school. She did not want Anu to feel that just because she had changed residence there was going to be any change in her responsibilities.

Kiran was already working as a lecturer in political science in Amritsar Khalsa College for Women. She taught there for two years, till selected for the IPS (Indian Police Service) in July 1972, the first woman to have made it! At the interview it was suggested to her not to pursue this career as it was a man's domain and she would find life very tough and very difficult. Nothing, however, could sway her from her determination. So, off she went to Mount Abu to the National Police Academy.

Here is one of the first interviews of Kiran as a police officer. It is indicative of her attitude to the service which hasn't changed once over the years despite all the upheavals and the storms....

IPS WOMAN BELIEVES IN PUBLIC SERVICE

Mrs Kiran Bedi, the first woman to enter the Indian Police Service, is used to limelight. An outstanding lawn tennis player, she always wanted to do "something outstanding," as she put it in an interview here today.

"That was why," she explained, "I did not take something ordinary. I had to have a challenging job." The Indian Administrative Service and the Indian Foreign Service were "flooded with" girls.

Asked if she wanted IPS to be flooded with girls, Mrs Bedi said she would strongly recommend the service to women who are physically fit and who are capable of independent thinking.

Speaking for herself, she said she had always been encouraged to think independently by her parents and the decision to go for IPS was also entirely hers.

She was confident that the IPS would give her a chance to show her qualities of taking up challenges and overcoming them to her satisfaction.

As such, she "loved public service" and believed that the IPS was the ideal public service as far as she was concerned.

Mrs Bedi, who married an Amritsar businessman last year, said it was possible for her to join the IPS because her husband encouraged her. "He is one of the most encouraging husbands one can encounter," she added, rather shyly.

How do they plan to bring up the family? She did not think they would have much difficulty in this respect as "neither of us has any inhibitions" about doing any sort of job.

As she has opted for the Union Territory cadre, Mrs Bedi knows it means staying away from home for long periods. She hopes that her initial postings will be nearer home. They plan to have a child after a year or two.

Playing tennis ever since her school days in Amritsar, she had made her name (née Peshawaria) hit the headlines of sports pages quite frequently. In fact, her strenuous tennis sessions have helped her to take the rigorous physical training of the IPS course at Mt Abu.

She has been selected along with two other Indian women players to play against Ceylon in Colombo next month. Her job in the IPS, she believes, will help her in promoting tennis among women at the district level.

A topper in MA (political science) from Punjab University, Chandigarh, Mrs Bedi thinks women officers will be an asset to the police force as they are "basically sympathetic and loving."

(The Hindustan Times, 20 July 1973)

Once she was into the midstream of her career, however, both Kiran and Brij realised that it would not be possible for either of them to make compromises with their work and so decided to live their lives independently and remain soul companions even though they would live physically apart. Kiran's mother-in-law gave her tremendous support during this period as well as boundless love till her dying day (19 May 1994). After her death Kiran brought her spectacles with her through which she used to see her with all her love and concern.

5

Her Real Life Roles

Kiran has become the role model for a number of movies. 'Kartavyam', in Telugu (later dubbed in Tamil under the title, 'Vijayashanti I.P.S.'), starring actress Vijayashanti in the role of a Kiran Bedi clone, even won a national award. Kiran was present at its *mahurat* and even gave a few tips to the actress on how to appear immaculate in her uniform. As the title of the film indicates, it deals with an officer's sense of duty and dedication to the service. The movie was well made and deservedly won an award for itself. There were other movies such as

'Tejaswani', and television serials, too, based on Kiran's life like 'Stri' and 'Inspector Kiran'. The movies and serials have been well researched by the directors through a study of writeups on Kiran in the press as well as through personal interviews with her. What she appears to the public at large is the impression that has been attempted to be captured on celluloid. The reviews as well as the public response provide ample evidence of her being accepted as portrayed in these films.

The sterling qualities that emerge from the movies/ serials centre around integrity. She has been projected as being an upholder of the law who is very impartial in dispensing justice to the offender. She has been shown to have been subjected to tremendous pressure by the nexus between the criminal businessman and the corrupt politician and to have successfully overcome all obstacles by her sheer determination, mental tenacity and an inflexible, uncompromising attitude when she knows and believes she is right. As far as emotions are concerned she has been shown to have tremendous restraint.

When asked what she herself thinks about how she has been portrayed, Kiran feels that barring a few exaggerations that are the wont of our film-makers, the portrayals are quite realistic. "They've even kept the heroines quite slim", she giggles, "but they seem to have an edge over me in their being very tough in the stunts they perform."

However, when she recalls her handling of situations in the past, she does feel that she could have been a wee bit more diplomatic and avoided some of the consequent stresses and pressures. In the case of the BJP incident at Delhi, for instance: "The leaders wanted to take a procession into the streets of the Muslim-dominated areas. I couldn't say I knew for sure there would be communal problems and the situation would definitely go out of hand. But I did think so. Maybe I could have told them to go ahead and then if there was any trouble I could have used police action. Maybe, I could have let it be a merely political incident and avoided the ensuing spate of protests and *dharnas.* Maybe."

Then, in the case of lawyers' strike, for instance (see also Chapter 11): she herself was nowhere in the picture to start with. The issue began with the demand for the suspension of a subinspector who, contrary to the court's earlier ruling not to use handcuffs, barring exceptional circumstances, had handcuffed a lawyer while taking him to the courts in a DTC (Delhi Transport Corporation) bus. Even her Additional Commissioner of Police, Rajendra Mohan, at that time, had recommended that she suspend the person and when matters cooled down somewhat she could reinstate him: a mature advice indeed. She, however, let her sense of fair play dictate her response. The subinspector, she maintains, was alone and there was sufficient proof of the offender's doubtful antecedents. He was travelling in a public transport vehicle and had no other means of ensuring the offender's presence in court except by handcuffing him. The court's earlier decision on handcuffing pertained to a threat perception and, in this case, according to the officer, it existed! She became adamant and very rapidly got sucked into the quicksand of the lawyers' agitation. It is a moot point that where she was being fair to one person she was also instrumental in causing large-scale suffering to hundreds of thousands of people whose cases were pending in courts across the country. The balance, one could say in retrospect, did not tilt in her favour.

One fact stands out clearly though. It was not for herself that she took the stand that offended the lawyers. It was for a junior member of her force whom her judgement had rendered blameless of any fault and any—mala fide intentions in the sincere execution of his duties. That, she has always believed, should never be punishable for whatever compulsion of expediency. It was the same in the case of the towing incident of the car belonging to the Prime Minister's Secretariat, which had taken place earlier. Then also she had backed the action of sub-inspector Nirmal Singh to the hilt. (See also Chapter 6.)

There seems to be an overriding element of compassion that dictates this quality of fair play in her. This feature can be seen by her response to the endless cases that people bring to her for justice even though she is not officially involved in them. Women keep visiting her house to complain of excesses committed by their husbands upon them. She is asked to intervene in cases of allegedly wrong arrests made by the police personnel who are not even under her jurisdiction. Small kids making a living by polishing shoes surround her during her rare shopping forays to Connaught Place and complain about how they are being harassed and prevented from plying their trade.

When Kiran was DCP(W) she had assured the people that she would ensure that not a single case of an unjustified arrest would take place in her area. One of the reformed and rehabilitated erstwhile criminals of the area had started to earn his living by selling vegetables. A dacoity was committed in the South District and, on the basis of this person's criminal record, the South District Police arrested him. His relatives came to Kiran and accused her of breach of trust. She explained to them that the matter did not fall under her jurisdiction but she would still conduct her own investigations to ascertain the truth. Her investigations revealed that injustice had indeed been done and that the accused person could not have possibly committed the crime. She approached the Commissioner of Police, P.S. Bhinder, with the details she had collected and requested him to review the matter in that light. Bhinder curtly ticked her off saying the case was not in her jurisdiction and charged her with interference. The DCP(South), Balwant Singh, Bhinder told her, had already submitted his report to him and he had, as a matter of fact, even commended him for his brilliant work over so short a period of time. According to the South District Police the case had been solved within 24 hours! The story of the South District Police did not prove reliable and the accused did get the benefit of Kiran's investigations, but after the loss of his wife, his child and his own liberty for some time.

The victim's wife, who was near delivery time, could not bear the trauma of her husband's arrest and died. The press, that had heard of Kiran's investigations, took up the human interest angle of the story and conducted its own investigations. The incompetence of the South District Police was exposed and the accused person was released.

Maybe it is this compassion that Mother Teresa saw in Kiran. During her tenure as IG (Prisons) the Mother called her up and expressed her desire to meet her. Kiran called on her at her ashram and got a couple of hugs from her. When Kiran was leaving and almost near the gate she heard the Mother asking her to wait. She turned round to see this frail and petite person come running to her, bare feet, and give her a third big hug. To Kiran's round-eyed look she merely told her that she had got this urge to just hug her once more. The Mother surely had sensed the compassion in Kiran!

6

'Crane' Bedi

The Asian games held in Delhi in 1982 symbolised a prestigious landmark for not just the capital but for India as a whole. The gala spectacle was bound to get tremendous exposure round the world through TV and other mass media and Delhi had started gearing up for the event years in advance. Kiran was posted as DCP (Traffic) in October 1981. She soon realised what a snarling bear she was required to grapple with in the form of Delhi traffic. To add to the chaotic traffic, nineteen sports stadia were being constructed all round and so were

Leading the Delhi Police Contingent on Republic Day, 1973.

Handling the Akali agitation single handedly.

Breakfast with Prime Minister Indira Gandhi after leading
the Republic Day Parade.

Receiving the Police Gallantry Award from Home Minister
Y.B. Chavan.

A rare occasion when she wore a sari

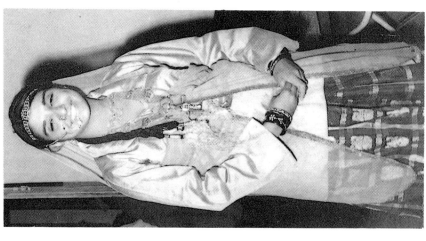

In a traditional dress to dance the *Gidda*.

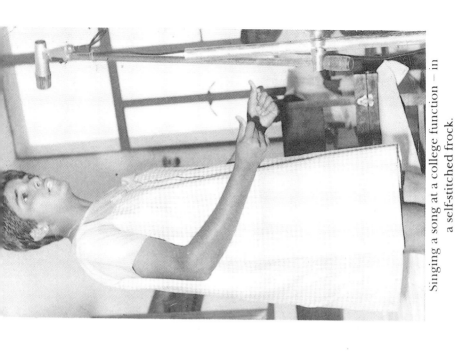

Singing a song at a college function — in a self-stitched frock.

Kiran with sister Anu.

The National Women's Tennis champ.

With father, Parkash Lal, after she won the
Women's Asian Championship.

Controlling Delhi traffic during the Asiad.

With actress Vijayashanti at *mahurat* **of film 'Kartavyam' – the film won a National Award.**

With husband Brij at Police Academy, Mt. Abu.

flyovers, thereby resulting in road blockages and diversions. Delhi traffic was haphazard as it was and all the construction activity had thrown it completely out of gear.

In order to meet the exacting demands of her job, Kiran would be up at 5 a.m. and settle down for her office work from 6 a.m. to 7 a.m. All letters to be issued from her office were dictated into a dictaphone and explicit instructions given for her staff. By 8 a.m. she would be making her rounds on the roads in her white Ambassador car that she had fitted with a loudspeaker. She then would check signal timings and note corrections on the spot. Any case of off-road vehicles needed on the roads would be inquired into and removals expedited. She would then check on her staff on duty and note explanations to be called for from absentees there and then. It became a common sight for the Delhi motorists to see Kiran Bedi on the road every day, pointing out traffic irregularities in specific cases. A woman's voice coming over the loudspeaker made an impression upon the motorists that a male voice could not have done. However, when she realised that so much of talking loudly was taking its toll on her vocal chords, she had to have her throat massaged every night by her mother and her daughter's nanny, and she asked an officer of hers, Shakuntala Khokhar, to assist her in issuing these warnings.

At 12.30 she would be back at her office and go through file work or hold interdepartmental as well as intradepartmental meetings, return calls and meet visitors. Those days the Municipal Corporation of Delhi (MCD) was busy with the construction of roads and flyovers; the Delhi Electric Supply Undertaking (DESU) was concerned with the erection of electric light poles and laying of cables; the Delhi Development Authority (DDA) was responsible for the land being used for the construction of roads and sanctioning of many projects. Over and above these bodies there was a professional consultant, D. Sanyal, from the National Transportation, Planning and Research Centre (NATPAC) who was coordinating all matters pertaining to traffic engineering, transportation planning and traffic management. Kiran felt that all these activities could not be effectively planned and executed by merely holding drawing room meetings and hence suggested that the actual behaviour patterns of the motorists could be seen and verified only on the roads. Everyone agreed.

The group would board a chartered bus and move from point to point; on-the-spot decisions were taken and corrections made. In this way this 'government on wheels' acted as a homogeneous team and the usual inter-departmental squabbles and lack of coordination were eliminated.

The same procedure was followed on an intra-departmental basis also. Heads of various sections would similarly move around together and coordinate the movement of various sections. Parking spaces, parking labels, advertisement space, and traffic training literature would all be earmarked or devised during these dry runs. She made her first audiovisual presentation of the Asian games traffic management before a select group of sponsors for raising funds for traffic guidance material. She was ably assisted by Achal Paul, an advertising professional then working with Clarion Advertising, and now with MAA. The sponsors responded generously by committing themselves to a variety of road safety and educational material worth Rs 35 lakhs. Prahlad Kakkar made a film on road safety entitled 'Who Saw the Zebra Crossing?', sponsored by Ramesh Chauhan of Limca. The Modis sponsored all the traffic booths which had traffic helmets, as headtops. The Pure Drinks group sponsored traffic islands. MRF provided road dividers and Apollo Tyres sponsored road safety literature. These dry runs and on-the-spot workshops, which were many, enabled her to put this money to the best use possible for the benefit of Delhi commuters.

If the sum total of her efforts for the preparation and the actual execution of her traffic plans for the Asian games of 1982 were to be expressed, it could be done so by using only one word — excellent.

The *Indian Express,* in its issue of 4 December 1982, reported:

GAMES A GRAND SUCCESS

...In the end, the greatest triumph was the way the traffic was kept moving during the Games, particularly during the closing ceremony and the opening day (Nov. 19). The police authorities deserve to be complimented.

The bane of Delhi traffic was (and continues to be) wrong parking and this one factor was (and is) a major cause of traffic snarl-ups. Kiran hit hard here and, after sufficient warnings to the public at large through the loudspeaker fitted to her car, she soon pressed several cranes into action in order to tow away the offending vehicles to the nearest police station. It was not long after this that she earned the sobriquet of 'Crane' Bedi.

Also, she insisted that offending vehicles would no longer be *challaned* but would be 'spot-fined'. The influential section of Delhi society had earlier never bothered about any *challans*. There were innumerable cases wherein these *challans* had been torn to shreds in front of the issuing officer with a 'do-what-you-want' attitude. But spot-fining, the people soon realised, was a different ball game altogether. No amount of influence and no friends, however highly placed, could help out here. Kiran had given clear-cut instructions to her men to stand by her orders and that she would back their actions to the hilt. She was not going to assess their work by the number of *challans* but by the quality of traffic management both in enforcement and regulation.

A lobby soon grew that resented her. After all here they were, affluent and with a lot of pelf, in the corridors of power, and there she was just a DCP and a woman to boot! It must have antagonised them no end.

She made no compromises and granted no concessions. In August 1982 even Prime Minister Indira Gandhi's car (no. DHI 1817) was *challaned* for wrong parking near a car repair shop in Connaught Place and the vehicle towed away by a crane. The action of the subinspector, Nirmal Singh, who was on duty, was backed to the hilt by Kiran Bedi, and her senior Additional Commissioner of Police, Ashok Tandon, whose support she enjoyed all along.

An interesting news item explains the situation:

PM's Car Held

When the deputy police commissioner (traffic) Mrs Kiran Bedi started a drive against wrong parking last year, no one could have imagined that even the Prime Minister's car would come into the dragnet. But the impossible happened. On 5 August [1982], when Mrs Gandhi and her family members were away in the USA, a traffic sub-inspector found a white Ambassador (DHI 1817), wrongly parked outside the Yusufzai Market, Connaught Circus, in the heart of the city. Only after he had made out a challan did he realise that it was the official car of the PM. The securitymen accompanying the car (which had gone there for repairs), pointed this out to the traffic officer. But he was adamant. Wrong parking was illegal, whether it be by a commoner or a VIP, he told the securitymen.

An enquiry has been ordered into the incident. As soon as the PM returned from her tour, the matter was brought to her notice. The scope of the enquiry is: how was there a lack of coordination between the VIP security and the traffic wings of the Delhi police? Mrs Kiran Bedi has, however, made it public that the question of putting the heat on an officer who was merely carrying on his duties did not arise. The incident, meanwhile, has exposed a chink in the Delhi traffic police. The shop to which Mrs Gandhi's car went, Handa and Company, belongs to a friend of a powerful aide of the PM. The shop deals in car accessories and upholstery. The popularity of the shop attracts many car owners. But to take a car to the shop also invites a traffic challan because of the shop's location. The car park on the opposite pavement is usually overcrowded (as a popular restaurant and hotel are located there). The traffic police have been refusing to recognise the fact that as long as Handa and Babbar Sons, two popular car accessory dealers, are located at the Yusufzai Market, car owners are bound to park their cars outside the shops and get the fittings done. Though the existing traffic rules prohibit parking in that area surely this reality has to be taken into account as well. Whether the incident involving the PM's car will awaken the traffic police to the realities of the situation or not is difficult to say. But Mrs Bedi's traffic drive certainly has reached the gates of 1, Safdarjang Road.

(Sunday, 28 August 1982)

Well before the Asian games Kiran had initiated the scheme of sponsorships. Those with money and political clout had taken it for granted that they would be able to corner the major share of advertising space, i.e., the numerous traffic islands, traffic booths and traffic bollards all over Delhi. Kiran, however, put a damper on their complacency by making a much more equitable distribution. Whereas her action was lauded by the many who got a fair share of publicity, it was taken as the arrogance of an upstart by the few.

Very soon she started to get 'signals' that she would be tolerated only for the duration of the games and not a day longer.

Many 'carrots' were dangled in front of her even during the months preceding the games. For instance, she was offered scholarships for courses in traffic regulation training in Australia and later in Japan. Naturally, she had no inclination to be away from Delhi for months while the ominous responsibility of regulating traffic during the games was upon her. Even while she was conducting meetings, where plans were being discussed, she would be called up on the telephone by senior ministry officials congratulating her and wishing her bon voyage. She could only refuse these scholarships as politely as she could.

"Was it because they wanted you out so that they could claim credit for the arrangements?"

Kiran responds: "I wonder what would have been done to me if the traffic situation had been chaotic during the Asian games. Could I then say sorry, I couldn't plan enough because I have just come back from Japan or Australia? To me these foreign trips at that point of time were out of place. I had only *one goal* and that was to achieve an orderly and organised traffic flow, to leave no one with a complaint that he or she could not make it because of traffic problems. We all wanted excellence in our arrangements."

Is Kiran being a bit spiteful, one wonders, but only for a moment. Forthcoming events underscore her belief.

The era of colour television came to India along with the Asian games. As is the practice before major events like the Republic Day parade and the Independence Day functions, the DCP (Traffic) is required to come on TV prior to the event and explain the traffic routes to the public. Kiran naturally had this responsibility. She said she would come immediately but was hastily informed that she could send a junior officer.

"There are nineteen stadia divided into nineteen zones," Kiran explained to the authorities concerned. "My juniors are each in charge of a zone and if you want I'll send them to you to explain the traffic regulations of their respective zones."

This explanation obviously had them stumped.

"Unfortunately, I am the only DCP (Traffic), there isn't even an Additional DCP. So how do you want it?"

She was told that there would be no prior recordings and she would have to go live on the air. If she made a mistake she had it. She did go on the air, ten times at that, and without a single flaw. The one officer whom some of her seniors were never tired of saying was publicity hungry got national and international coverage, in colour, ten times over!...by her own preparation, her own work, her own destiny !

7

Delhi to Goa and Beyond

The shift from Delhi to Goa was a traumatic experience for Kiran. She had put her heart and soul into her work as DCP (Traffic) and her '*junoon*' (passion) at that time was to succeed one hundred per cent. The Asian games traffic arrangements were quite indicative of the zeal that was firing her at that time. Yet even while she was in the thick of this cumbersome task, she was being sent 'signals' that she would be tolerated in Delhi only till the duration of the games! And so it was. She was transferred to Goa as soon as the games were over.

"Postings are a part of the job and they have to come sooner or later," says Kiran today. "I easily could have done nine months more. What did trouble me, though, was that my seven-year-old daughter was being treated for nephritis and needed me to be with her as much as possible."

At that point of time, Kiran's husband, Brij Bedi, being Amritsar based, was not in Delhi and the child had her supportive grandparents and her mother for comfort.

She appealed to the ministry for a delay in her transfer at least till her daughter's condition became stable. There was no response to her appeals and she was given no proper hearing.

In this context, let Kiran speak for herself:

I recall how I had to wait endlessly to even get an appointment with officers I thought could help. All I was hoping for was to make them feel the agony the dislocation would cause to my seven-year-old daughter and me. But I was expecting what does not exist in the Government, i.e., sensitivity. I also realised here and now that all along in my traffic work I had 'actually' made no friends in power. I had obliged no one then by working for equal enforcement of law. On the contrary, I had placed myself in a very vulnerable situation where those who had got offended by my 'arrogance of equal law' alone could help. I found them 'attempting' to teach me my first lesson – 'favour' your seniors blindly, if you want 'favours'. It was a humiliating and repelling atmosphere in the corridors of bureaucracy. I could not bear it any more. I decided to leave for Goa.

But I left my heart and soul behind.

In May 1983 a well-known Goan journalist Mario Cabral e Sa interviewed Kiran, who could not hold back her feelings:

I FEEL BANISHED

"Yes in a way I feel banished in Goa," Kiran Bedi, the high profile former Delhi 'supercop', told this correspondent. *"Banished in the sense,"* she hastened to qualify, *"that I have been separated from my only daughter who had to be kept back on serious medical grounds in Delhi with my mother".*

The little girl suffers from nephritis and after one year of all available allopathic treatment she is now in the hands of a good Delhi homoeopath Dr. P.S. Khokkar. Mrs. Bedi was posted to Goa recently for a three-year period.

She will not admit that her sudden transfer to Goa had anything to do with the 'famous' traffic ticket issued to Dhirendra Brahmachari in Delhi. *"We never know what happens in those circles",* she said, asserting that she does not go by rumours and Goa was just another posting and a beautiful place too.

Only she sees no way of keeping herself away for three years from her ailing daughter. *"My daughter needs me,"* she kept repeating.

Right now she is well on senior police officers' necks deep in CHOGM [Commonwealth Heads of Government Meet] retreat, planning the traffic and security.

(The Daily, 11 May 1983)

Kiran remembers that on the publication of this interview she was asked to offer her first explanation to the then Chief Secretary of Goa, K.K. Mathur. "This was a case akin to an injured who is expected not to speak of the pain but remain injured", says Kiran.

"Goa as a place of work is beautiful. Its people are relaxed, warm and disciplined," Kiran recalls with fond feelings. "I reached a place which had a heart of its own! Beautiful, noble and warm! I could spend a lifetime at the Aguada Beach, or driving past the tall coconut trees. I drove past innumerable churches and holy crosses. They reminded me of the holy pictures of my school days. I knew I was in another home of God, and I felt comfortable."

Her 'Crane' reputation had preceded her, much to her surprise. There were expectations of repeat performances! Citizens of Goa started to state their problems in traffic regulation and expected one and all to get disciplined just because she had landed there.

But what were the resources with which she could provide the 'best'? A total force of twenty-five traffic officers for the whole of Goa? The capital, Panjim; the busy market centre, Margao; the busy port area that also had the airport, Vasco da Gama; and yet another business centre, Mapusa. Each of these centres had serious traffic problems.

Right through her NCC days in college Kiran had been very proud and fond of her uniform. And in Goa she found that the depleted force at her command was used to working without a uniform. The reason was simple enough. The people of Goa did not respect them enough for, as it is, being so few in number they couldn't do much at all. Hence it was almost a case of having given up. Without any 'visible' demonstration of traffic control, the roads were free-for-all highways of death and destruction.

The sparse force found it prudent to remain in the background.

The very first meeting she called of the Goa traffic police could very well have been a cameo from one of the run-of-the-mill Hindi movies. Belts slipping beneath paunchy waistlines, shoes like they'd been fished out of the sea, and dirty uniforms and headgear crying out for replacement. Twenty-five such men standing in a group not just reeking of Fenny (a very potent and popular Goan brew made out of coconut) but also demonstrating its aftereffects, looking in awe at the trim and immaculately uniformed officer addressing them.

"As it is I am allergic to strong perfumes, and this 'aroma' was almost making me nauseous," recalls Kiran, with an 'ugh'.

She explained to her men the benefits of becoming 'visible'. They should be proud of their uniform, she told them, and should wear it with pride and dignity. They had not opted for this job to lurk around in streets in civvies like discards of society. They had joined this profession to come forth and help the administration to sort out the problems of society, and, more importantly, to be seen to be doing so. The lecture was long and sincere and ended with her requesting them not to carry the tell-tale signs of Fenny with them, at least while they were on duty.

The traffic squad, inspired by their new leader, became a rejuvenated force. For the first time in years, the Goans saw traffic police in uniform constantly on the roads and actually helping in untangling the snarls that were the order of the day for Goa traffic. The gesture was sincere and executed earnestly and the community responded to it. They let the SP (Traffic) know verbally and through letters that they appreciated her sincerity of purpose and that they would do their best to cooperate with her. Various meetings were held regularly with different groups of the community to identify their problems and involve them in their solution. Several new features were introduced, such as clearance drives, systematisation of traffic flow, community interaction with market and institutional associations, open house meetings, prosecutions and educational and awareness programmes in collaboration with the Rotary Club.

The Goa traffic department soon became a no-nonsense, highly effective force. Their rapid movement on motorcycles all over the state soon put fear into the hearts of the erring motorists who promptly started referring to them as 'hell's angels'. Over 3000 traffic cases were booked within a period of six months.

Even while the community was appreciating and responding to these new measures wholeheartedly, the administration revealed its greater-than-thou attitude. A report was received at the traffic control room that the footpath below the State Secretariat was being used as a car park for VIP vehicles. The traffic officer who reached the spot for investigation asked the drivers of the vehicles to clear the area but got no response from them. He then issued a warning to them that their vehicles would be *challaned* if they did not do so. A photographer of a local newspaper was on the scene and he took a picture of the cars that were parked there. The picture showed even the IG's car, but it left just before the warning was issued.

The press played up the incident and, as in Delhi, so in Goa, Kiran was hauled up by the Chief Minister's office. She was told to issue a correction to the press and to withdraw the police action. She refused point-blank saying that if there were any clarifications to be sought they should be done from the Secretariat. The traffic police action, she maintained, was correct and any compromise on the initiative taken by the officer concerned would demoralise the entire force and stall the momentum created in traffic management and would make the force lose all the credibility it had striven so hard to build up in the eyes of the community. With some sort of a vague warning, she was curtly asked to leave.

The Goa administration had provided the SP (Traffic) with one black Ambassador car and the DSP with a jeep. The car was in a mess and since there was no DSP Kiran got the jeep overhauled and had it painted white with fluorescent red stripes. A loudspeaker and a siren were mounted.

"The siren was not to clear the way for VIPs but for the common man, to feel good that we were on the road for him", she declares with her characteristic impish grin.

The day Kiran reached Goa from Delhi, while on her way to Panjim from the airport, she had to cross the Zuari river by ferry as the bridge was just nearing completion. A few months later the bridge was ready. Yet it still remained closed for the public who continued to use the ferry. The administration had been trying, desperately to invite a VIP from Delhi to inaugurate it but no confirmation of dates had been secured. The bridge therefore had to remain closed. Kiran was patrolling in the area one day and saw a huge snarl-up at the ferry point. She decided to drive over the bridge and with the help of her operator and driver she removed all the blockades and crossed over. She then diverted the waiting traffic over the bridge, thereby 'inaugurating' the bridge with a down-to-earth approach. The people of Goa loved her for this gesture.

"The bridge was inaugurated by a person on duty for whom the people always came first," she says mock-sternly and then laughs, "and today it does not have an inaugural stone and goes by its own name and not that of any VIP." Obviously, the administration realised it would make them look foolish if they re-inaugurated the bridge. Surprisingly, this is one of the few incidents of its kind in her career where she was not hauled up by the bureaucracy or the politicians. She, however, gave them another chance.

The Exposition of St. Xavier's body used to be a momentous occasion for the Christian community of India. The body of the Saint is preserved in a reasonably good condition and exhibited to the public in a glass case on the occasion of the Exposition. Some years back, however, it was discovered that such exposure was affecting the condition of the body and so the practice has now been stopped. Thousands upon thousands of people would flock to Goa on the occasion. The inflow of traffic from neighbouring Karnataka would be almost non-stop. Such an influx would certainly put immense pressure on the road traffic, specially around the church area. The worst affected were naturally the pedestrians, of whom countless numbers suffered physical injuries by being scruffed by the cars that insisted on driving right up to the cathedral gate itself. The traffic too remained locked for days together.

On the occasion of the Exposition the scanty Goa traffic police would be bolstered by a few imports from the Karnataka traffic police. But the purpose of this bolstering was clearly that the police should ensure that the VIPs' cars reached the cathedral gates. "VIPs never got to see the chaos. The police are content with saluting their bosses and giving them special right of way. VIPs considered this privilege their right, the police their duty and the people their destiny," explains Kiran today.

But this time things were *not* going to be the same. It was going to be the people's turn to avail of their right for a safe, obstruction-free pedestrian passage and parking space with uniformed men to regulate the flow of traffic and pedestrians. The VIPs were to be given a nearby parking lot from where they would have to walk to the gate. This would eliminate the problems the pedestrians faced due to the VIPs and police vehicles. The people loved the arrangement and the VIPs resented it. As Kiran puts it: "The people appreciated it but the VIPs called for my apologies and explanations."

One of the senior ministers of the Goa cabinet visited the cathedral. His car was stopped at the parking lot meant for VIPs and he was requested to walk the remaining few yards to the cathedral gate. This was never heard of in the Goa VIP circles and the matter was taken up with Chief Minister Pratapsingh Rane.

Kiran was summoned to the CM's office and asked to tender an apology to the concerned minister.

She replied: "Is the honourable minister not well, Sir?"

"The minister has the honour to drive to the gate. You must correct your traffic arrangements."

"You may be aware, Sir, of the people's appreciation for this arrangement?" Kiran had the courage to ask the CM.

"Never mind the public. Ministers must be allowed to drive right up to the gate," he insisted.

"But that would mean having no traffic arrangements at all."

"Who made these arrangements?"

"I did, Sir."

"Did the IGP (Inspector-General of Police) approve of them?"

"Yes, Sir."

"Then I will speak to him. I shall tell him to change the arrangements."

"You may do so, Sir. But then may I request to be relieved of traffic duties."

"We'll see about that," said the CM, ending the meeting.

The CM, it appears, never spoke to the IGP. The public was extremely appreciative of the relief its members got. They could park their vehicles properly, walk to the church and return in an orderly way. They could pull out their vehicles without waiting for hours for others to give way. The police were there for them. But this was not the way the ministers wanted things to be. They perhaps never forgave Kiran for treating them as equals!

But there were others who were treated as equally important who would never forget the November of 1983. That was the time when the Commonwealth Heads of Government Meet (CHOGM) was being held in Goa. This was a great event for the region. A number of benefits that would have taken years to materialise came instantly: Total lighting of the new airport road; electronic telephone exchange; road carpeting; bridge repairs; wireless equipment; and many other facilities. Three defence helicopters were pressed into service for road clearance. Cranes were brought in from Delhi. A signals system was incorporated to assist traffic policemen, constant air surveillance was provided and, best of all, over 1200 students of Goa colleges joined in for traffic duties.

All these 'bonanzas' were made possible by the then Lt. Governor of Goa, Daman and Diu, K.T. Satarawala, and Kiran Bedi's strong belief in community cooperation. Regular meetings were held with businessmen and heads of institutions to discuss and plan out traffic management methods and the community responded in a very generous way. Goa came on the world map with all its bounties of nature.

The Commonwealth Heads of Government were housed at a top-notch hotel, called Fort Aguada (of the Taj Group), located on the Aguada beach, one of the most beautiful beaches of Goa. The meeting of these heads was also scheduled to take place in the same hotel. Special cottages had been constructed for the visiting dignitaries. Prime Ministers Indira Gandhi and Margaret Thatcher were the star attractions, besides Queen Elizabeth herself. Amongst the men, the most sought after was Prime Minister Pierre Trudeau of Canada. The route from the airport to Fort Aguada was 40 km long and the VIPs had a choice between driving or flying by helicopter. Some chose to travel by road. This meant giving them a total right of way all along the 40 km route. The route was one long stretch, with only intertwining small lanes. Since the motorcade would be expected to be driving past very fast, it had to be ensured that no vehicle or pedestrian came in the way. Therefore, it was all the more essential for all these small lanes to be physically manned by vigilant cops at the point where they met the main VIP carriageway. Where was the manpower to come from? The 25 Goa policemen were far too inadequate to meet the traffic requirements for the airport route, for the places where the functions would be held and for normal traffic outside as well as within the four towns of Panaji, Margao, Mapusa and Vasco da Gama. Kiran drafted a few policemen from Karnataka who had reported for duty. But they were not trafffic trained.

CHOGM was one great occasion for the Goans to participate in. But alas! It was to be an all-VIP function that had no place for the common man. The people of Goa would only hear the helicopters flying over their heads and the zooming of the speeding cars on their roads! Security regulations required them to be kept away. But not necessarily from traffic arrangements. Kiran required many hands for making route arrangements, and discovered this was a great occasion for legitimately involving the young Goans and at least letting them become witness to some of the goings-on so that this young generation could carry forward the memory of the event. She decided to involve all the NCC cadets of Goa in traffic regulation, all along the VIP route.

Goa's youth participated enthusiastically in CHOGM, and not merely as spectactors, but as trained police cadets. All the 1200 youngsters recruited for the job turned out in white and blue dresses, red lanyards, whistles, white socks and PT shoes. All of them sported golf caps. Girls had tied their hair, while the boys had theirs neatly trimmed. These youngsters had been trained over a period of six Sundays in traffic drills by Kiran Bedi and her team of officers; her Delhi Police junior colleague, Subinspector Sarabpal Singh, who was a great asset for her during the Delhi Asian games, had been specially called for duty for this purpose. The cadets had learnt to regulate traffic and salute smartly! It was these youngsters who managed the bylanes, which otherwise would have been unattended. While doing their duty they also waved at the dignitaries driving past who saw strings of students dotted all along the 40-km route. It was a rare sight to see! The students attracted the attention of one and all. President Trudeau and Mrs Gandhi stopped their motorcades to say 'hello' to some of them. This gesture delighted the Goans.

Each of the Goan youngsters took home not just a visual memory but a beautiful certificate of gratitude given by the police. In many homes these certificates still stand displayed. Even the Governor of Goa, as if not to be left behind, sent an appreciation letter to the police.

Once CHOGM was over, Kiran rang up her house in Delhi, and her daughter Saina, also called Guchoo, answered the phone. It was daytime and Kiran wondered why she had not gone to school. She replied, "Mama, it's a holiday". Kiran's mother came on the line and told her that she should return to attend to Guchoo for she needed her total attention. She told her that all along, because of the exigencies of her work, they had held back the information on Guchoo's deteriorating health from her and that it could no longer be risked. Guchoo's nephritis had gone beyond control and she needed immediate hospitalisation.

Kiran put in an application for leave on the ground of her daughter's serious condition. The leave was recommended by her IGP, Rajendra Mohan. The date of departure as requested in her application arrived, but there was no response from the Secretariat as yet. Meanwhile, she came to know that a particular BSF (Border Security Force) plane which had flown in with the BSF equipment for the CHOGM arrangements was flying straight back to Delhi. If the leave had been formally sanctioned she could have gone on the same plane and saved three days and nights if she had to travel by train. She was out of money to fly as she had to maintain two establishments, not to mention the enormous medical expenditure. She was in mental agony as to how to reach her daughter, and decided not to wait for the clerical approval. She did not have the confidence that the IGP would have the courage to permit her to go despite his recommendations to the Government. She decided to risk her posting in Goa and left for Delhi to face a tougher challenge: the risk to her daughter's life.

The Dornier aircraft in which she flew was piloted by Inspector-General (Air), the late Tarlok Singh Dhaliwal, who was on CHOGM duty. Those five hours in the aircraft were long hours. Kiran reached home just after sunset. Her daughter was thrilled to see her, totally unaware of what she was looking like. Her face was swollen and her stomach bloated; her face had a double chin and her eyes had become Mongoloid because of water retention and protein shortage in her body. Kiran took her straight to AIIMS (All India Institute of Medical Sciences), New Delhi, where she was admitted under the personal care of Dr Veena Kalra and Dr R.N. Shrivastava, both specialists in nephrology. Kiran's daughter stayed admitted for a week, after which she was allowed to go home. The child needed all possible care.

Kiran sent a request for leave extension; instead of granting it, she was declared absconding and absent without leave. It seems the CM made a statement to the UNI (United News of India) in Goa. The UNI in Delhi got back to her and asked her what the matter was and whether she was really absconding. She told them that she certainly was not and that circumstances had compelled her to be with her daughter. She told them that if they wished they could come and see for themselves, and they did. On seeing her daughter's condition, the UNI, Delhi, wrote a strong rebuttal of the Goa CM's statement. It put the record straight, but it did expose the Goa administration, and made its members even more hostile to Kiran. They refused to sanction any leave at all. Here is a news item which appeared in this context then:

LEAVE LANDS KIRAN IN TROUBLE

"What use is this job if I can't attend to my suffering child", laments a harassed Goa police chief Kiran Bedi, who is accused of absenting herself from duty once the CHOGM retreat responsibilities were over.

On learning that her child, Guchoo, was suffering from acute kidney infection, Mrs Bedi proceeded on 15 days' leave from 5 December [1983]. Since then she has been at her child's bedside in the Capital.

A former Delhi Traffic police chief, Kiran Bedi was posted to Goa in March last year [1983]. She says: "Even then I had to rush back to the Capital as the child had developed kidney problem".

This time, she claims, Goa Inspector-General Rajendra Mohan had sanctioned her leave initially for 15 days and later extended it on the ground that the child required constant attention.

When asked about the explanation the Goa administration had demanded of her, she described the case as "unique in which the IG sanctions the leave of a senior police officer and the State administration cancels it".

Medical Report

"No mother would ever tell a lie about her child's illness... I have sent them medical reports and certificates only to make them realise the gravity of the situation," adds Mrs Bedi,

who is in a dilemma whether to resume duty or attend to the suffering child.

Guchoo is suffering from "nephritis" and is undergoing homoeopathy treatment, while the medical examinations are conducted both by the AIIMS and the Willingdon Hospital.

When is she expected to resume duty?

"Whenever my child is fully recovered... I have sent a personal letter to the IG and a detailed explanation to the Goa administration about the circumstances in which I am on leave."

She says that during the eleven years of her service, this was the only occasion when she went on leave. "Otherwise my leave always lapses.... There is plenty of leave in my account."

Ever since she proceeded on leave on 5 December last, there has been no objection from the Goa administration and she presumed that her leave had been sanctioned. "I am not absenting myself from the duty... I am on leave for which I am entitled."

(Patriot, 30 January 1984)

Reproduced now is a handwritten letter that Kiran wrote to Rajendra Mohan, her IGP (Goa):

To,   25.1.81

Shri Rajendra Mohan
IGI, Goa

Sir

I received your telegram, in which
I have been informed that even my
first 15 days leave has not been sanctioned
and therefore extension asked for, obviously
is not sanctioned.

The leave for 15 days which
I had asked for, and applied for
around 29th of Nov — apparently
according to the telegram has been
rejected being turned down after
One Month and a half. If I understand
Correctly, my leave application has
been decided after a month and a
half —!

Sir I had applied for
leave on medical grounds of my
daughter — I stated that in my
subsequent telegram also
My daughter has Nephrotic Syndrome.
When I returned she was under a
severe relapse. — My parents
deliberately did not inform me earlier

is that I do not get disturbed
impending / during Chopu — But
soon after that my Mother told
me the _truth_, and I flew back
"It is extremely important for me
to attend to my daughter during the
period — and it took her
more than a month to improve —
I was never in a position to leave
an ailing child behind —
She is still not back to normal
and is still off school again
we have changed to another doctor
again, — since Allopathy has really
no cure, except to give CORTISONS —
She still has a lot of swelling, —
She is still retaining Urine —
& therefore ancillary reactions —
I am still not in a position to say
when would I be in a position to
return — since as a Mother —
I am not in a position to leave
her alone

I too shall be greatful Sir, if the Administration takes a humane approach to my problem

I am an officer who is most ill at ease without work —, and I will never feign sickness for my child, who is dearest to me —

In my $11\frac{1}{2}$ yrs of service I have not availed of more than three $\frac{1}{2}$ mths of earned leave so far —. Since I just did not need it —.

I shall be grateful, if the Administration helps me tide over my present problem. I shall return to duty, as soon as I am in position to leave behind my daughter

I shall be grateful, if my prayer relieved, since I am in need of funds too. Hoping & believing the Administration will appreciate my difficulties, thank you. Your's etc —

Kisan Rao

For six months Kiran was not given any assignment. Whatever she may have thought about this sudden void in her career, it certainly gave her plenty of time to spend with her daughter and to bring her back to a normal, stable condition. It was only during this stage that she sought an audience with the then Union Home Secretary, T.N. Chaturvedi. He lent a sympathetic ear to what she had to say and had her posted to the Railway Protection Force (RPF) as an Assistant Inspector-General of Police working at headquarters.

Kiran was extremely relieved on leaving this position, short of six months. She recalls her stint here as follows: "Since I was in the headquarters dealing with personnel matters and directly assisting the Director-General, a number of rank officers who had a grievance would come to see me. I heard them out and then responded as per their needs. After due examination, I put up the files to my boss, but then I realised that nothing would come back. After a reasonable period of waiting, I went to my senior to ask for a decision on the files I had sent. To my surprise I was advised not to be positive, and that I ought to have learnt my lessons from Delhi traffic and Goa! I felt suffocated! I was facing not only a big wooden table but also a wooden heart. Such a person, I feel, has no moral right to be occupying a position which decided the fate of thousands of men and women posted all over the country, for ensuring the security of the Railways, the passengers and the freight."

Next, Kiran was posted as Deputy Director in the Directorate General of Industrial Contingency (DGIC) under the Department of Industrial Development. This department was expected to closely monitor industrial relations and send out intelligence and analysis reports. Its head office was located at Delhi, with zonal offices in Delhi, Bangalore and Patna.

This assignment at DGIC was on an all-India basis and gave Kiran a wide jurisdiction. Her bosses in Delhi were Brijinder Sahay and Bob Murari, both senior IAS officers, in the Department of Industrial Development.

Kiran found working with them, and in this non-police department, refreshingly different. She added to her daily newspaper reading *The Economic Times* in order to pick up the relevant industrial news and also to stay up to date with the latest developments and to target priorities. She reorganised her office to meet the requirements of her assignment. She sent a note to her seniors on her first three weeks in office, which ran as follows:

1. *The officers performing field duties have been found to be rather vague as regards knowledge of their actual duties. They are not even aware of the exact responsibilities assigned to the DGIC. Thus due to lack of information with the field officers there has been diffidence in their working.*

2. *Records maintained are incomplete and vital aspects of information non-existent; e.g., items of production which would need preference in production in the eventuality of strikes.*

3. *Monitoring is being done of some public sector units and a very large number of private sector units, whereas the assigned task is primarily of monitoring of labour relations of public sector units and important private units. There is no existing system for a concentrated and*

selected monitoring, more so in view of manpower resources available.

4. *Contents of the model contingency plan offered to the undertakings so far are the same as drafted in 1971.*

5. *The offices in this unit have never had an opportunity to get exposed to any training in labour laws which they are required to refer to in different situations.*

6. *The weekly digest which we were circulating was merely a cyclostyled copy.*

7. *This office which issued the important weekly digest, reporting on labour situations, has not even a cyclostyling machine of its own. Presently the work is got done from outside.*

8. *The staff on field duties are not provided with advance TA [travelling allowance] and thus the field staff feel very handicapped in incurring expenditure first and reimbursement later.*

Efforts Underway

1. *A three-week course on labour laws for the officers and staff of DGIC has been arranged with the Labour Institute, Safdarjung Enclave, New Delhi.*

2. *The officers have been read over and shown the annual report of the Department of Industrial Development wherein the responsibilities of the DGIC have been written.*

3. *The card index system has been started and a separate card for each establishment being covered has been opened. A red card attachment system has been systemised to immediately identify the unit having labour/production problems. This will facilitate concentrated monitoring of units requiring greater attention.*

4. *The weekly digest has now a new appearance and a wider circulation.*

5. *Coordination has been made with the Labour Ministry and the Bureau of Public Enterprises. In coordination with the Bureau of Public Enterprises, zonal meetings are proposed to establish a direct communication and encourage a discussion/session on the issues which should form part of an ideal contingency plan, which is practical and useful. After that all establishments could be given time to prepare and send to DGIC the contingency plans so prepared. These meetings will help DGIC achieve in a month what in a normal course would take a year's time.*

6. *The object of this interaction is also to introduce the officers of the DGIC to their counterparts, facilitating future functioning.*

7. *Welfare aspects and purchase of an electronic typewriter are under active progress.*

She next set about correcting the basics of the DGIC functioning. Alongside, she began travelling to the various industrial units to see for herself the ground realities. On the basis of her findings, she produced certain reports for circulation, some of which were trend-setting in nature (given later in this chapter). The main objective was to bring about coordination both at the state and Central levels according to the demands of the situation so as to effectively respond to industrial unrest or breakdown.

The following press report sums up the developments succinctly:

FLEXING THE CORPORATE MUSCLE

Five minutes of warm up exercise before the start of work and having the same meal in a common canteen can do wonders for accelerating growth and increasing industrial production.

This seemingly ordinary formula for increased production has been suggested to industry by the Directorate General of Industrial Contingency (DGIC), a wing of the Industry Ministry. DGIC has circulated a special report on better industrial relations and management practices to over a thousand industries in the public and private sectors.

The report, prepared by DGIC officials after conducting a field study for three months, advises industry to maintain healthy industrial relations and management practices, as these necessarily lead to growth and increased production.

Besides warming up exercise and a common meal,

the report suggests that practices such as the wearing of a uniform by the workers and the managerial staff bring about a sense of cohesiveness and unity in an organisation.

The report indicates that better leave facilities with incentives and observing national holidays and national festivals can help avoid a situation of devious behaviour. Bonus incentives linked to those not availing of any casual and earned leave for a quarter ensure regular attendance.

It also observes that units having an "open way" of working function more efficiently. Moreover, training for managerial personnel has an excellent effect on productivity. Similarly, streamlining of operational procedures (like giving workers their wages at the place of work) motivates them to function better.

The report notes that discussions on and providing solutions to quality control problems by workers have a direct bearing on improving quality and productivity in a unit. Introduction of suggestions scheme and giving rewards for any suggestions accepted can lead to a sense of recognition and involvement among workers.

Several industries have shown interest in the DGIC report as they want to incorporate the suggestions in their day-to-day functioning.

DGIC functions as the "security adviser" to the Government, suggesting steps for the proper protection of installations so that accidents are prevented.

(Financial Express, 5 October 1985)

It is interesting to know how she enlarged the scope of her learning. She and her team visited those industrial establishments which had a reputation for effective management as well as those which did not enjoy such a reputation. They met cross-sections of people, shared their canteen meals and held discussions with them. After that, they produced objective reports for countrywide circulation. Some of the reports are now reproduced.

I. SPECIFIC PRACTICES

We in the Directorate General of Industrial Contingency (hereinafter called DGIC) regularly visit public and private sector undertakings to observe practices in industrial relations management. We have found that the growth of an industry of any sector or size is directly linked with industrial management practices. The healthier the environment through its communication system, the more prosperous it would be, benefiting all concerned.

Some of the useful practices which we came across during our visits to growth-oriented industries, we would like to share for information and adoption wherever required.

Practices such as:

Wearing of Uniform by One and All

This practice is found to have brought about a sense of cohesiveness and unity in the organisation. The uniform was seen to be worn from the shop floor worker to the top manager. It was seen that the worker was feeling a sense of pride in wearing his uniform, even while commuting in it.

Practice of Warming-up Exercises before the Start of Work

It was observed that a five-minute workout as a group before the start of work was proving useful. Since all levels of workmen and management participate in the activity, it was found very productive for the industry. It was bringing in a feeling of team spirit, brotherhood and oneness, besides the main benefit of physical fitness, leading to fewer health problems.

Same Meal in the Canteen for Workers and Management

This is the practice where all ranks of the industry queue up to eat the same meal together at a common place. We found that such sharing of food was instrumental in bringing about team spirit and a further sense of pride and participation in the workers as it made them feel no less important than any other person in the management.

Suggestion Scheme Linked with Industrial Recognition and Rewards

We came across a documented hand-out which spelt out the suggestion scheme. There were formats and reward schemes linked with accepted suggestions. There are gold, silver and bronze cards for categorisation for accepted suggestions. Presentation of certificates and cash rewards is made by the officer signing the card. For instance, if the gold card has to be signed by the Chairman or Managing Director, the presentation shall be made by him alone, amidst all the workers of the unit. We found the organisation where this practice is being followed, and it made the workers feel not only as workers only but as "think-tanks" of the organisation. The workmen knew that their suggestions had a value for their organisation and that these shall benefit all, besides providing individual recognition. The scheme seems to have a total involvement of the workers and the management.

Constitution of Quality Circles

A practice of groups of workmen at the shop floor level discussing the problem of quality control and providing solutions to improving this has found to have a direct bearing on regular monitoring of quality and productivity in these establishments. Efforts made in these quality-circle meetings and results thereto were linked with status awards, which were found to be extremely attractive wherever observed.

Immediate Supervisor of the Workmen Better Trained than the Worker and Capable of Replacing the Worker in Case of Unplanned Absence

It was found that if the supervisor (his designation may be anything) is capable of both instructing and actually doing what he is supervising, this has an excellent effect on productivity. This makes the supervisor command both respect and authority.

Delivery of Workers' Dues at Their Work Place

The workers in the units where this care is taken did not have to line up for getting their pay and other dues nor are they required to fill up any forms or claims, etc. The procedure is so simplified that all deductions or additions are made at the source, without workmen having to send reminders.

No Work on National Holidays as well as on National Festivals with Incentives Leave System

It was observed that this practice had reduced absenteeism in the organisation to a negligible percentage. National festivals, which workmen anyway would want to go to celebrate, are treated as block earned leaves for everybody, thus avoiding a situation of any deviant behaviour. This period includes the days of national festivals and the single working days falling in between. There were bonus incentives also linked with those not availing any casual leave or earned leave for the quarter, while there was also the provision for leave encashment for 2/3 earned leave and casual leave with provision for accumulation facilities up to 180 days of earned leave. This practice had enabled the company to ensure regularly 96 per cent attendance.

Moderate, Neat and Similar Office Layout for All Ranks

It was observed that in some of the units all managerial levels had an open way of functioning with no additional frills attached to their respective offices. Each manager could see the other while sitting on the same type of furniture. There were no heavy carpets to lead to the offices of the top management. There were hardly any individual telephones. There was no system of peons to carry files or bring cups of tea. The seating plan was in such a manner that the file would be moving to the correct hands with minimum loss of time and effort....
We all know that prevention is always better than cure. In matters of industrial relations, cure comes only at a very heavy price.

II. CONSTITUTION OF A QUALITY CIRCLE

A Few Details

As already discussed under the head "Suggestion Scheme Linked with Industrial Recognition and Rewards", discussions in groups at the shop floor level are encouraged and are limited to a particular department. But in constitution of quality circles the scope for thinking of these groups becomes wider and is made at the level of the plant as a whole. Quality circles consist of:

(a) Group leader.
(b) Secretary.
(c) Treasurer.

Group leader: *He is the person who helps in implementing the suggestions in the unit. He also gives his guidance to the group and helps in bringing better ideas.*

Secretary: *He is responsible for preparing minutes of the meetings and considering the views of all members.*

Treasurer: *He keeps the record of rewards received by the group. He also organises how the money received through rewards is to be spent in the group. To strengthen group feeling, outings or picnics are arranged by him for enjoying collectively the reward money.*

Functioning

Meetings of quality circles are held after office hours only. For overstaying in the office, workmen get Rs. 3 per hour as canteen money for refreshment.

Quality circles are free to give suggestions in any part of the unit, i.e., for any department. Suggestions of the group are conveyed through suggestion forms and the minutes of the meeting are sent with the form.

Recognition of Group Circle Office Bearers

Colour photographs of the leaders are hung at the shop floor level at conspicuous places to give due recognition to the workmen putting in their extra effort for the benefit of all.

Advantages of Group Circles

By conducting such type of group activities talented workmen/ supervisors are spotted and a healthy competition begins amongst groups of workmen, thus keeping them mentally and physically engaged in thinking for the growth of the company.

The foregoing reports presented a brief, crisp and precise analysis and the relevant suggestions for tackling specific problems. They just could not be ignored. The DGIC was now making its presence felt, and those organisations which did not come out in a good light started questioning the legitimacy of the DGIC's jurisdiction. Such questioning was firmly and effectively replied to by Brijinder Sahay (Kiran's boss). This step strengthened DGIC work even further.

All reports of the DGIC, such as the special report and the intelligence bulletin, were being sent to the concerned decision- makers and needed due coordination. The objective behind this exercise was to achieve a collective focus on the problems without loss of time. Kiran made it a point to ensure that all important reports reached the Prime Minister (Rajiv Gandhi) directly. In the left-hand corner of each report, she used to write in her own hand (usually on single page reports) 'Mr. Prime Minister'.

Kiran learned a lot about the 'ins and outs' of management through first-hand observation. It came as pleasant surprise to her when she got a call from her DG, Brijinder Sahay, that she should fly out to Bokajan (Assam) to try and resolve the strike at the cement plant there. She eagerly accepted this opportunity. Kiran, along with S. Manoharan, the District Deputy Commissioner, went to the unit and succeeded in signing an agreement within 24 hours, ensuring that the workers' demands were satisfactorily met and they returned to work.

Some of the major units covered by the DGIC include Bokaro Steel Plant, Bharat Leather Corporation, Cochin Refineries and IDPL (Indian Drugs and Pharmaceuticals Limited) (Gurgaon).

It is interesting to learn that the DGIC, after Kiran left in October 1985, was wound up as part of an economy drive by the Government of India. Certainly, some degree of saving had been achieved, but, at the same time, 'inquisitive' police officers like Kiran would not get a chance to scrutinise carefully the functioning of the public sector industrial units.

According to the grapevine, the opinion was that the DGIC did not work before Kiran Bedi came, so what will it do after her? So let it be closed down.

8

Novel Methods, Novel Results

In 1980 bootlegging was rampant in Delhi, with a cartel of big-time smugglers and wholesalers getting liquor from across the borders and peddling it on the streets of Delhi. The 'Sansi' were a criminal tribe, declared as such during the British days, and had been traditionally involved in bootlegging. The members of this community were the people used by the cartel to further their criminal business. As Deputy Commissioner, West District, Kiran Bedi interacted with these tribals and involved herself in the process of their rehabilitation in non-criminal fields.

With patient and persuasive counselling and by winning the confidence of the community, this menace was successfully removed from the streets of Delhi. This, in fact, was her first exposure as a correctional police officer at heart. Incidentally, the Ramon Magsaysay award citation begins with the correctional work done as a police officer.

Reproduced below is a news item which appeared in this context, which is very explicit:

REFORMED SANSIS HELP BRING DOWN CRIME RATE

Incidence of bootlegging in west district appears to have declined following the "voluntary" decision by the Sansis of Madipur some months back to give up liquor distilling and to take up "legal" profession.

Though no planned jobs have been created specially for them, many Sansis have begun taking up new trades. According to Mrs Kiran Bedi, Deputy Commissioner of Police, West District, the fall in bootlegging had resulted in an appreciable drop in related crimes.

The problem of "connivance" still poses a major problem as even well-planned and executed schemes imposed from the top can run aground due to dishonesty in some pockets, she said. "Policemen are not all that innocent."

In the last few months, according to Mrs Bedi, about 10 officers and constables, detected while accepting "protection money" or believed to be conniving with illicit still operators, had been suspended. "These things cannot exist without police connivance and it is here that rooting out of bad elements must begin," she said.

(The Times-of India, 1 November 1980)

For effective interaction between the police and the public a system of setting up beat boxes was introduced in the west district of Delhi. Each constable was allotted a beat box of his own to be used as his 'office', i.e., in his own area under his responsibility for the benefit of the residents of the area who therefore did not necessarily have to come to the police station but instead could go to the beat box to seek help from the beat officer. The beat constable became a sort of community leader or elder and the distance between the public and the police was narrowed. Various petty offences could be reported to him and matters could be sorted out at the beat level itself. Not only did this system reduce pressure on the police stations but it also saved the public a considerable deal of harassment. The beat boxes themselves were erected with community sponsorship.

BEAT BOX: A POPULAR MOVE

In sharp contrast to the bruised and battered image that plagues the police force in most parts of the country, the police of Delhi's populous West District have of late been consciously turning out in their Sunday best, as it were, and wooing the public in a way that, with encouragement, could become a trend-setting move in cooperative peace-keeping.

Kicking off with a widely attended oath-taking ceremony on New Year's Day in which the entire staff of the West District police swore "to help anybody in need", this year [1981] alone more than 100 open-house public meetings have been held to encourage a dialogue with the community and to evolve effective methods of law enforcement.

The latest, and the most popular move has been the

setting up of the beat box
system, a significant and
wholly indigenous concept in
neighbourhood policing. In less
than a month, more than 100
blue and white beat boxes have
mushroomed in the West
District, funded entirely out of
neighbourhood donations.
These are manned for three
hours everyday by the local beat
constable, bringing police
assistance almost literally
within yelling distance of the
whole neighbourhood.

Effective   Security:
Backing this up is an intensive
system of monitoring with the
beat box constable being briefed
and debriefed every day by the
SHO [Station House Officer].
More significant is the sense of
security that the beat boxes
have brought, acting as
deterrent   scarecrows   to
prospective law-breakers. Said
Harbanslal Khurana, a
resident of Tilak Nagar:
"There was a great deal of
goondagardi in this area
before the introduction of the
beat boxes. Girls were harassed
and people felt very insecure.

But things have improved a
great deal now."

But the most important
result of this system is the
policeman's debut in the civic
arena, as an arbiter and peace
counsellor. Of the more than
800 complaints that are
processed by the beat box
constables every day, several
are of a nature that would
draw a blank at the police
station.

Community members often
seek out the beat box constable
to settle petty disputes between
squabbling   couples   or
neighbourhood brawlers. As
constable Rameshwar Dayal of
Mongolpuri resettlement area
said: "I have been sorting out
all sorts of problems --
husband-and-wife problems,
drunkards, women squabbling
at the water queues and so on.
We are like a sarpanch in a
village and people treat us like
that."

The beat box system seems
to have paid off with a major
psychological coup for the
constable as well. His new-
found role as a community

leader, with the full backing of the neighbourhood, serves not only to motivate him but also does wonders for his sagging self-esteem.

Clean Home: *Said Kiran Bedi, the dapper, rakish, Deputy Commissioner of Police, West District, and the moving force behind the experiment in cooperative peace-keeping: "Who would not accept a policeman who is ready to help? I would, if I were a citizen." With a woman's home-making instincts Bedi has set about putting her house in order, with a zeal that brooks no barriers. "The beat constable has started thinking that the beat is his home. Just as his home has to be kept clean, so has his beat to be kept clean," said Bedi.*

Behind the zeal is a conviction that any social scientist will share — that combating crime and keeping the peace is an activity which involves the entire community, and the police can only be effective so long as they enjoy

the support and cooperation of the community. By making public relations the bedrock of peace-keeping and law enforcement, Bedi has scored where strong-arm methods have failed. But support is slowly gathering. Says P.S. Bhinder, the embattled Commissioner of Delhi Police: "We have always felt that fighting crime is not just a police effort, but also a public effort. Nowhere in the world are criminals fought by law alone."

Public support seems to be one reliable factor in this move. Bedi put it this way: "We have found that if the police take one step forward, the public responds by taking five steps forward." But given the politicisation of the police, given the paralysing wage structure of the policemen and the rot within the law enforcement system, that one crucial step which could transform the police from a goon force into a peace force might just be insurmountable.

(India Today, 1-15 June 1981)

Kiran Bedi relates an interesting anecdote regarding these beat boxes. "The Lt. Governor of Delhi (S.L. Khurana), in a meeting with the Commissioner of Police and the various District Commissioners, asked us separately as to the number of beat boxes we had put up in our districts. One said five, another seven and so on. I told him I had 165. So he asked the Commissioner of Police, P.S. Bhinder, why the other districts could not have as many. Mr. Bhinder told him that if he were provided the finances he would be able to ask them to do so. The Lt. Governor then asked me how I had managed to get the finances and I told him that it was all through community effort. Mr. Bhinder apparently never forgave me for that. He thought I had upstaged him. I had no intention to do so."

In a concerted effort to prevent crime a ready reckoner of the criminals of West Delhi was published with the names of more than 3500 men and women (in an alphabetical order) having a criminal record since 1970. This 266-page manual, giving the criminals' past records, the area in which they lived as well as the *modus operandi* of their crimes, was distributed to all the nine police stations of Kiran's district to enable the duty officers to immediately check the antecedents of the criminals being brought in. The net result was a drastic fall in the crime rate.

The concept of a ready reckoner of criminals was carried forward during her tenure later as DIG (Range) in Mizoram (see Chapter 12 for details). However, this concept now evolved into a system of participative policing. Local leaders were given these lists so that people would be able to identify the criminals and help variously in detecting or rehabilitating such people. And this is how it was used.

CRIMINALS UNDER THE THUMB

The West District police has compiled a ready reference of criminals for use by police stations in the district.

The reference, which contains the names of 3522 persons with criminal records, runs into 266 bound pages. The names of the persons are listed in alphabetical order under the various sections of the Indian Penal Code.

Mrs Kiran Bedi, Deputy Commissioner of Police for the district, said that the ready reference would help policemen to ascertain immediately if the suspect had any previous record.

The ready reference will supplement the one prepared and circulated by the central crime record office at R.K. Puram. It will be updated from time to time.

(The Times of India, 12 July 1981)

In 1988 she took over charge as Deputy Director of the Narcotics Control Bureau (NCB). During this tenure she again hit the headlines. In a lightning swoop she made from Delhi into the verdant hills of Chakrata *tehsil* in the interiors of north-western Uttar Pradesh, she physically supervised the destruction of almost 12 hectares under illegal poppy and cannabis cultivation. This task she undertook in spite of the fact that it was the constituency represented by a powerful sitting Member of Parliament, Brahm Dutt, of the then ruling Congress Government.

There appears a discernible transparency in her work, especially in organisations which had otherwise been kept under a cloak of confidentiality. That not once was security relaxed only exposes the fact that it was only the fear of accountability that had given the guise of confidentiality to these organisations.

At every stage there was a keen interaction with the community which participated in a magnanimous way. Such confidence and faith exhibited by the community in a serving person can only be gained through honesty of intention and the will for achievement on the part of that individual.

In 1985 the reputation of the Delhi police was at an all-time low and the law and order situation was being condemned by one and all. The press was lambasting them left and right. Prime Minister Rajiv Gandhi called up the Commissioner of Police, Ved Marwah, and told him to do something about it. The CP replied that there was nothing much he could do about it as long as he did not have the right officers with him. Rajiv Gandhi told him to ask for any officer and that person would be given to him. The CP asked for Kiran Bedi and found himself stonewalled. The antipathy towards her on the part of the PM's office still continued and Rajiv was quite aware of it. The situation continued to deteriorate and after a month and a half the CP was called up again. This time, however, his request was granted and Kiran Bedi was transferred to headquarters as Deputy Commissioner of Police. Bedi found herself inundated with files, files and files. The table tops were overflowing with files and drawers were jammed shut because of them. Kiran adopted the policy of taking spot decisions and would dispose of the file there and then. The staff under her was a demoralised lot, burdened with problems ranging from lack of accommodation to lack of promotions. She wanted a large map to be displayed that showed the various police apartments lying vacant in the various districts. The allotment of these apartments had been used as a lever of influence to establish authority and to curry favour. The staff members were called to be interviewed before their posting so that, wherever possible, the officers could be accommodated nearer home, and they did not have to continue travelling 40 to 50 km daily. Lack of convenient accommodation had been one of the chief grouses of the police personnel and also one of the reasons given for their inefficiency. History was created at police HQ when 1600 promotions were made in a single day. These had been pending for the past six to seven years and no one had shown any concern for them. Kiran attributes the results to the dynamism of Ved Marwah and his impatience for getting results.

The drivers in the HQ pool were inspired by Kiran's problem-solving approach and took their case to her. They maintained that from the day they joined service to the day they retired they remained constables without any promotion whatsoever. Bedi took up their case and recommended a three-tier promotion system for them to the Home Ministry. She suggested that they should be promoted from constable to head constable and finally to subinspector. The Home Ministry merely sat on the file. Bedi then told the drivers to file a writ of mandamus in the Delhi High Court and to make Police Headquarters (PHQ) a party. The court took up the case and summoned her. She, of course, said that PHQ agreed completely with the drivers' cause and that the Commissioner of Police had recommended a three-tier grade. The court then directed the Home Ministry to look into the matter of the drivers' promotion and that is how today many police drivers retire as subinspectors. Kiran's driver who was a constable in the late 70s is today a subinspector.

Standing instructions were issued by Bedi to her office staff that if any file was not cleared within three days the person concerned would be called to personally explain the delay. They realised she meant business when they saw her clearing the tremendous backlog that she had inherited, and put their nose to the grindstone. Ved Marwah had reason enough to pat himself on the back for the choice of officer he had made to the Prime Minister. Kiran, on her part, gives the entire credit for work to Ved Marwah who allowed the expression of leadership qualities and encouraged work based on integrity.

The question of pending file work came up again when she took over charge of Tihar Jail. There were 140 files concerning vigilance matters pending at HQ as also a large number of prison staff under suspension for the past six to eight years or even more. These cases mostly pertained to an attempted escape bid through a tunnel that was later discovered to be a very old and forgotten sewer. A large number of the jail staff was suspended pending enquiry and investigation. Many of them were not even on duty when the incident occurred but, regardless, they were also punished. She kept on hearing the bogey of 'tunnel case, tunnel case' whenever she took up the issue of the pending files and decided to attack the issue head-on. She remarked in Punjabi: "*Keda* tunnel case, *le ao to sahi, paddhien te sahi*" (What tunnel case, bring it to me so that I can at least read it). There she discovered that a Bakshi Commission had already looked into the matter and found no evidence of any mala fide intentions on the part of the suspended staff. With that as sufficient evidence, she cleared the mess in one stroke.

When queried, "Did you do it because you thought the staff would be grateful to you and work with you under a feeling of obligation?" she replied: "The suspended staff was already on more than 75 per cent of the salary, so why should I continue to waste manpower which is being paid anyway – and for so long! I also did it on the individual merits of the case seen in the light of the Bakshi Commission Report. Remember, I was there to take decisions and not to postpone them. You see, as head of the department if I do not solve problems then I myself would become part of the problem."

The North District was one of the six police districts of Delhi, and Kiran was Deputy Commissioner Police, North District, in August 1986. This district was one of the largest in area terms, around 412 sq. km with a population of over 1,900,000 then. (Delhi is now divided into nine police districts.) There were 83 villages in this area that bordered the neighbouring state of Haryana. The district was (and continues to be) communally very sensitive and highly crime-infested. Dacoities, burglaries, pick-pocketing and drug-peddling were rampant when Kiran took over charge. In a record time she made 1033 externment proceedings and placed all of them under rehabilitative surveillance. The heinous crime rate dropped rapidly with regular spot arrests and swift investigation. Community help again came to the fore with the residents very forthcoming in their assistance. *Chowkidars* of different localities would be called to the police station for a monthly parade conducted by the Station House Officer (SHO). They were

briefed about the activities in their respective areas and
given necessary information about notorious criminals of
the area. The *chowkidars* became an extension arm of the
police force and were treated as such. This feature gave
their morale a big boost and contributed greatly to their
efficiency and discipline.

By sifting through the mass of statistical data it was
discovered that one particular region was contributing the
maximum to the field of crime. This was known as the
Yamuna Pushta Jhuggi area, with a population of around
1,25,000. The area suffered from abject poverty and lacked
even the basic amenities such as drinking water and
domestic electricity. Drug peddling was rampant amongst
these people and women played the more active role in
this activity. Kiran held a public meeting in the area and
informed the residents that no form of criminal activity
would be tolerated by her force. Man or woman, no one
would be spared. There certainly would not be any
unjustified arrests to harass them, but then their criminal
activities would in no way be condoned.

This warning was backed up by immediate action. A
number of spot arrests were made daily and many were
sent out of Delhi. Such action had an electric effect upon
the people and the large turnout at the next public
meeting was a good indicator of this effect. The women
again represented the more vociferous segment here. They
admitted that they indulged in criminal activities like drug
peddling but what alternative did they have? They lived
in such poverty that they had to resort to such means to
get even one square meal for their children. What
alternatives was the DCP (North) going to offer these
hapless women so that their children would not starve?

What answer did she have to their problems? Here was a matter of ethics that could counteract the noblest of intentions.

The Assistant Commissioner Police, D.L. Kashyap, and Station House Officer, M.D. Mehta, assured them that the police would extend to them all help but that they must first establish their bona fides. Thus was a pact of understanding and mutual trust born that day. But such things are easier said than done. However, as with most of her good intentioned commitments, help was not far to seek. A philanthropist of Delhi, Padam Sen Gupta, offered generous help in the form of sewing machines for the women of the Yamuna Pushta Jhuggi area. With festive fervour the '*Apradh Sudhar Silai School*' (Criminals Reform Centre) was launched. The very first job entrusted to these women was the stitching of hundreds of green shirts for the porters of the Chandni Chowk area. Needless to say, the number of women drug-peddlers and petty criminals came tumbling down. Today, in the same area, she, through her organisation Navjyoti, benifits around 5000 children, men and women through education, vocational training and health care.

Such has been the hallmark of Kiran's crime prevention activities. These activities have always been tempered by humanistic considerations and are based on ground realities. It is only for these reasons that the community responds to her appeals for help in furthering her people-oriented programmes. Again, on the basis of the aforementioned considerations, she has made a very broad appeal to the business tycoons of the country for the big industrial houses to adopt one village each.

9

Acts of Conscience?

Kiran has always viewed the role of the police as being primarily one of prevention of crime and criminality and then of detection and prosecution. There are many instances that convince one of her conviction. As mentioned in Chapter 8, in 1980, for example, when she got rid of the menace of bootlegging.

In August 1986, she was appointed Deputy Commissioner Police, North District. In 1980, when she was DCP (West), the crime scene had revealed that illicit brewing and bootlegging were prominent. For her now it was the sale and consumption of 'smack' (a street name for heroin) that was the focus of criminal activities. One reason for the drop in bootlegging could, of course, have been the increase in official liquor vending as the Delhi Administration became a bit more liberal in its prohibition policy.

As she got more and more physically involved in checking drug-related criminality, she got mentally involved with the problem too. It was apparent to her that drugs and crime went together and she became intent on pursuing the subject of cause and effect even academically. She delved into books on the subject and found that though some work had been done on this subject in the West, there was very little available in Indian literature, and on the Indian scenario. Cursory findings revealed that a majority of drug abuse cases led to crime in the form of domestic violence, and not just verbal abuse, but to a great extent mental and physical torture as well as physical violence.

What was surprising was that such violence was rarely directed towards the fathers or the brothers of the male addicts but almost always towards the mothers and the wives. They were 'soft targets' from whom money, jewellery and even clothes could be extracted to sustain the habit.

Section 47 of the Delhi Police Act is not often put to use. And yet, it empowers the DCP with scope for punitive powers permitting him or her to use persuasive correctional methods and, if he or she is so inclined, a lot of correctional reforms. In keeping with her inclinations Kiran made effective use of these powers.

Armed with such powers she could initiate externment proceedings against anyone who had breached the law three times and whose being at large was a threat to general peace and security of the area. She could ask the person concerned to show cause why he or she should not be asked to leave the city premises. This would perforce compel the person to live in unfamiliar environments, away from his or her area of influence. He or she, then, would have stood essentially and effectively uprooted. Yet, such an individual could be permitted to stay in the city as long as he or she was not found to be violating the law. This threat certainly did dissuade many drug pushers. The brillance of this scheme was that without a single person being uprooted, *all* of them came under social control and the residents heaved sighs of relief.

The extent to which she used the aforementioned powers, during her tenures as DCP(West) and DCP(North), was apparent from the crowds of 250-300 people who would attend the 'court session' at her office daily from 2 p.m. to 5 p.m. Such people would gather in connection with a wide range of issues, such as fixing hearings for jailable offences, seeking bail and asking for general counselling. Her staff members would accept the applications from the people and prepare the required reports for Kiran to study. There never was any need for a lawyer. It was this single-minded and determined performance of her duties that may have antagonised the lawyers of the Tees Hazari courts. Keeping litigation going to the extent possible apparently constituted some of the lawyers' 'bread and butter'. Kiran had, unwittingly, but nevertheless rudely, snatched this 'right' from the lawyers. However, she was to realise the extent of their antagonism only later, i.e., when she found herself caught up in the imbroglio resulting due to the lawyers' agitation which paralysed the legal machinery all over the country (for details see Chapter 11).

In the 'social justice system' adopted by Kiran, the accused would be 'show caused' with his or her specific offence(s) and then be asked to fetch his parents or close relatives or even neighbours to her 'court'. These people were given the responsibility of ensuring that the culprit desisted from his or her criminal ways or else he or she would no longer be able to live with them because he or she would be externed for a year or two. Such a situation put the onus on the culprit who felt that he or she now owed something to the family and neighbourhood for allowing him or her to stay with them, and this also brought families closer. Somehow, they could not get around to breaking the faith reposed in them by Kiran. Incidentally, the beat constable too was keeping up his home visits. Kiran has that special something about her that she probably derives from her honesty, hard work, goodwill and compassion. The fluctuating graph of arrests relating to when she was in charge and when she was not speaks volumes.

These sittings in 'court' as DCP(North) were different from those as DCP(West) in that here every second offender was a drug addict. The parents would reveal that despite all the pressure that they could lay on, even going so far as to tie up their sons, they could not get them out of the habit.

"I was shocked," exclaims Kiran. "Here I was trying to act the policewoman when what these youngsters actually needed was pharmacological and community management!"

The enormity of the situation struck her when her academic pursuits told her that as a matter of fact only four per cent of such cases, including mother and wife beating, were reported to the police! And when 94 per cent of the families were affected by domestic violence.

In 1986 there was only one centre in Delhi for the treatment of drug abusers and that was 'Ashiana', established by the NDMC (New Delhi Municipal Corporation). The menace of drug abuse could be controlled only if more centres were established where the abuser would have to stay away from his or her family and from accessibility to drugs and get a package for therapeutic treatment. She began looking for such a place and she did not have to look far. There it was in front of her: her own police station. There and then the concept of 'Navjyoti' was born, i.e., in June 1986. She appealed to the community at large for help and, as always, it was forthcoming and in abundance. Beds, blankets, *durries*, televisions, fans, doctors, yoga teachers, and medicines came in a flood. Food usually came from the patients' homes or from nearby hotels. At the launch, Ved Marwah and Rajendra Mohan were present and were very supportive of the rehabilitation work. This social work of Kiran finally consolidated itself into a registered foundation called Navjyoti Delhi Police Foundation for Correction, Deaddiction and Rehabilitation. The Commissioner of Police is its ex-officio President and Kiran is the Founder General Secretary and continues to work as such.

The Navjyoti centre soon became popular and, with the amount of community assistance that the programme was receiving, five more such centres were developed within a year. Of the 19 police stations under her charge, six were running drug abuse treatment centres. Although each centre was primarily meant for thirty patients, the programme was so popular and so necessary that, at times, one centre had to cater to 100 patients at a time.

The Narcotic Drugs and Psychotropic Substances (NDPS) Act came into force in 1986. Section 27 of the Act provides that one does not have to be shown to be in possession of drugs but has merely to be an admitted abuser, or have complaints lodged against him about his abuse, or be proved medically to be an abuser, to come under the purview of the Act. Such a person, if he volunteers for medical treatment, may be legally referred to treatment centres. It is only under Section 21 of the Act, where one has to be shown to be actually in possession of drugs of specified quantity notified under the law, that criminal proceedings are initiated. 'Navjyoti' was a registered voluntary organisation and those booked under Section 27 of the NDPS Act were sent there.

In December 1994, an arrest in which she was involved in 1987, while she was DCP(N), made news in the dailies. She had arrested two people with 90 kg of *charas* in their possession. The case was presented in the Sessions Court and the Sessions Judge was satisfied with the investigation and the presentation of evidence and convicted the duo. After that, the two accused appealed to the Delhi High Court. In December 1994 they were acquitted and the judge strongly indicted the arresting officer Kiran Bedi in words she believes are unwarrantedly derogatory and also almost defamatory.

The NDPS Act provides for the presence of a gazetted officer, besides the arresting officer, at the time of an arrest under the Act. A newspaper file picture showed the duo being arrested by Kiran Bedi along with subordinate members of her staff. There was no sign of any other gazetted officer in the picture. This technicality was taken by the High Court judge to be sufficient to warrant an acquittal. And in the order the honourable judge indicted Kiran for being a press-hungry officer.

Kiran retorts indignantly: "This was certainly not warranted. Whenever there is a major operation by the police the press call us up at odd hours to confirm the story. So, instead of waiting to answer these inevitably forthcoming calls, I released a press statement. That does not make one press hungry. And, if this technicality about the photograph could warrant such derogatory comments for me, then what about the Sessions Judge who convicted the two? And what about all the press conferences which senior police officers hold, from time to time, and instantly on any important arrest? Are they all publicity hungry, or are they performing a duty of informing the people? What is to my mind important is what should I reveal without compromising the interrogation. The display of seizures by the Income Tax Department, Customs, Narcotics and Police is usual. What was unusual in my case?"

That Kiran is press hungry and wants to be in the limelight are oft-repeated charges against her. In 1989, while she was the Deputy Director of the Narcotics Control Bureau, she was part of the NCB team which swooped down on the verdant hills of western Uttar Pradesh, in the Chakrata and Tuni *tehsils* of Dehra Dun district. Poppy was being cultivated extensively in the area by innocent agriculturists who were being compelled to do so by big landlords with powerful political connections. Members of the press also accompanied the NCB team. This team was split into two, with one group going up to Chakrata and the other moving further ahead to Tuni. Ajay Goyal, photographer of this book, expressed his keenness to accompany Kiran to Tuni, and she certainly did not mind. In Tuni she had the *Patwaris* organise the uprooting of the poppy plants from the fields and Ajay took a beautiful picture of her standing in one of the fields with a bouquet of poppy flowers in her hands.

She had to get back to Delhi because she had to appear before the Justice Wadhwa Commission and so left earlier than the rest of the NCB team. A few days later the dailies splashed her 'poppy field' picture in their pages along with the Tuni story. The story, of course, was reported from Dehra Dun. The NCB officials' hackles went up. Had she come back to Delhi earlier than the others so that she could hog the limelight? Anyway, from that day onwards, she was never given any operational assignment throughout her stint at the NCB.

As a matter of fact, she was never ever sent out on any foreign training assignment either, whereas every year at a conference at least two or three such opportunities would arise. Once, a file was put up to Prime Minister Rajiv Gandhi for sending an officer to Kuala Lumpur, Malaysia, to address, and participate in, a world conference on the drug abuse problem in schools. Rajiv Gandhi was quite aware of the   work she had done in this field, especially after the setting up of the 'Navjyoti' centre. Therefore, he wrote 'Why not Kiran?' on the file. That was how she was informed by the PM's office, just two days before the conference, that she was being sent to Malaysia.

Besides being dubbed a 'publicity hound', Kiran has also been branded as a controversial officer. Is her being controversial a mere myth or is there something about her and her mode of functioning that lends any credibility to such an accusation? One of her first acts that was viewed in this light was her arrest of a sitting MP's (J.S. Baraia's) private secretary, A.P. Karunakaran. He was held on charges of possessing a diamond ring suspected to be stolen during an armed dacoity in Delhi in December 1980. In this context, a dreaded criminal revealed that he had been harboured by the abovementioned private secretary who even sported a ring that had been given to him from the loot of that particular dacoity. Kiran and her officer in charge, special staff, Gian Chand, then kept watch over the secretary's residence. They covered themselves up in crude blankets and moved around the premises, as if they were watchmen, in the dark, late one night. As the opportunity presented itself the person was arrested and sure enough he was wearing the ring given to him as informed. The news of his arrest was widely reported in various newspapers on 24 and 25 April 1981.

The Commissioner of Police, P.S. Bhinder, took umbrage at this arrest and ticked her off in no uncertain terms. Did she not know, he asked her, that the arrested person was a sitting MP's private secretary? How dare she take the initiative into her own hands? he demanded. She should have consulted him first and sought his permission before taking any action. Even at that early stage in her career she stood by her decision and left the onus of taking any action against her on the police chief himself.

Her act of leaving Mizoram in the dead of night was also controversialised. Kiran had been threatened by the Minister of Law that if she did not surrender her daughter's medical seat in writing, then there was the possibility of the agitating youth surrounding her house and the State Government would not take responsibility for the consequences. In a place far away from home, all alone, with threats to her life and no assurance of any protection from the state machinery, she had no option but to fend for herself. Consequently, she drove to the Governor's residence and informed him of her decision based on the exigencies of the circumstances. The Governor (Swaraj Kaushal) gave sanction to her decision and only then did she leave the state for Delhi. (See Chapter 12 for details.)

As already described, her exit from Goa had also been because of compulsions of threat to life. In that case, however, the life in question was that of her daughter. Because of the inordinate delay in sanctioning leave that had been approved by her senior, the IGP of Goa, she had rushed to Delhi to take into her own responsibility her daughter's medical treatment. For that she had been declared to be absconding from duty, a charge, had it stuck, would have put paid to her career.

During her tenure as IG (Prisons) another uncalled for controversy, which was made to develop, was on distribution of condoms to prisoners. A doctor visiting the prison as a part of the Health Care Day went off his designated work and, on his own, questioned a few adolescent prisoners on the subject of homosexuality. He managed to confuse the scene and, thereafter, the following day, gave an interview to the press that the prison had 90 per cent homosexuals. This news went all over the world to the extent that even the BBC lapped up the item. For days the matter dragged on. Now here was a subject where Kiran least wanted to be a party to ! She realised that if she did not clarify the professional stand, the doctor would continue to have a field run, just what he wanted. So she decided to clarify — and she had to do so any number of times ! Once that started, it led to a 'controversy', including a petition to the court challenging the validity of the law against homosexuality in the Indian Penal Code. Kiran Bedi's professional stand was as follows :

(a) The problem of homosexuality persists but not as made out by the doctor who issued a statement without an academic study.

(b) His observation, as he himself admitted, was on the basis of speaking to a small group of young boys only — how could that be treated as 90 per cent 'affected'?

(c) Homosexuality as per Indian law is an offence and the prison cannot promote it by giving condoms.

(d) The problem of homosexuality in Tihar Jail was well contained and therefore should not be encouraged with free availability of condoms.

(e) The majority opinion was against the practice as per surveys done within the prison.

(f) The relations, particularly wives, protested against the suggestion of condom distribution as they did not want their husbands to become homosexuals due to the environment which may foster this habit.

(g) Adequate provision had been made for dealing with individual cases of homosexuality, and, therefore, the status quo did not require a change.

(h) The excessive overcrowding gave no place or occasion for privacy in the prison.

But Kiran till now continues to refute the suggestions made by a supposedly qualified doctor! And it adds to her bank of controversies ! Some pressed this issue further and

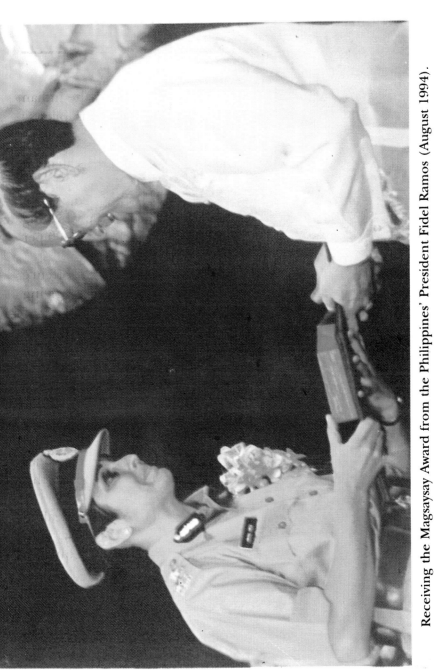

Receiving the Magsaysay Award from the Philippines' President Fidel Ramos (August 1994).

At the Magsaysay Award Ceremony at Manila (August 1994).

Addressing an audience in Manila.

With Cops on the Block, Manila — flanked by Indian Ambassador
Shyamala Cowsik and a senior police officer.

Doing a jig the Filipino way (1994).

The four Peshawaria sisters — Kiran, Anu, Shashi and Reeta.

Sweet moments between father and daughter.

Policing requires a fit body with a fit mind — yoga at home.

insisted that although she may consider homosexuality a vice, yet world opinion on this subject was changing and that she had merely been imposing her own cloistered views and they were not necessarily right. Should we not also consider, then, the denial of rights to heterosexuality in prisons? After all, the jail is a place where certain rights and privileges are withdrawn from the inmates. The objective behind the far-reaching correctional reforms that have taken place in Tihar is to ensure that energies are not idled away but are directed towards constructive, creative and wholesome activities. It is this determination that has brought about such remarkable changes in the mind-sets of the inmates that it is only by seeing the ground situation for oneself that one can believe it.

Another controversy related to Kiran's clash with members of the legal profession. In 1988 Kiran came into conflict with a section of lawyers and even while the Justice Wadhwa Commission (enquiring into the matter) was still compiling its report, she was ignominiously transferred to the CRPF (Central Reserve Police Force) as a commandant. Such a post is given to an officer of eight years' standing, but as she had already put in 16 years, it was obvious that the lawyers' lobby had succeeded in 'punishing' her. Rajiv Gandhi, then Prime Minister, read about this and sent for her. Kiran met the PM. He straightaway asked her where she wanted to be posted. Narcotics ? Kiran said that would be good but in the soft area of correction. The PM said no, she should go for a hard area. She should get these drug traffickers, all of them and go all out ! Kiran was amazed to get her new orders within 24 hours. She left for the NCB office after one day's work in the CRPF office. The lawyers, of course, were stumped.

10

Optimum Output

During her stint in the NCB she was exposed to the drug scenario at both the national and international levels. She was working at the national level and also attending a lot of seminars and talks on the problem. She was also interacting with international agencies like Interpol and with the respective country's drug liaison officers (DLOs) and the picture of narcotics trade and drug abuse became clearer in her mind. Also during that period she was pursuing her doctoral studies on 'The Performance Appraisal System'. With this newer and closer involvement she changed her topic to 'Drug Abuse and Criminality'. She was getting access to the best of teachers, to the best of knowledge and, moreover, to the most authentic documentation. However, she did not get time to write her thesis because she was travelling a lot in the course of her duties and also attending and addressing a lot of meetings and seminars on the subject. Moreover, she was spending a lot of time in courts because of the proceedings of the Wadhwa Commission. But she did manage to collect a lot of material on the subject which was to be organised and collated at a later and more convenient time.

Meanwhile, the 'Navjyoti' programme was working wonders and had made an impression internationally for its pioneering work in drug abuse treatment. This programme was honoured by a number of national and international awards, which encouraged the mushrooming of drug victims' treatment centres all over India. The feedback from many of these centres helped in keeping her attention focussed on the treatment programme. Although Kiran could not take time off to write her research papers, she did manage to chalk out interview schedules and formulate questionnaires in connection with her research work.

Kiran's next posting took her to the north-eastern state of Mizoram. In contrast to her tight NCB schedules, here, Kiran had a lot of time on her hands. She, therefore, decided to commence writing her doctoral thesis. She realised that it would be difficult and time-consuming to trace the drug abuse-related criminals whom she had come across as DCP (North), and moreover they would not now be as forthcoming with their information when she was no longer in charge of that area. So she wrote to the then IG (Prisons), Delhi, H.P. Kumar, requesting his permission to let her interview the drug addicts (around 250) in Tihar Jail. She was very happy that a police officer was holding that charge and explained how the work she was engaged in was something which was very much related to crime and the police. It would assist greatly in crime prevention if one were aware whether drug abuse was followed by crime or vice versa. On one of her visits to Delhi she visited IG(P) Kumar in his office to follow up on her letter. He did not even ask her to sit down and after some time when she reminded him about what she had come for, he brusquely told her to leave her application with his PA. And that was it, the end of the interview. She had earlier met the superintendent of the jail regarding the same issue and he had told her that there would be absolutely no problem and that she would have to just take the IG's permission, which was a mere formality. She left her application in the IG's office. When quite some time had elapsed and she did not get any reply to her application, she checked back with the superintendent. She was shocked to hear that the IG had not only refused to give permission but had also declined to put it in writing. She was told that he had this habit of 'killing' an issue by not responding at all.

Kiran, therefore, once again changed the topic of her research work. This time she decided to work on 'Drug Abuse and Domestic Violence'. The number of people already treated, as also those undergoing treatment, at 'Navjyoti' centres became her data for study. They were very forthcoming in their responses and were very eager to participate in these interviews and fill in the questionnaires which almost became platforms through which they could express their gratitude. Every time she went to Delhi from Mizoram she would meet batches of twenty or so of these people. That is how her work progressed.

Kiran's posting in Mizoram contributed greatly to her pursuit of studies in drug and alcohol abuse prevention. Unlike her postings in Delhi, here, she had plenty of time on her hands. Mizoram had undergone a long period of insurgency and had become accustomed to a curfew environment. Then again there was not much street lighting available and life on the streets after 5 p.m. was virtually non-existent and all social activities were over by 6 p.m. Kiran just did not have any official work after 5 p.m. every day, which must have been quite a pleasant surprise to a police officer used to working 16 to 18 hours a day! Such a situation gave her plenty of time to sift through her research material and do a lot of writing. But Kiran gives the entire credit for her Ph.D. work to the institute where she was a scholar, i.e., the Indian Institute of Technology (IIT) Delhi (Department of Social Sciences). She says the faculty allowed her freedom to think and plan her work, which was essential for creativity. The IIT provided the best guides in the form of Dr K.L. Nadir, a management expert, and Dr Anuradha Sharma, an expert in the field of psychology. Both were aware of Kiran's potential and, all along, guided her in pursuing her academic work. Anuradha Sharma proved to be a true friend and guru to her. A computer expert and social scientist, Dr B.S. Nagi, of the Council for Social Development, helped her analyse her data by applying the latest statistical tests. Kiran was eventually awarded her doctorate for her thesis on 'Drug Abuse and Domestic Violence' in September 1993.

Consumption of alcohol is very common among Mizos. Many houses brew liquor from rice, called '*Zu*', for domestic consumption and sale. The Mizos are voracious meat eaters, with pigs and dogs treated as delicacies. Basically, the Mizos are not cultivators. The abundance of rice, however, is because of the plentiful subsidies provided by the Central Government. Though the state is officially 'dry' yet '*Zu*' is available in plenty. Many of her junior police officers were alcoholics. In the beginning she would get nauseated by the reeking odour in her office but then she had to gradually get used to it. Anyway, it was alright as long as they were sober on duty. But they just could not remain like this for more than a few hours at a stretch, sometimes not even for more than two hours. She was not going to interfere in their cultural habits but it did hurt her to see her forces being incapacitated in this manner. She was also trying to investigate the antecedents of the repeat criminals and discovered that most of them were alcoholics. She did not possess any special powers like in Delhi and so the strategies that worked so wonderfully there could not be applied in Mizoram. She, however, opened an indoor treatment facility for the treatment of alcoholic policemen — and it did yield results. Besides this, the younger generation, mainly twelve to thirteen-year-olds, were on to drugs. Proxyvon was very common and so was heroin. And, worse, when the kids could not get either of these drugs they would inject liquor intravenously, which resulted in a number of deaths. Most certainly this activity is the cause for the incidence of AIDS being so high in those areas. Drug abuse was rampant in the tribal belt of Manipur, Mizoram and Nagaland. In Assam, too, it was prevalent but not to the extent as in this belt. The local culture, and the lack of any barrier at the Indo-Burma border, gave the population easy access to heroin and other drugs. She realised that this was the area she would have to concentrate on, once again, in prioritising crime prevention. (See also Chapter 12.)

11

The Lawyers Strike – at Kiran

Perhaps the most tense, tiresome and nerve-racking time that Kiran had to endure during her term of service was during the lawyers' strike that commenced in January 1988 and continued through June that year. However, the legal battle in and out of the courtrooms ended only in April 1990.

The events which triggered off the strike were as follows. Around 2 p.m., on 15 January 1988, Ratna Singh, an English honours student of St. Stephen's College, New Delhi, came out of the toilet of the ladies' common room and saw a man wearing a green checked coat dashing away from where she had left her handbag.

Sensing mischief she gave chase and shouted for help. Kavita Issar, also an English honours student, saw her chasing the man in the green coat and joined the shouting. Anand Misra, a second-year chemistry honours student, heard the two girls shouting and caught the person whom they were chasing. The group was joined by Anand Prasad (second year history honours) and Manjusha Damle (final year Sanskrit honours). Ratna Singh checked her handbag and declared that Rs. 110, a cassette tape and her doctor's prescription were missing. The items were found on the person of the man they had apprehended. The college authorities were informed and the Vice-Principal of the college Horace Jacob duly notified the Roshanara Police Station. A subinspector of police, Kawal Singh, soon appeared on the scene. The culprit accepted his crime and maintained that he was an educated unemployed youth and had therefore resorted to stealing. He also admitted, in his own handwriting, to having stolen some money from girls' handbags a day earlier in the same place. A DTC bus pass in the name of Manjusha Damle was also recovered from him. He gave a written statement wherein he stated that his name was Rakesh Kumar and that he lived at E-40, Model Basti, Delhi. A first information report (FIR), No. 9/88/U/ S380/111/IPC was lodged with the Roshanara Police Station. During his stay at the police station, however, he gave another name and address.

The investigating officer apparently knew that the apprehended person had been giving false names and addresses and so the former felt that the latter might try to give him the slip. However, since he was taking the accused in a DTC bus (which is always very crowded) he took the extra precaution of handcuffing him for the period till he produced him before the court. At the court, however, all hell seemed to break loose. Some of the lawyers present there recognised the handcuffed man to be one Rajesh Agnihotri, a lawyer practising at Tees Hazari courts. The investigating officer was manhandled and shouted at. On learning the identity of the accused he, however, promptly removed the handcuffs. Metropolitan Magistrate, Pradeep Chaddha, dismissed all charges against the accused on grounds of lack of evidence. He also directed the Commissioner of Police, Delhi, to take action against the concerned police officers.

"This was a surprising decision, as the production was not for a judgement but only for remand or bail. This was a clear judgement of 'NOT GUILTY', without looking at the evidence," says Kiran.

The very same day, 15 January 1988, the lawyers of the Tees Hazari courts struck work. Hari Chand, the President of the Delhi Bar Association, declared that Rajesh Agnihotri had been falsely implicated by the students of St. Stephen's College. This was because Rajesh Agnihotri had been involved in a scuffle with the students in a university special bus over the occupying of seats reserved for ladies. These students, Hari Chand claimed, beat him up and took him to the college hostel where he was illegally confined for a number of hours. On a subsequent date, when he had come to the college to visit his father, who was a reader there in the Department of Botany, he was apprehended by the students and implicated in a false case. The then President of the St. Stephen's Students Union Society, Rajit Punhani, has said: "The incident [lawyers' response to their colleague's arrest] erodes the confidence of the students in doing what the law requires them to do." The Magistrate held that there was no prima facie case against the accused and therefore the case should be immediately dropped by the police. The Metropolitan Magistrate recorded his views as follows: "There's hardly any material placed on record which should justify further detention of the accused or his trial. Nobody has actually seen the accused taking out money and also no recovery was effected. Hence, prosecution and trial will serve no purpose...." (signed Pradeep Chaddha, Metropolitan Magistrate, 16 January 1988). What interest the police had in pursuing the case was, however, not a matter he would care to look into. Over the days the strike gathered momentum and on 21 January, the lawyers formed a protest procession and marched, shouting slogans, to the office of the DCP(North), namely, Kiran Bedi. The protest marchers straightaway forced entry into her office and tried to get at Kiran. She was at that time in a meeting with all her district gazetted officers, reviewing the preparation for the forthcoming 26 January parade. All of them, sensing the intrusion, sprang to their feet, and immediately came between the lawyers and their DCP and succeeded in physically pushing them out. While doing so, they bolted Kiran in, protecting her from being attacked. The Additional DCP, M.S. Sandhu, being seniormost on the spot, took charge. Other officers with Sandhu were Prabhat Singh, Assistant Commissioner of Police (ACP), D.L. Kashyap, Vinay Chaudhury, Ram Kumar, S.B.S. Tyagi and others.

The lawyers, for hours, remained menacing, shouting filthy slogans. Sandhu continued to tolerate them, avoiding a confrontation with them as far as possible. But while he could tolerate the lawyers, some constables could not. When some lawyers started to pull out the name plates and berets of some constables the latter hit back, and all hell was let loose. Some lawyers were injured, as also some policemen. Photographers' cameras were smashed. It was all very wild. But the lawyers' biggest grouse was that they could not do to Kiran what they had come for. Now they wanted nothing short of her 'head'. They went on an indefinite strike and demanded her suspension. They alleged that Kiran ordered a lathicharge on them and made sure that they were injured. They demanded compensation for the injuries they had received, but nothing short of suspension. The incident had eyewitnesses at different stages of the rapidly changing scene. Therefore, the next day's newspapers reported on the versions of all sides: the injuries, the smashing of cameras, the filthy slogans and what have you!

It was clearly evident from published accounts in the newspapers that the lawyers wanted to humiliate the gender in the service and perhaps send out a larger message. Otherwise how does one explain the language and aggression displayed? After all, if it was only a matter of the accountability of a senior officer, then, by the same token, the Commissioner of Police could also have been gheraoed and harassed. There perhaps was something about Kiran's way of functioning that had raised the hackles of the lawyers. Up to 7 February, they did not have anything substantial against her and so somehow she had to be suspended and dismissed. This was effectively achieved by playing up the handcuffing incident to create the bogey of 'police high-handedness'.

In retrospect, one wonders whether the crime prevention activities undertaken by Kiran under the commissionerate powers entrusted to her, wherein she was holding her own courts and consolidating effective crime prevention through externment proceedings, did not provide the real reason for the lawyers' ire. After all, she seemed to have effectively curbed the role of some of the lawyers and typists as middlemen whose primary source of income was the seeking of bails for petty criminals involved in picking pockets, stealing from their own homes or those of others and delving in crimes related to their drug habits. One really wonders.

On 22 January 1988, the Lt. Governor of Delhi, H.L. Kapur, ordered a magisterial enquiry into the entire incident. The enquiry report was to be submitted within a week.

The lawyers, however, would have nothing to do with this enquiry and continued to insist that they would not compromise on anything short of the dismissal of Kiran Bedi.

By effectively utilising the system of associations and unions that are so prevalent in the country, the Delhi lawyers succeeded in persuading five lakh lawyers all over India to join their strike. A strike of this dimension constituted a record in the history of the legal profession. Yet, the amazing fact about this bushfire strike was that it was not engendered by any noble principle or constitutional crisis but was based on a one-point programme, i.e., the dismissal of Kiran Bedi from service. And that too on the issue of the handcuffing of a person who kept changing his name and address and was caught red-handed by the students and handed over to a police officer for legal action. The main difference was that this person happened to be a lawyer too !

On 4 February 1988, the magistrate in charge of the enquiry submitted his report. He maintained that the sequence of events led him to clearly believe that Rajesh

Agnihotri was definitely involved in the crime of theft and that he was rightly arrested by the police of the Roshanara Police Station. However, he maintained, Rajesh's being handcuffed was not warranted.

The lawyers immediately demanded that the concerned subinspector be suspended and disciplinary action taken against him for the reason of handcuffing !

Meanwhile, a judicial enquiry had been instituted into the 21 January case of lathicharge on the lawyers outside the office of the DCP(N). The enquiry was to be conducted by a retired judge of the Delhi High Court, Justice P.N. Khanna. He was instructed to submit an interim report within a week and the final report within a month. But this wan't enough for them. They wanted an enquiry only by a sitting judge of the Delhi High Court. And they had their way.

On 7 February, the lawyers of the Supreme Court called off their strike. The lawyers of the lower courts, however, were in no mood to compromise on their one-point stand, i.e., the dismissal of Kiran Bedi, before they would take any further action on the issue.

Fifteen members of the Action Committee set up by the lawyers of the Tees Hazari courts started a relay hunger strike to get their demand fulfilled.

The courts thus remained paralysed. On 17 February, the Tees Hazari courts complex witnessed an unprecedented riot. People from distant places such as Samaypur and Badli and also from adjoining areas came in trucks and tempos to protest against what they considered to be an unlawful and baseless strike. They raised slogans against the striking lawyers. The lawyers formed an opposition group immediately and slanging matches and brickbatting became the order of the day. In the ensuing mêlée several persons (belonging to both groups) as well as bystanders were injured. The police had to intervene to separate the groups and restore order. A number of arrests were made, the most prominent being that of a Delhi Municipal Councillor, Rajesh Yadav.

Such a situation naturally stoked the fire of the lawyers' agitation. They were quick to scream themselves hoarse that Kiran Bedi had engineered the whole scenario and declared that they would stop short of nothing but her blood!

The interesting thing about the whole episode was that the lawyers themselves were divided about the course of events. Almost all the senior lawyers of the Supreme Court as well as the Delhi High Court were strongly opposed to the strike, whereas the junior lawyers were adamant that they would not rest till Kiran Bedi was dismissed. The senior lawyers insisted that secret balloting be held to determine the true opinion of the majority regarding the continuation of the strike. Under vehement protests and demonstrations such a secret balloting was held in the premises of the Supreme Court Bar Association Library. Govinda Mukhoty, the President of the Delhi Bar Association Action Committee, assured one and all that there would be no force used during the balloting and that if there was, then, he would resign from his post. Ballot boxes, however, were hijacked. The Supreme Court Bar Association President, M.C. Bhandare, condemned this hijacking and declared it to be highly undemocratic and an act of cowardice. "Those who fight for human rights should see to it that others' right to vote should not be frustrated. The silent majority of the Supreme Court has decided to lift the siege from March 7," he declared.

If telling evidence of hijacking were needed, the photographs published in some newspapers showed a group of lawyers carrying away ballot boxes from the Supreme Court premises. Prominent among them were the President of the New Delhi Bar Association, Thakur Onkar Singh, and Rajesh Wadhwa, a member of the New Delhi Bar Association. The two, however, denied that the pictures were theirs but admitted that they did have a remarkable resemblance. Govinda Mukhoty stated that there was 90 per cent evidence of his 'boys' having been involved in the ballot-box hijacking and in the general disruption caused to the voting process but maintained that as there was still a margin of 10 per cent proof of certainty, he would not resign. Later, however, he changed his stance and said he would resign. This was enough to drive the Chairman of the Delhi Bar Association, Daljit Tandon, to tears and declare that once again money power and adverse publicity were out to stifle their efforts.

In another significant development, a lawyers' delegation approached Home Minister Buta Singh, and demanded the suspension of Kiran Bedi. The Home Minister rejected their appeal and requested them to call off their stir pending the report of the high-powered commission that was looking into the matter. While the striking lawyers then demonstrated against the Home Minister, women's rights activists, women's groups and university students held a massive rally to support Buta Singh's statement.

While the lawyers in Delhi continued their agitation, several high courts across the country condemned it and declared it to be illegal. They maintained that such gross dereliction of duty should be severely punished. They declared that lawyers had made it a habit of striking work on the flimsiest of pretexts without any responsibility towards their commitments, leading to the harassment of the people at large. Lawyers' strikes had been sparked off by inane things like a judge objecting to not being addressed as Your Honour; cases being dismissed because the pleader came in late; and political demands for the formation of a separate Telangana Pradesh.

Meanwhile, the office of the Administrator of Delhi conceded to the demands of the lawyers and issued orders countermanding the enquiry by Justice Khanna. It felt that a fresh commission should be constituted to look into the entire matter from its genesis onwards. As a result, a two-bench commission, comprising Justice N.N. Goswami and Justice D.P. Wadhwa, was set up.

The Goswami-Wadhwa Commission was asked to give an interim report within a specified time. It did. It held Kiran Bedi guilty on all possible counts. Soon after that Kiran was transferred to the Central Reserve Police Force, an order to be reversed within twenty-four hours by the personal intervention of none other than Prime Minister Rajiv Gandhi. He had called her for a personal meeting in which he suggested that her talents would be better utilised in interdiction of drug trafficking. (See also Chapter 9).

But little did the Prime Minister or Kiran realise what a marathon legal battle lay ahead. Kiran used to start the day in the lawyer's chamber, if she was lucky to have a lawyer, then go to the courts for her hearings that had assumed the shape of a public trial, then go to attend office in the Narcotics Control Bureau and then return to the lawyer's chamber to prepare for the next day's hearings or prepare herself with her colleagues, namely, M.S. Sandhu, S.B.S. Tyagi, Vinay Chaudhury, Prabhat Singh, Jinder Singh and others, all serving officers of the Delhi Police. There were days in which Kiran had to be physically present in three courts, that is, before the commission of inquiry, the Delhi High Court and the Supreme Court. She was appearing in person, defending herself, while the seniormost of the counsels, K.K. Venugopal, would be on the opposite side to argue against her. Kiran lived by the hour then, as she says, morning, afternoon, evening and night. Her day, she says, was divided into four major portions when scenes changed and so did the priorities and strategies. The slogan of a section of the lawyers was a "fight to the finish! We must get Kiran Bedi's scalp". This was a battle where one woman was visibly pitted against a large organised union of lawyers. Both had their grievances, without a doubt but, who was the accused and who the accuser? Kiran for the first time became a lawyer for herself and filed a petition for herself before the apex court. She recalls the help given to her by a friend, Anil Bal. He introduced her to a senior advocate, Gopal Subramaniam, who gave all possible legal guidance and staff assistance which enabled her to prepare her petitions and appear before the Supreme Court in person. The rulings given by the Supreme Court in her case are already part of legal history and are quoted as landmark judgements delivered by Mr. Justice E.S. Venkataramiah, Mr. Justice M.M. Dutt and Mr. Justice N.D. Ojha. Kiran had gone to the highest court, questioning her status of accused before the commission of inquiry and therefore seeking the right to defend herself. When the commission of inquiry had asked her to take the witness box to be examined, she took the stand and said, "I do not wish to make a statement, your lordship. I beg leave to state that." The judges did not say anything for some time and only then did Justice Wadhwa suggest that she take a chair while he consulted his colleague. "I am used to standing for long periods," answered Kiran.

"Are you advising your client not to take oath?" Justice Wadhwa asked G. Ramaswamy (Kiran's counsel). "She can be prosecuted for contempt of court," he was told.

"I am only asking that my client be given an opportunity to defend herself, your honour," said her counsel. "You cannot force her to take that opportunity without examining the witnesses first."

Ramaswamy then asked the judges to overrule his plea if they so thought fit so that "we can move the higher courts".

Here is what appeared then in the press which indicates the situation in the courtroom.

KIRAN BEDI REFUSES TO TAKE OATH

Mrs Kiran Bedi refused to take oath before Justices Wadhwa and Goswami on Thursday. She was asked to show cause by Friday why she should not be prosecuted for contempt of court.

Subinspector Jinder Singh, who was to have been cross-examined before the panel on Thursday along with Mrs Bedi, did not turn up in the court. He was issued non-bailable warrants to appear before the court on May 23.

Mrs Bedi's counsel told the two-judge panel that he would move higher courts against their ruling. The Tis Hazari Bar Association, meanwhile, filed petitions before the High Court and the Supreme Court to prevent any ex-parte stay of the proceedings.

Mrs Bedi's refusal to take oath came after her counsel had argued that, virtually being an accused before the committee, she was not bound to take oath. The judges, however, ordered that she be cross-examined. "I beg leave to state that I do not wish to make any statement," Mrs Bedi said.

The courtroom erupted with cries of "contempt". The show-cause notice was later served on Mrs Bedi as the court adjourned.

Simultaneously, the court ordered that Mr Ved Marwah, former police chief, and Mr M.S. Sandhu, ex-additional DCP, be present on Friday for cross-examination.

Dozens of lawyers had crammed the courtroom on Thursday to witness Mrs Bedi's testimony. Five minutes after the judges had taken their seats, there was a buzz of excitement. Mr G. Ramaswami, additional solicitor-general, walked in to defend the police department. His appearance on Monday had generated a spate of objections from the bar associations.

Mr Ramaswami first made his own position in the matter clear. He said he was duty-bound to accept the brief since the Government had ordered him to do so. "The lawyers did not discuss any of their confidential case strategy with me. My conscience is clear," Mr Ramaswami said.

Mr Ramaswami then addressed himself to the case. He said the present inquiry was not just for fact-finding but for probing specific charges against specific individuals. "Mrs Bedi is almost the accused before this committee," he said.

Mr Ramaswami said that if a person refused to testify before the committee when he was called as an ordinary witness, he could be penalised. But, he said, a virtual accused could not be compelled to depose.

Mr Ramaswami cited the case of Mrs Indira Gandhi who had refused to depose before the Shah Commission under similar circumstances. "The high court upheld her right to stay away from the witness box," he said.

"Are you saying Mrs Bedi will not take oath?" asked Justice Wadhwa. Mr Ramaswami said she would appear later, after he had had a chance to cross-examine those who had deposed against her.

The judges ruled there was a fundamental difference between Mrs Gandhi's case and Mrs Bedi's case. Mrs Gandhi had not filed an affidavit before the commission while Mrs Bedi had done so: "She is only being cross-examined on her own affidavit," said Justice Goswami.

The judges asked SI Jinder Singh to take the box. The sub-inspector was not present. Non-bailable warrants were issued for him to appear on May 23.

Mrs Bedi was then called to the box. "Mrs Bedi, have you filed an affidavit?" asked Justice Goswami. Even as she was replying, counsel for bar associations, Bawa Gurcharan Singh, asked her to take oath.

The reader asked Mrs Bedi to repeat the oath after him. "I do not wish to make a statement, your lordship. I beg leave to state that," Mrs Bedi said.

"Contempt, contempt," shouted the lawyers. "She cannot be compelled to take oath," said Mr Ramaswami.

The judges did not say anything for some time. "Take a chair," Justice Wadhwa told Mrs Bedi as he consulted his colleague. "I am used to standing for long periods," Mrs Bedi told him.

"Are you advising your client not to take oath?" Justice Wadhwa asked Mr Ramaswami. "She can be prosecuted for contempt of court".

Mr Ramaswami told the judges that he only wished to read out an extract from the judgement in the Indira Gandhi case to them. "After that, your lordships, I will advise her to take oath if you overrule my contention," he said.

The judgement was read out. Mr Ramaswami said the accused was only being given an opportunity to defend herself. "You can't force her to take that opportunity without letting us examine their witnesses," he said. When Justice Wadhwa mentioned the affidavit, Mr Ramaswami said: "If you are going to get technical, I will be super-technical."

Mrs Bedi, at this stage, asked if she could state on oath that she would not make any statement. "That would be tantamount to contempt," Justice Wadhwa said.

Mr Ramaswami asked him to overrule his plea "so that we can move higher courts." "What further overruling do you want," Justice Wadhwa said, and served notice on Mrs Bedi to show cause why she should not be hauled up for contempt of court.

(Indian Express, 20 May 1988)

It was on this issue that Kiran went on special leave petition before the Supreme Court vacation judge on three counts :

(1) She wanted to know what her status was before the commission of inquiry: was it that of an accused or not?

(2) If she was an accused then did she have the right to defend herself and examine the witnesses before she herself could be cross-examined to know the allegations against her?

(3) She requested that the prosecution that had been launched against her in the court of Chief Metropolitan Magistrate R.L. Chugh be quashed.

Mr. Justice K.N. Singh (the vacation judge), before whom her petition was presented, gave relief to her on all counts. In a packed courtroom, the vacation judge also directed the Goswami-Wadhwa Commission to reconsider its decision regarding the order in which the police and the Delhi Bar Association witnesses would be examined.

Later, however, the same matter came before the regular bench comprising Justice E.S. Venkataramiah,

Justice M.M. Dutt and Justice N.D. Ojha. They made several observations of great consequence which led to strong reactions. They ruled that since Kiran Bedi was the sole object of attack by the Bar Association before the commission of inquiry, she was the "fittest person to come under Section 8 (B) of the Commission of Inquiry Act". In other words, she should get the rights and privileges of an accused along with its responsibilities. They also quashed the prosecution's contempt of court proceedings in which she was already on bail, based on a complaint of the commission. The apex court also categorically stated that Kiran Bedi was discriminated. Further since her prosecution was not based on the order of law the prosecution against her should also go. Various national dailies recorded and reported the event, which was history in itself.

PROTECTION UNDER SECTION 8 (B)
KIRAN BEDI WAS 'DISCRIMINATED'

Justice E.S. Venkataramiah, the presiding judge of the bench hearing the Kiran Bedi case, observed on Thursday that the commission's order naming only four persons entitled to the protection under Section 8B of the Commission of Inquiry Act was discriminatory on the face of it as Ms Bedi, former DCP (north), was left out.

"Either the order must go or they must write a fresh order," the judge explained. If the commission judges had given reasons for this discrimination this appeal would not have come to the Supreme Court, he observed.

Since Ms Bedi is being prosecuted on this point, the judge doubted the validity of the prosecution also. The court had earlier stayed her prosecution for not taking oath before the commission.

Her counsel and Additional Solicitor-General, Mr G. Ramaswamy, said that she had not refused to take oath but only maintained that the stage has not come to put her in the box. Even the commission's order had stated that Section 8B witnesses would be examined at the end of the proceedings. Therefore, her prosecution was not proper, counsel submitted.

Moreover, the lawyers cannot intervene in the prosecution as they have no locus standi in it. It is entirely between the court and the accused, he argued.

Justice Venkataramiah asked counsel to read out the order of the commission which purportedly discriminates against Ms Bedi. He then observed that the parties were not dealt with even-handedly. When he indicated that the prosecution is liable to be set aside, Mr K.K. Venugopal, counsel for the lawyers, said that the order should not be set aside on a "technical" ground.

The judge insisted that it was "substantial" ground.

Most of the day on Thursday was taken by Mr Ramaswamy summing up his arguments of the last two weeks, and reading out well-known judgements on the procedures of commissions of inquiry.

Justice Venkataramiah strengthened his arguments occasionally by quoting judgements. Reading out the judges' case of 1980, he remarked that the loss of reputation is worse than death for anyone. The judge also stressed that the procedures followed by tribunals must be fair and reasonable under Article 21 of the Constitution. Agreeing with Mr Ramaswamy that the lawyers must lead evidence first, the judge said that the principle of burden of proof must be followed.

The hearing will resume on Friday. The bench hearing the appeal of Ms Bedi challenging the procedures adopted by the Goswami-Wadhwa

Committee inquiring into the lawyers' strike in Delhi also *consists of Justice M.M. Dutt and Justice N. D. Ojha.*

(Indian Express, 29 July 1988)

SC MAY QUASH BEDI'S PROSECUTION

The Supreme Court today indicated that the criminal prosecution of Mrs Kiran Bedi and Mr Jinder Singh for declining to take oath prior to deposing before the Goswamy-Wadhwa committee would be quashed since the two police officers were not dealt "even-handedly" by the fact-finding committee.

A three-judge bench comprising Mr Justice E.S. Venkataramiah, Mr Justice M.M. Dutt and Mr Justice N. D. Ojha also hinted that they might ask the police to lead evidence before the committee investigating the incidents starting from handcuffing of a lawyer to a mob attack on the striking lawyers in the Tis Hazari complex on February 17. In that case, Mrs Bedi, the

former DCP (North), who is now deputy director of the Narcotics Control Bureau, will have to come in the witness box in the last.

Arguing for the police officers, Mr G. Ramaswamy contended that the petitioners had not been treated fairly by the two-judge Delhi High Court committee comprising Mr Justice N.N. Goswamy and Mr Justice D.P. Wadhwa. Counsel submitted that Mrs Bedi only declined to take oath because she had no other alternative.

During the hearing, Justice Venkataramiah remarked that from the facts of the case it was very difficult to say that Mrs Bedi did not come under Section 8 B of the Commission of Inquiry Act. Under the circumstances, the committee would have to extend provisions of 8 B which gives the person covered by it the right to cross-examine the opposite party's witnesses, observed the court. Following an indefinite strike by the lawyers demanding action against the police for its alleged excesses on them, the Centre set up the two-judge committee.

The court also observed that Mrs Bedi was the fittest person to be covered by 8 B as her case of being the sole accused was stronger than the case of the three police officers, who had been issued notices under 8 B by the committee.

Mr Justice Ojha noted that the Bar Association allegation against Mrs Bedi had a direct bearing both on her conduct as well as on her reputation.

In another significant observation, the judges said that courts (committee) should act in a "restrained manner" while ordering prosecution of an individual. The committee was at fault in rejecting Mrs Bedi's request to make statement before being asked to depose on oath, the judges noted.

Counsel for the Delhi Bar Association, Mr K.K. Venugopal, after hearing the observations made by the court, pleaded that at this stage the judges should not decide the case. He also contended that the criminal prosecution of the two police officers could not be quashed by the court hearing the petitions challenging the procedure adopted by the committee.

(The Times of India, 29 July 1988)

Disagreeing with the counsel's contention, Justice Venkataramiah questioned the commission's haste to recommend Kiran's prosecution and also found fault with it on a few other counts. This observation was sufficient for Mr. Justice Goswami to put in his resignation from the commission of inquiry. To this Mr. Justice Venkataramiah expressed his regrets stating in a letter that when the discussions were going on in the Supreme Court during the arguments the members of the committee were never in his mind. They (the three-judge bench of the apex court) were only concerned with the commission's 29 June order that was placed before them.

Cross-examination of Witnesses
Wadhwa Panel Should Set Aside Order: SC

Justice E.S. Venkataramiah, the presiding judge hearing the Kiran Bedi petitions in the Supreme Court, on Thursday reiterated that the order of the Goswamy-Wadhwa Committee regarding examination of witnesses should be set aside.

He observed during the hearing that he was repeating his view for the third time — "that let the order be set aside, let the commission take a fresh look and make a fresh order which does not look discriminatory."

The judge said that if this had been done earlier, the court need not have spent the seven days in arguments. "Otherwise

we will have to think over it overnight."

Justice Venkataramiah also remarked that the lawyers were not really a party in the case. "We are hearing you only as friends of court."

For most of the day, Mr K.K. Venugopal, counsel for the lawyers, was reading judgements from English courts affirming his views that there was no accuser or accused in the case and a commission of inquiry can ask a person to depose whenever required.

Counsel also stressed that the argument over Section 8 (B) of the Commission of

Inquiry Act was not contemplated when the commission was deciding the basic issue. It was an afterthought to delay the working of the commission, he said.

The lawyer for Mrs Kiran Bedi, former DCP (North), however contradicted the statement and said that it had been raised several times earlier.

The arguments will continue on Friday. The bench consists of Justice Venkataramiah, Justice M.M. Dutt and Justice N.D. Ojha.

Mrs Bedi has challenged the procedures of the commission and her exclusion from witnesses given the protection under Section 8 (B). She has also challenged her prosecution for not taking oath before the commission.

(Indian Express, 5 August 1988)

Kiran was greatly relieved at all this and was back before the Wadhwa Commission. She appealed for another member to head the commission and for a change of venue as also for a lawyer. While the first two requests were not conceded the third one did mature. K.T.S. Tulsi, a senior advocate of great repute, practising primarily in Chandigarh and a university friend of Kiran, volunteered to take her case. In fact, his was one of the first voices, as a lawyer, to speak against the lawyers' strike.

But not before Kiran, once again, had to face another situation of declining to come to the witness box. This was because her earlier lawyer, P.P. Grover, had been 'hounded' out. An earthen pot with garlands around its

neck, making it appear like an 'urn', was placed at the Tees
Hazari courts complex. It was placed there, ostensibly for
'collection'.

The eve of the Delhi Bar Association elections today (Friday) saw [an] earthen pot put up at the Tis Hazari courts complex in the Capital, ostensibly to collect funds in aid of Mr P.P. Grover, advocate, who is representing Mrs Kiran Bedi and other police officers in their case against the lawyers before the Wadhwa Commission – an act which according to Mr Grover has made him the butt of ridicule by other lawyers.

(The Statesman, 16 December 1988)

The trial before the commission moved briskly after
the arrival of K.T.S. Tulsi on the scene. Kiran stood for
cross-examination after the lawyers and she faced the
barrage of questions for a full week in the dock.

In the end the commission gave its report in April
1990, finding fault with Kiran, all police officers involved
and the lawyers who had gone on strike as well as with the
politicians for their motivation of the crowds. The matter
today rests at this stage. Kiran moved soon thereafter to
Mizoram (a hard posting), the policemen said that they
were not much bothered by all this and the lawyers (some
of them) continued their strike now for other reasons.
Justice Wadhwa returned to his bench to the relief of the
waiting litigants.

No Punitive Action Proposed
Wadhwa Panel Censures All

The much awaited Wadhwa [Commission] report, set up to go into the events leading to the longest ever lawyers' strike, is believed to have censured police officers, lawyers and politicians but has recommended no punitive measures against anybody.

Its findings assume significance especially after the latest incident in which a police officer allegedly misbehaved with an additional district sessions judge, sparking off a strike in the lower courts in the Capital.

The Wadhwa Commission which submitted its final report last month is yet to be made public and is likely to be placed before Parliament in the forthcoming budget session.

Mrs Kiran Bedi, then DCP (North), is learnt to have been indicted for her role in the lathicharge of lawyers, which took place outside her office on 21 January 1988, when lawyers collected, protesting against the handcuffing of a colleague.

The report has also found the role of certain lawyers suspect and adverse comments have been passed also on Mr Rajesh Agnihotri, whose arrest was the genesis of the strike.

Some politicians, both from the Congress (I) and the Bharatiya Janata Party (BJP) have also been named for their involvement in the 99-day strike by lawyers, sources said.

Police officers have been censured for dereliction of duty when crowds from Samaypur Badli entered the Tis Hazari court complex on 17 February 1988 leading to violence.

The report, which is reportedly exhaustive, has gone into all details of the lawyers' agitation in 1988 but has not recommended any punishment, sources claimed.

The two-judge commission was set up by the Lt. Governor, under an administrative order, to go into events leading to the *lawyers' strike which began on 15 January 1988.*

In April 1988, the commission had submitted its interim report to the Lt. Governor, which was duly placed before Parliament. It had recommended the transfer of Mrs Kiran Bedi and four other officers, in the interest of investigations. What it had also recommended was that a CBI inquiry be initiated to go into events of the lathicharge and the violence in the court complex.

The final report does not include the findings of the CBI inquiry. It was to be headed by a DIG, Mr Jaspal Singh. The findings of the CBI investigations could be contrary to the Wadhwa report.

"There has been no severe indictment on anybody but aspersions have been cast on several persons' conduct," sources said.

Lawyers have been demanding that the report be made public as it was constituted by an administrative order and not set up under the provisions of the Inquiry Act.

One of the panel members, Justice N.N. Goswami, had resigned in September '88 when a Supreme Court judge passed observations on an order he had passed.

(Indian Express, 10 March 1990)

• •

The counsel for Kiran, K.T.S. Tulsi, was later appointed as the Additional Solicitor-General of India. Bawa Gurcharan Singh, the counsel for the Delhi Bar Association, who is on record (*Newstrack,* June 1990, a video news magazine of Living Media Ltd.) as saying that "Kiran's career is finished for ever", was murdered in his chambers by one of his clients. Swaraj Kaushal, another lawyer-friend of Kiran who helped her to prepare to plead for herself before the courts, became the Governor of Mizoram.

12

North to North-East

The Narcotics Control Bureau posting had started to become somewhat of a drag for her. There seemed no effort forthcoming from the NCB for initiating growth and development. The functioning was all 'closed door' with no attempt to make it transparent. Some of the top brass had prioritised their own foreign travel plans in order to attend conferences or seminars and kept whatever information they acquired there to themselves. Nobody else was given that information, so that only those who had it could stake a claim to follow it up by attending more conferences. The NCB Director-General, M.M. Bhatnagar, wanted to keep the trips for himself alone but there were times when two conferences took place simultaneously and he could not possibly attend both. Bitterness among his subordinates had to creep in. However, there were amusing moments also when Kiran Bedi saw the chief receiving the invitations to conferences and recommending his own name for them on the files. The record of all such correspondence was kept strictly in his personal custody and no one knew the details. It was only when she would inquire about some inspector or the other, who was not present on duty, that she would be told that he was out arranging the visa and making travel reservations for the boss. Only then would it come to light that the chief was going abroad for a conference. Kiran rationalises that the country does need to be represented at such conferences and that the head of the department is to a great extent the best representative. What irked her, however, was that whatever information was presented there, and whatever was acquired there, was never shared. As Kiran succinctly puts it: "We only got to know about bits and pieces of it when the chief wanted to show himself off as the sole repository of all knowledge, and therefore most appropriate to continue to represent the country." One can quite understand her frustration at that time.

Kiran somehow completed her two-year stint at the NCB and asked for a change, even if it meant going out of Delhi, and she did put in a written request to be sent out to the furthest place possible. Little did she realise the consequences....

Mizoram is a part of the union territory cadre to which Kiran Bedi belongs. The state lies thousands of kilometres away from Delhi and all the knowledge she had about Mizoram was what she had acquired from the weather bulletins over Doordarshan and the bamboo dances on

Raj Path during the Republic Day celebrations. She had had enough of soft postings for a while and opted for a hard posting. She wrote to the Joint Secretary (Union Territories) that she would be grateful if she were sent to the Andamans, Arunachal Pradesh or Mizoram. There was no response to her letter and so she went to his office. She was assured that the matter was under active consideration and she would be informed soon. For quite a while though, nothing happened. She visited his office again and was told that the schools in Aizawl (capital of Mizoram) were bad and that she should reconsider her request. Her daughter Sukriti (also called Guchoo) had completed her tenth standard from the Convent of Jesus and Mary, New Delhi, and so she consulted officers who had served in Mizoram about the real situation regarding schools there. They told her that although there was nothing much to write home about, yet it was manageable. Armed with this knowledge she went right back to the Joint Secretary's office and told the officials concerned that she had reconsidered her request and stood by it. There was still no response from the Joint Secretary's office for another long period and then finally they communicated to her that they could offer her the post of Vigilance Officer of the Delhi Transport Corporation (DTC). The Joint Secretary's office was, therefore, obviously a dead-end and so she wrote to the Home Secretary about her request. The Home Secretary, Naresh Kumar, informed the Joint Secretary that if she was volunteering for the hard area posting then he should rightly accept her offer and send her there. Meanwhile, feelers were sent to her that if she had no objections she could be sent to Jammu and Kashmir because they needed women officers there to handle the women agitators. The obvious gender bias towards an officer who had put in 18 years of service was very offensive and she conveyed a polite 'no' Finally a batch mate, Parminder Singh, and a common friend of Kiran and the Joint Secretary persuaded the latter that, whereas officers who were given the Mizoram posting refused to accept it, here was one who was volunteering for it and the official was not letting her go. After that, she received her orders to report to the Mizoram Government on 27 April 1990. She left immediately.

She had wanted a change and a change she most certainly did get. A change from the pollution, over-population and noise of Delhi to the serenity of open tracts with pure air and plenty of space; from the sequence of one tightly scheduled day after another she could now get back to the tidiness and purposiveness of regular office hours; from precious moments snatched for reading to ample time for leisurely indulgence in books; and from early morning newspapers to no newspapers at all!

It was indeed a much required change. For the first time in her 18 years of service she was having regular lunch with her family and also returning home at 5 p.m. sharp. Essentially a home-loving person, she was enjoying the closeness of family life almost for the first time in her career. There was a tennis court at a walking distance and the office was only 20 steps below. (The house was on a hillock.) There was not much scope for shopping and she could even economise a little.

Vegetables were very difficult to come by because (as already stated) the Mizos are essentially meat-eaters and thrive on pork, beef, mutton, poultry, fish and dogs. They can comfortably manage without vegetables, milk and milk products. Kiran and her family gave up eating chicken only when they realised that they could not get a dressed chicken there. Once they had asked the cook to prepare chicken and learnt this fact when they saw him dressing the chicken at home. That effectively put an end to their chicken lunches and dinners.

The area of Mizoram is vast and the terrain rugged. The state is sparsely populated and because of lack of any good system of roads it is highly inaccessible. Because of this lack of interlinking roads very little ethnic bonding exists among the tribals living there. Moreover, economic development activities and facilities for education are almost negligible. The people living in the interiors and the remote villages are, by and large, very discontented with their lot. Such areas provided the ideal breeding grounds for insurgency and terrorism and Mizoram had an unduly large share of the ravages that such activities bring about. Suffice it to say that Aizawl has the dubious distinction of being the only place in our country that has been bombed by its own Air Force.

The Hmars constitute that group of the Mizos which had been the most prominent one in the insurgency operations. They exist in relatively larger numbers than the rest of the tribes and since they also speak a very different dialect from the rest they could form a very cohesive group. The army and the police, therefore, had quite a parcel on their hands in dealing with the Mizo hostilities in the area. However, through sustained and coordinated efforts, they could ultimately manage to contain the situation and bring the Hmar Revolutionary Council (HRC) from a position where it could dictate terms to one where it sought surrender and rehabilitation. The only alternative for the HRC members would probably have been decimation. Unfortunate as most such conflicts are, the Mizos had lost a lot by then.

Mizoram signed the peace accord after several years of insurgency. By the time Kiran was posted there as Deputy Inspector-General (Range) [DIG(R)], the overall situation had already limped back to near-normal. Since there was no electricity in most of the areas and because of the years of curfew conditions that had prevailed, the Mizos were quite used to waking up with the sun and going indoors at sunset. Gradually, however, the situation started to change and the evenings, specially during summer, saw groups of young boys and girls sitting outside their houses and singing to the accompaniment of guitars, or leisurely strolling down the streets. The Mizo community is quite liberal in its social norms and there is free intermingling of boys and girls without any parental frowning on their activities. The youngsters choose their own marriage partners, and divorce is not uncommon.

As already mentioned, Mizoram has a very porous eastern border and drug abuse is rampant among its youth. This factor, combined with the general air of permissiveness amongst its youth, has made Mizoram one of the states with the highest incidence of AIDS. Mizos do not grow enough quantities of rice and the Centre has to provide large subsidies for this cereal. However, a lot of this rice gets diverted to brewing the local drink called *Zu* in Mizo language. The incidence of alcoholism, too, is consequently very high.

As with any newly formed state the Mizos are very suspicious of non-Mizos. They call foreigners '*Vais*' and their distrust borders on hostility. Given the foregoing conditions in Mizoram, the non-Mizos have a very difficult time there. The majority of criminal offences are directed towards the latter. They are repeatedly looted and are afraid to make formal complaints lest they be further harassed. Most of the lower ranks in the police are made up of Mizos and, given the close community links, they are somehow or the other related to most of the local families. The '*Vais*', therefore, have very little chance of seeing justice done and prefer to bear their fate stoically. A number of them are married to local girls but have not been accepted by the Mizo community. They naturally let things be in the hope that they would be spared in the future for being 'good boys'. Yet they continue to stay on because they would rather not face the trauma of relocating their homes.

Without getting into the political dimensions of the Chakma (refugees from Bangladesh) problem, one can quite realise the cause of the enormous aggression shown to them, with murder, arson and pillage being the norms of the day.

Mizoram has but one law and order range. The tasks of its Deputy Inspector-General (Range), DIG (R), therefore, include looking after the law and order situation, crime prevention, protection of the people and public property, management of traffic and checking the menace of drug abuse by destroying the drug sources all over Mizoram.

Kiran's first priority was to gear up the resources at her command, in the form of the police force. When she took over, things used to move at a very personal level rather than at a professional or institutional level. Consequently, she tried to reform her force; at least those personnel working at the headquarters. An almost abject laxity marked the pattern of working, especially the keeping of records. Consequently, every case had to be taken up from scratch each time. Kiran took several steps to rectify this situation.

Kiran's approach has always been to take the initiative to prevent a crime rather than merely catching and punishing the criminal. In Mizoram also, she resorted to her time-tested method of seeking community participation for preventive policing. With regular updating of the scanty record system, her office was able to attain a position where it could keep track of criminals through their antecedents and ascertain whether a particular culprit was still traceable and whether he was still active in a life of crime or had given it up. A list of people with known criminal records was drawn up, which was circulated amongst the community at the village level and also amongst the village defence parties (VDP) and the YMCA. Such open identification helped deter a lot of criminals from carrying on their activities. Another benefit gained was in the form of information given by the criminal caught, which helped in the arrest of those who persisted with their old ways.

The language problem was resolved as her staff officer, Lalhuliana, was fluent in both English and Mizo. Through him she could reach out to her officers and other staff at different levels of understanding, commitment and motivation. The briefings were held so often and so regularly that the staff officer gradually did not even have to be explained in English but would rattle off the needful in Mizo straightaway to the groups. If it was to be a lecture on 'management' then all he required to be cued in was to be merely told the subject and off he would go.

"It is very important that the staff be given direct access to their seniors to promote motivation, involvement and innovative experimentation in the ranks," believes Kiran.

Her constables were the happiest with her because of this belief. As a matter of fact, wherever she has served, her constables have always sworn by her and are very forthcoming in telling one and all that they feel secure under her leadership. Obviously, there was a marked change in their attitude and performance. And as there were discernible improvements in the scruffy looking Goa traffic police force, so also in Aizawl.

The beat system that had been implemented in Delhi was put into effect in Mizoram too. The lacklustre, lethargic Mizo cop suddenly found he could wield authority in his beat. Also, he realised that along with this authority came responsibility too and the lure of the one motivated him to aspire for the other. Thus, the Mizo cops began policing their beats under their own initiatives, taking their own decisions. The all-too-new briefings and debriefings and the regular roll calls each morning and evening made them alert to the responsibilities related to the incidents and inhabitants of their respective areas. With the ready reckoner of criminals that had been prepared and the new-found responsibility they felt towards their beats, policing did indeed become more effective.

What greatly assisted in this positive development was the fact that probably because of their nature, but certainly through circumstances, the Mizos are a very organised community. Almost everyone belonged to some organisation or the other. The existence of these organisations helped the force a lot as their support was very forthcoming. For instance, there were the village councils, village defence parties, youth wings and the women's organisation, the MHIP [Mizoram Women's Association (translated from Mizo)]. Over and above such organisations, the churches to which the Mizos belonged drew their own affiliations. And then there were the affiliations to the political groups and parties like Congress (I), the Mizo National Federation or the Janata Dal, all of which had fairly committed policies.

Although it was the aforementioned organisations and groups that extended wholehearted support to her idea of community policing, one cannot deny the fact that it certainly was Kiran who had taken the initiative. What probably convinced the Mizos so soon and so effectively was the fact that her in-house cleansing programme was so visible. There had been common public discontent that while drunkards in civilian dress were regularly arrested and punished, those in uniform were allowed to move about scot-free. The beat system had become very popular with the constables and Kiran ensured that no constable with an alcohol problem be given the responsibility of a 'beat'. This deprivation hit their self-esteem. It was not difficult, therefore, to persuade them to undergo treatment at the Mizo Armed Police (MAP) Hospital that had been set up to treat alcoholics. Such a salubrious development not only helped the personnel of the force within but also sent out healthy signals to the community.

The persons involved in the commercialisation of the home-made '*Zu*' were also dissuaded from the practice through counselling and, more importantly, through rehabilitation. Such a procedure had proved very effective with the 'Sansi' community in Delhi as also with the women of the Yamuna Pushta Juggi area there. It proved very effective in Aizawl too. The spate of traffic accidents in Aizawl during Christmas is always a measure of the unregulated fondness the people there have for liquor. The records of road accidents and brawls that took place during the Christmas celebrations during 1990 and 1991 are indicative of the steep decline in the abuse of alcohol while driving. The records of the emergencies at the local hospitals as well as the FIRs lodged in the police stations also vouchsafe this fact. The best part was that the entire exercise was 'people managed' with police supporting them – the key to any such situation.

Traffic asssistance cards were widely circulated amongst the public at major entry and exit points to Aizawl. These cards provided an opportunity to bus and taxi passengers to report against overspeeding, consumption of alcohol by the driver, carrying of excess passengers, and overcharging. Such cards also helped in getting information on luggage left behind. The cards were similar to postcards with the postage paid by the police department. On receipt of such complaints, after verifying their genuineness, the police would initiate action on their own. These cards exerted a great deal of psychological pressure on the erring drivers and irregularities were considerably reduced. And this feat was achieved without taxing the department financially as the project had been funded by the local sponsors of the area.

The Mizos form a very religious community and this trait was put to effective use in the prevention of crime. With the help of an enthusiastic Mizo police officer, Hriua (pronounced *shroya* in Mizo), subdivisional police officer, Aizawl township, regular prayer meetings (known as '*Reh*') of the listed persons were held in the police station confines along with the Mizo police staff. Hriua arranged for a priest to be present and, to the accompaniment of a guitar, he would lead these prayer meetings himself. This message of a rehabilitative and correctional approach for the community soon reached the ears of the Mizo cable TV network and the programme soon became the talk of the town.

The Aizawl District SP, L.S. Sailo, a Mizo himself, however, did not appreciate these goings-on and soon created a lobby of local citizens and activated a part of the press to protest against the interference of a '*Vai*' in local customs. Such a move put paid to the prayer meetings. Kiran remembers she was advised by the Home Secretary, S.L.R. Siama, to work less, and let things take care of themselves. He, of course, said it in good faith, for he cared for Kiran and did not want her to be misunderstood.

By nature, Mizos are strongly biased against the people of the plains, the '*Vais*', but in Kiran Bedi they saw a person who was working *for* them and their Mizo Council. They began to appreciate and accept her. The common man was the beneficiary of her actions and he was gradually reaping the benefits. The state officials, however, looked on this with some degree of scepticism, and their attitude was quite understandable. It was probably for the first time that they were seeing a police officer interacting with the public beyond the usual levels of search, arrest, prosecution and punishment. But this interaction required a lot of persuasion from, and coordination with, the supporting agencies and the community. It is this constant interaction with the community that has been the hallmark of Kiran Bedi's mode of functioning. The fact that such positive interaction has inevitably, as in the case of Mizoram, been viewed with suspicion of her intent discloses the tendency of our bureaucracy to alienate the people.

● ● ●

On the domestic front, Kiran Bedi underwent an agonising experience. Her father was enjoying the salubrious air and climate of Mizoram and indulging wholeheartedly in his favourite pastime of tennis during this period. One morning he complained of a sharp pain on the side of his abdomen and was taken by his wife to the hospital. Kiran also reached there and was told that some pathological tests were being done and that there was absolutely no cause for concern. A few minutes after she had returned to her office the doctors informed Prem Lata Peshawaria (Kiran's mother) that her husband had to be immediately operated upon for an appendicitis as the appendix could burst any moment. As the doctors and the staff of the hospital spoke only the Mizo language, she could not get to understand much but her husband, being in great pain, signed the documents for the operation. It would take only half an hour, they assured her. The operation, in fact, lasted four hours. Prem Lata Peshawaria was joined by her daughter and after a while by Swaraj Kaushal, the Governor of Mizoram. Kaushal appeared stupefied that in a place where people rushed to Delhi in case of even a minor cough or infection, Kiran and her mother had agreed to a major operation! After the operation they were told that the patient was not suffering from appendicitis but that he had tuberculosis of the intestines and that the entire maze of intestines had to be brought out, cleaned, checked and placed back.

It was discovered later that while conducting such a check a portion of the intestines had been nicked. This negligence brought Parkash Lal Peshawaria almost to death's door. Acute infection and damage to major organs resulted and a severe bloating of the stomach commenced almost immediately. The principal of the Government Hospital in Silchar Dr. Barua was contacted. A helicopter was requisitioned by Swaraj Kaushal, Governor of Mizoram, and a university friend of Kiran, who had great regard for Kiran's parents. The copter brought in the doctor. He examined the patient and administered a cut on the side of the abdomen. Copious quantities of bile and noxious fluids poured out. Swaraj Kaushal was the one in real agony! He had sensed total danger in case Kiran's father was not sent to a properly equipped hosptial. He again requisitioned a helicopter to fly out Kiran's father to Silchar, along with the doctor, and Kiran and her mother followed by jeep. In Silchar no other course of treatment was suggested or given except the draining of the abdominal fluids. Parkash Lal's weight slumped from a healthy 58 kg to 36 kg. An intern, from amongst a number who visited him as a test case for research, suggested to Kiran that as there were just no facilities in the hospital she would be best advised to shift the patient to Delhi. When the principal was requested for a discharge he had no objection and even agreed to send a doctor with them in a helicopter Swaraj had arranged for. Yet again, now, they had to fly straight to Guwahati to be linked with an Indian Airlines flight. The helicopter pilot informed them that no women were allowed aboard. The matter was referred immediately to his superiors who were told that since the Peshawarias did not have any sons they would have to make do with his daughters Kiran, Reeta and Anu, who had all come together at this moment of crisis. Permission was granted by Air Headquarters (Delhi). But Mizoram Raj Bhawan did not sleep that night till it got the clearances! Kiran says she can't thank her colleagues enough: for instance, Prabhat Singh, Amodh Kanth,

Joseph and many others who went out of the way to help her in that moment of crisis.

The pilot contacted the captain of the Indian Airlines flight from Guwahati to Delhi, requesting him to hold the flight for an emergency case. Kiran's batch mate, G.P. Srivastava, waited anxiously at the airport. The flight was ready for take-off when they landed and even the Governor of Assam was waiting. Captain Kaul, on the Indian Airlines aircraft, assured Kiran that he would ensure a smooth flight to Delhi.

At Delhi airport friends of the family, Kiran's brothers-in-law, colleagues and few others immediately took Kiran's father by ambulance straight to the operation theatre of the All India Institute of Medical Sciences. Dr. S.N. Mehta, a brilliant surgeon, now in the Middle East, took charge. He told Kiran that he was very sorry to say so, but the condition of the patient was very bad and that all they could do was hope. Since her father was in a critical state, another operation could not be conducted. Consequently, he was put under medication and all that the family members could do was to pray that the nick in the intenstine would heal on its own.

After four months, with the family's savings almost finished, not to comment on the toll it took mentally and physically of the parents and their four daughters, Parkash Lal could get back on his feet. Today, at 80, he still plays tennis at the Chelmsford Club courts. He loves, lives, eats, reads and dreams tennis.

Back in Mizoram after a long leave, Kiran gradually settled back into her daily routine as a police officer. She learnt then that while she was with her father in the hospital at Silchar, the IG(P), Lal Chhanga, various ministers and officials in Aizawl had been trying to discuss with the Governor the list of the persons whom they would have to inform for the funeral in case it had to be organised there! It was immediately after this that the Governor had told Kiran to rush to Delhi with her father in yet another helicopter arranged by him with reservation connections through Guwahati. Kiran calls Swaraj her brother today! "A friend in need is a friend indeed," and Swaraj proved this beyond imagination!

13

'Road to Freedom'

Kiran's daughter, Saina, had done her 10th from the Convent of Jesus and Mary in New Delhi. She did her 11th and 12th, the most important years of schooling, from the Kendriya Vidyalaya in Aizawl. This effectively debarred her from taking her pre-medical examination from Delhi which required a mandatory condition that the concerned student should have done 11th and 12th from Delhi itself. This debarment left her with the option of appearing only in the all-India examinations. Because of the comparable differences in the educational facilities between Delhi and

Mizoram, this option again required that she be in Delhi, which of course was not possible, given the exigencies of her mother's service conditions. In the course of a conversation with her friends at school, Saina learnt that as she was studying in Aizawl she could compete for the medical seats allotted by the Centre to Mizoram. The ranking done on the merit list of the 12th standard examinations would be the deciding criterion and she plunged herself into studies despite the lack of sufficient guidance at the school at Aizawl. The school was deficient in teachers. She cleared the board examinations admirably well, securing 89 per cent marks, the highest among the non-Mizo students. Interestingly, the two Mizo girls above her in the merit list had done their schooling in Madras. To apply for the medical seat quota Sukriti had, however, to attach her domicile certificate. Kiran requested the District Collector for this certificate but was told in no uncertain terms that she would not be given one. She then explained to one of her officers that all she wanted from the DC was a certificate stating that Sukriti had been domiciled in Aizawl for the past two years, that was all. The officer asked her to speak to the DC on the telephone and explain the situation to him. The DC agreed to consider the matter and later this same officer collected the certificate of residence. This certificate was despatched along with the application and marksheet to the relevant authorities who asked Saina to appear for an interview. At the interview she was asked for her choice of medical college location and she left it to the board to decide.

For a long time, no list was announced and nothing made public. Everyone kept guessing about the government's intention. As regards other seats, for other courses, the lists of candidates, selected on merit, were duly announced, but not those of the medical course Such an announcement, apparently, was the prerogative of the Chief Minister.

An interesting event that took place during this period of waiting was that the non-Mizo doctors' lobby in Mizoram, which was always close to the powers that be, started pressing for the selection of non-Mizo students for the reserved quota not on the basis of merit but on the longer period of domicile. Politics was apparently at work, dividing the non-Mizo community, small though it was.

As per the Government of India rules, Sukriti was eligible for, and deserving of, her seat on three counts. First, by virtue of her domicile and having acquired her higher secondary education in Mizoram; second, by virtue of her being the daughter of an officer of the union territory cadre posted to the state of Mizoram; and third, and the most important, by virtue of her merit in the board examinations. The Central Government had allocated thirteen seats to Mizoram and there was no way anyone could deprive Saina of her due. This sense of surety went a long way in diluting the harassment of a long wait for both the mother and the daughter.

The order of 4 August 1992, for the Central pool MBBS and BDS seats for the state of Mizoram for the year 1992-93 clearly states "... that the States/UTs should nominate their candidates on the basis of the merit system devised by the Government of India; the children of all-India service officers would also be eligible to participate in the said merit system."

On his basis, Saina was allotted a sent on 11 August 1992, which was subsequently notified to be cancelled on 15 September 1992.

Word got through to Kiran Bedi that Chief Minister Lal Thanhawla was apparently angry with her and, therefore, as a form of punishment, he was in no mood to grant her daughter her due. This development gave a new turn to the whole incident and Kiran would wonder as to why on God's earth the CM was annoyed with her. Grapevines function for just this sort of a situation and the reasons soon reached her.

Kiran had discovered exemplary qualities in an officer under her charge. In her view he was the most outstanding of all the police officers in her range. She found him to be alert and quick to grasp strategies, possessed initiative and exhibited good leadership qualities. Over and above these features, she also found him to be highly welfare-oriented. In one of her monthly meetings with officers of her range, where this particular officer was representing his battalion, he mentioned to her how he was being harassed and mistreated by his SP. The DIG (Range) called up the SP and asked him for an explanation. Because the young officer concerned was a non-Mizo, the SP was quick to proclaim to one and all that discrimination was being exercised against a Mizo official by a non-Mizo superior. The SP who had earlier shown contempt for her concept of introducing prayer meetings for Mizo criminals was quick to join forces on the issue. They took the matter up to their political bosses.

Yet another incident seemed to irk the Mizoram Government. The Additional SP (Prosecution), a Mizo officer this time, was supervising court operations from his office located at some distance from the courts. His Deputy SP, who functioned from the court office, was therefore his own boss and had, consequently, lowered efficiency to an extremely low pitch. The Additional SP could not do much about such a situation due to lack of proximity. Bedi advised him to shift his office to the court so that a modicum of efficiency could be restored. This step was not in the least appreciated by the DSP who suddenly realised that he was now expected to not only attend office regularly but also to actually work. He also joined forces with the aforementioned SPs and added a new dimension to the entire episode; i.e., Kiran not just discriminating against Mizo officers but also taking on powers of the Government in transferring an Additional SP. The CM promptly issued orders that the Additional SP was to revert to his earlier office. A hapless and much harassed ASP came back to Bedi and expressed his annoyance. She told him to go and explain to the CM that he had never been transferred in the first place but had merely been required to shift his office in order to ensure proper surveillance and efficiency in the disposal of court cases. He did so and was told that if that were the case then he should do what he had been advised. When the two SPs and DSP trio realised that the Additional SP had also met the CM, it took the wind out of their sails.

What is even more interesting is that the Chief Minister did not choose to refer back to his DIG for information or confirmation but rather chose to become angry with Kiran. And so, her daughter Saina was not to be allowed her due.

(In passing one may mention that after Kiran's transfer from Mizoram not much later, the non-Mizo DSP mentioned earlier was suspended from service.)

Kiran decided to meet the Health Minister Vaivenga and ask him directly about the progress of her daughter's case. The Health Minister suggested that she try to somehow wangle a seat from Delhi because it was going to be very difficult to do so from Mizoram. "Why should I?" she demanded, and asked him to give her daughter's standing in the merit list that was on the Minister's table. He looked at it and merely suggested that she speak to the Chief Minister.

Instead of the CM, Kiran decided to look up the Chief Secretary, Pahnuna. She thought that because he was the chief of administration he would at least possess some concern for merit and fair play. She explained to him that although her daughter belonged to Delhi she could not appear for the examinations there because she had not done her higher secondary schooling from there and that although she had done her higher secondary from Mizoram she could not appear from here because she was not a Mizo. She then posed the question as to where did the Chief Secretary think her daughter should appear from? The Chief Secretary gave this matter a little thought and suggested that she meet the Chief Minister.

Not deterred by this reply Kiran decided to meet the CM and personally explain her daughter's case. She decided to first have some other Mizo officer outline the case to him and then seek permission for an interview. The interview was granted soon enough. She put her case forcefully enough. She first showed him the application form as it had come back after being rejected from Delhi (to appear from there). She then recalled for him the recent Guwahati High Court judgement regarding seat allotments on the basis of merit. And then, in the form of a *coup de grâce,* she reminded him of the colossal and callous bungling of her father's operation because of ill-equipped and substandard hospitals in Mizoram. The family bore it out with fortitude and never once complained. Had they done so, Kiran was quick to inform him, she and her three sisters would not have to work all their lives in order to earn money.

The position of the Chief Minister was clear. If he himself did not clear the list then Kiran had enough justifiable documents to have the courts direct him to do so. Then and there he issued orders for the allotment of Saina seat in the Lady Hardinge Medical College at Delhi.

She rushed to Delhi the same day to get her daughter admitted.

The first child from either the Peshawarias or the Bedis entered a medical college on 14 August 1992.

While she was in Delhi, Kiran was informed that people had held massive demonstrations in Aizawl and that they had launched an agitation there against her. Despite her parents' attempts to stall her departure, she went back to rejoin duties. Aizawl greeted her with black banners, placards and shouts of "*Kiran Bedi Go Back*".

Her decision not to lead the police against the agitationists from the front is quite justifiable seeing that her best of intentions could be construed as biased. This was also in keeping with the views of the Chief Secretary, although there were many who insisted otherwise. The general attitude of the authorities was one of toleration and restraint. Under the circumstances it was as expected that the agitation grew from bad to worse. Riots and arson were the 'order' of the day and, by and large, the agitating students had a free hand in what they were doing.

She received an invitation from the Indian Institute of Public Administration, Delhi, to attend a seminar there for a week. Sending her there for that duration would have been sound strategy and could have diluted the agitation somewhat, but the authorities thought otherwise. The IG(P), Kulbir Singh, who was a non-Mizo, suggested to the Chief Secretary that he should allow her to go, but the CS told him that regrets had already been sent on their own.

Without any will or determination on the State Government's part to check the agitation, the situation had gone totally out of control. It was at this stage that Kiran was called to meet the Law and Education Minister, Dr. Thansanga, in his office at 7.30 one evening. She took a Mizo officer she could trust with her and drove to the minister's office on that dark, rainy and chilly evening. Both the Law and Education Minister and the Health Minister were present. It was explained to her how grave the students' unrest had become and what did she suggest be done? She told him that matters had to be taken in hand and a will to control the agitation must be shown. Unfortunately, she observed that there was nothing of the sort visible. On the contrary, the magistrates were shying away from their jobs and were not present at scenes of law violation. They allowed small groups of 50 to 200 to swell into mobs of 1500 to 2000 and, consequently, declared that the law and order situation was completely out of control. A couple of such crisp volleys by Kiran and the minister's changed course. They suggested to her that the only way out of the situation was that she should surrender, in writing, her daughter's seat allocation. The admini-stration, they contended, could do nothing about the situation and if she did not heed their advice then the matter would rest in the hands of the students who could even kill her. "Kill me?" asked Kiran. "Kill you", said

Dr. Thansanga. She requested time to discuss the matter with her daughter and her family and was granted time till 8 a.m. the next day. With that the meeting was over.

Promptly at 8 a.m. Dr. Thansanga called her residence. She told him that she was still trying to get across to her family in Delhi over the telephone. At this she was told that in defiance of the prohibitory orders, the students would be collecting at 10 a.m. and that if the information on the withdrawal of seat allocation was not given to them, then they would take matters into their own hands. She decided to take shelter by driving to the Raj Bhawan, the house of the Governor, Swaraj Kaushal. Frantic calls were made to her office and residence to trace her whereabouts from the Chief Minister's office downwards. It was only when she informed the IG (P) that she was at the Raj Bhawan that the calls stopped. With the approval of the Governor, Kiran Bedi drove out of Mizoram for good at midnight.

Back in Delhi, Kiran told *The Sunday Observer* (27 September 1992):

Controversies, troubles, brickbats, fierce opposition ... all these are not new to me. When I devoted my life to the Indian Police Service (IPS), I embraced all these and more, as part and parcel of my fate. Remember the Akali agitation when thousands of Akalis brandishing naked swords had charged towards the police in a frenzy, and I clashed with them with only a danda (baton) in my hand? Well, I forget the exact date when the incident occurred, but in retrospect, I am sure that it was not physical force but a psychological pressure from my side which made the crowd flee. My attitude to the incident, as my attitude towards anything, was simple. There was my target, and here was I. That I had to succeed was the only thought at the back of my mind, and whatever I did thereafter, was a reflex action. My motto in life is that nothing is impossible, no target unachievable − one just has to try harder and harder.

I had somewhat similar experience during the raid on drug traffickers in the UP hills when I was with the Narcotics Bureau. What I want to point out − and this has been my stance during the lawyers' agitation too − is that I have never been cowed down, or accepted defeat or tolerated injustice in my over 20 years of service. So why should I bow to a totally absurd demand made by the Mizoram chief minister now? People have often wondered how I, being a woman, can combat certain things. My answer to all of them have [sic] been, that it is wrong to think that just because a certain person is a woman, she is delicate. I am not delicate − maybe that's why

one does not get to see me in a saree − I feel the saree is for delicate people.

Anyway, in the context of the present situation, the ongoing controversy about me and my daughter, Sukriti, I'd say that we are absolutely on the right. My daughter gets the seat for two factors. One, that she is the daughter of an IPS officer who is serving on a "hard area" posting, and as per the Central Government guidelines the children of such officers are entitled to certain benefits. But, this is the secondary factor in Sukriti's case. She got the seat on her own merit − by dint of getting the highest marks among students who took the exams from Mizoram. Now what I'd like to add here is that I did not ask the government to give me a posting in Mizoram, the government wanted my services there. Since my daughter stays with me, she went to Mizoram too with me, and studied in the Central School there for two years. So now that she has studied there, why should she take the exams elsewhere? The chief minister says that he does not want non-Mizos to get seats from Mizoram because they are not going to return to the state. I ask him, what gave him the idea that they are not going to return ? All the other four non-Mizo candidates who were selected -- all on merit — are children of people who are integral part of Mizoram. One student's father has been a civil servant in the Mizo government for almost two decades and is going to retire in the same capacity, another's father is a doctor there, the third student's mother is a Mizo woman... I ask where will the children of these people go? After all, they are a product of the place. I am fighting on this issue because if this is allowed to go unprotested, tomorrow nobody will be willing to go and serve in Mizoram, and then some time later other states too might follow suit. This would be a big blow to our country's unity, national integration, demo-cracy and all that we stand for. I wonder how a state government can bow to such unjust and discriminatory demands.

For that matter, what guarantee does Mr Lal Thanhawla have that the Mizo students who do their MBBS are going to serve in Mizoram? Have all the Mizo students returned to the state in the past? Can they be compelled to do so? India after all is a democracy, not a dictatorship — you cannot curb a citizen's freedom to go and work wherever he feels like, so what is the big point? And besides, the seats of doctors in the state are not vacant because of want of availability of doctors. If the chief minister says so, I challenge him to prove it.

The third question I'd like to ask is, what if tomorrow the same treatment is meted out to Mizos in Delhi? What if they are told that they will not be considered under the scheduled caste or scheduled tribe category in Delhi, and so they should return to their states and apply under the special slot there? Well, don't misunderstand me. I don't want that to happen. I am not a Mizo or non-Mizo, a Hindu, Sikh, or Delhiite — I am an Indian, and I look upon every individual in India as an equal, so whatever happened has hurt me extremely. I have become a victim of an anti-Indian, anti-national feeling. Till my actions like controlling the drug problem there, has [sic] benefited the society there, I was accepted, but the moment matters came to Mizo-non-Mizo sentiments, I was made to feel that I was an outsider.

I was asked in writing to meet the chief minister and discuss this issue with him in the evening on September 12. There, I was categorically told: "Your daughter is the only one who is coming in the way of normalcy in the state. Withdraw your daughter or bear the consequences ...". No, I don't want to go into full details of this meeting because I think it does not behove my position, but they tried their best to do a little more than intimidate me. Thereafter, in my wisdom, I thought it best to leave the scene. I thought it might help the law and order situation. People say that I ran away — well, actually, I sped away, and that too in the dead of the night. Circumstances had got beyond control and I realised that if I informed anybody my departure would be made impossible. I had earlier asked for leave, but this was not accepted. So, I left without asking. I left a letter saying that I was leaving under compelling situations and that I would be away for as long as the situation warrants, so that I may please be granted leave. I regret leaving a place like this. My term was over four months ago, and I had wanted to leave, leaving goodwill behind. It is very unfortunate that all my slogging, struggling and hard work there, had to get lost in one Mizo emotion.

I had no option but to resort to this. During my police training we often sang the

'Hum honge kaamyaab' song. *I stand by this. I will not surrender to injustice. They say that they will take stronger action. Well, I am ready. The ball is in their court. My daughter shall continue attending classes and I shall not meet people here or lobby for my case. I am claiming something on merit which, I believe, speaks for itself. If it ultimately does not, I shall do whatever I can, to protect my daughter's career. I have seen her slogging to make it. How can I, as a mother, take away what is the rightful fruit of her labour? It's the question of her career, her life. There's something called natural justice in law — this is on my daughter's side. What these people will be doing if they try to have my daughter thrown out is to go against the law — break it. I don't think they will dare do that. I am sure that justice will prevail. It must prevail. I am here to ensure that it prevails.*

(The Sunday Observer, 27 September-6 October 1992)

Once the students of Mizoram realised that she had actually left, they called off their agitation immediately. The state promptly issued orders for the cancellation of allotment of a seat to Sukriti Bedi. The Lady Hardinge Medical College, Delhi, however refused to give cognisance to such orders on the ground that they had no reason to expel a student registered on their rolls.

The State of Mizoram tried to file a petition in the higher courts. But the Supreme Court was not even willing to consider it. The matter rested at the contention that "seats allocated by the Government of India are not for Mizos but Mizoram, that is a state of India."

14

Freedom from Fear

The course of her career clearly reveals the qualities Kiran Bedi has imbibed through the formative years of her childhood, in school and during her preparatory years in college when she was intensely involved in studies, extra-curricular activities and, of course, the tennis courts. As situations demanded throughout her career, she drew on her reservoir of resources some qualities that came naturally to her and some that she diligently and assiduously developed herself. In the interaction between her values and actions she matured along with the passage of time.

The jagged edges that she had developed, mainly because of the exigencies of her circumstances, were gradually and steadily smoothening themselves against the tide of experience. Yet, if there was satisfaction at one moment, there soon followed an irritation at the circumstantial curbing of potential. She seemed to feel that though she had imbibed, learned, and experienced so much, yet she was not being given an opportunity to express herself fully.

The opportunity to really prove herself came when she was posted as IG (Prisons), Tihar Jail, New Delhi. This posting represented a colossal challenge for her; verily, it entailed the cleaning up of the mythological Augean stables. The results are there for everyone to see!

At this stage, it would be relevant to provide some background information. The establishment of the Delhi jail can be traced to the British rule in India. During the Mughal times, close to the Khooni Darwaza (or Delhi Gate, located near Lal Qila), one Farid Khan had built a large inn for travellers passing through Delhi. When the British took over power, they requisitioned this inn and converted it into a jail, mainly for the locality. However, as the Indian freedom movement gathered momentum from 1919 onwards, it led to the arrest of a large number of political prisoners whom the British had to accommodate. Thus, the local jail was upgraded to a 'district jail' in 1937. After India gained independence, this jail was shifted to a place near Tihar village, then on the outskirts of Delhi. A few years later, the jail was further upgraded to the status of a Central jail, which it still retains. However, its size and capacity have changed dramatically over the years. In 1958, Tihar Jail covered an area of 170 acres. Today, it houses over 8500 inmates against a sanctioned capacity of 2500.

It was only as late as 1965 that Tihar Jail came under the control of the Delhi Administration. Until then it had been controlled by the Punjab State Police. Even when Delhi took over control of this jail, it was the Deputy Commissioner of Delhi who was the ex-officio IG of prisons, and the superintendents and other executive staff still came on deputation from the Punjab State Police cadre.

The present post of the Inspector-General (Prisons) is an ex-cadre post occupied by an officer of the Indian Administrative Service, or the Indian Police Service. The Deputy Inspector-General (DIG) is from the Delhi and Andaman Civil Services (DANICS). The superintendents of the prison also belong to the same services. The personnel of the Tihar Jail cadre are the deputy superintendents, assistant superintendents, head warders and warders. This is a very neglected cadre, where hardly any attention has been paid to promotional growth or service conditions. Consequently, there exists in this cadre tremendous frustration, low morale, exploitation and poor integrity. They are also not transferable out of Delhi, the capital being a city-state anyway. This implies they are on prison duty at Tihar as long as they are in service — perhaps twice the 'life imprisonment' term compared to a normal one of fourteen years.

Kiran went to Tihar with mixed feelings. In the eyes of the public, the post was not a highly esteemed one. Even in the service it was considered to be a 'dump' posting. She had come from a 'hard' posting and was entitled to get back to the Delhi Police. But apparently there was no place for her. On return from Mizoram she sat in Delhi for over nine months and it was now becoming difficult for the government to justify no posting for such a long period. The Tihar post was lying vacant and Kiran was 'adjusted'. However, inside her she found this to be an opportunity to further the cause of correctional reforms and crime prevention! There were around 8500 people there to whom she could bring her correctional methods and attempt their rehabilitation. She was being destined to do what she would most willingly have done voluntarily.

Tihar was exactly as she could have expected it to be. Its working was completely shrouded in secrecy. The entire area was closed to visitors for fear of exposure to the fact inmates were being treated like animals, the prisoners were uncared for and disorganised and possessed a mob mentality and were being tackled by mob management tactics. To say it was totally disorganised would be an understatement.

The jail staff was typically colonial in their outlook. In her initial visits to the jail they would precede her with batons in their hands, clearing the way for the IG. And their language? It was crude and offensive towards the inmates. The inmates would all crowd around, wondering why a senior officer had come visiting the jail. The earlier practice was to have the prisoners locked up whenever an officer visited the prison. For security reasons, the authorities claimed. There was an absolute fear psychosis prevailing. There was no communication between the IG and the prisoners. Everyone faced problems in plenty but no solutions were forthcoming because of this lack of communication. Individual attempts were made to sort out problems, but there certainly was no collective effort in this direction. As a police officer Kiran was quite used to moving amidst aggressive crowds and so she had no problems moving amidst the prisoners, although the magnitude certainly was greater. The environment posed no threats for her and she was very comfortable standing or sitting amidst large groups of prisoners to discuss their problems with them. This close contact with the inmates revealed that they were totally disorganised and disoriented. The purpose behind such meetings was not so much as to offer immediate solutions as soon as problems were stated but rather to make the staff, along with her, become aware of them. Because she had been there with them she could later ask her staff to analyse the problems that had come up in these meetings with the prisoners and suggest collective measures to overcome them. This approach helped greatly in their participation in, and involvement with, the prevailing situation.

The word 'inspection' has become obsolete in prison parlance. It was suggested that the staff members try and observe the causes and consequences of their actions and to see if they had a clear conscience about what they had done. This suggestion led to a lot of introspection amongst them, and corrective measures for problems arising out of their own mistakes were freely offered. As a matter of fact, the officers were very forthcoming on the rectification of their errors. This was a very good sign and it paved the way to progress much faster than one would have thought.

'Anger' was the operative word for the earlier mode of action adopted by the staff. They were habituated to using force whenever they encountered any form of indiscipline. Their actions were all geared to put the fear of authority into the prisoners' minds. They probably

Breaking eleven days' 'noble silence'.

Back in Tihar from Manila — responding to the inmates' jubilation.

With a bouquet of poppies while destroying illegal poppy fields in the Chakrata *Tehsil*.

Making a point at Prison Headquarters.

Paying homage to Mahatma Gandhi inside Tihar (October 1993).

Christmas day performance by jail inmates (1994).

Sitting amongst a large group of inmates — watching a function in jail.

Being hugged by foreign inmates in a gesture of thanks for making life better.

A French class being conducted by a foreign inmate.

A Persian class in progress.

Raksha Bandhan inside the jail.

With prisoners' children in jail — children up to four years can stay
with their mothers.

Even the aged prisoners take to the literacy programme.

Women prisoners do export jobs and earn money for themselves.

A glimpse of the crowded conditions in Tihar (Tihar houses four times its capacity).

Listening raptly to complaints of the shoeshine boys at Connaught Place, New Delhi

never even thought of trying to create respect for authority. It seemed that there were two antagonistic forces present there: the prisoners on the one side and the jail staff on the other. There was a sense of mutual distrust. Therefore, the staff probably felt that fear was the key. The enire environment exuded an aura of negativism and the culture of working towards gaining respect was nonexistent.

Kiran herself sums up the situation lucidly:

I was quite conscious of one fact that could prove very detrimental to my efforts. I was aware that my staff knew that I did not belong to the prison cadre and that they had to bear with me only till such time as I was posted here. In the Delhi Police the situation is very different, because there they know that we could be working together on posting after posting. In Tihar most of the staff members were not even from the prison cadre and they knew that our association may not last for very long. Another inhibiting factor was that they were not used to serving under a woman officer and therefore felt they could not communicate with me as they would with a man. I was aware of these things and I had to face them.

The prison cadre is non-transferable, and so I could not use the threat of transfer for disciplinary purposes. I was short on staff and I needed whatever staff I had. I had to convert them to a positive line of thinking. The staff I had was by and large inadequately trained; some of them even had no training at all, they were close minded, habituated to an earlier regime of repression and force, and quite a number of them were much older to me. The plus side was that they immediately understood that I was a no-nonsense person, that I would not indulge in dishonest means and that I would never sanction force and beatings.

The jail superintendents had, for long, kowtowed to the junior staff because they did not have the backing of their own superiors and also because the junior staff had been here for a very long period. Whatever the superintendents had to do had to be got done by the lower staff and therefore they had to make a lot of compromises. Because of individualised functioning a lot was happening that should not have been allowed at all. But then, they were working within their limitations. The problem itself was clear to see. The lower staff did what they liked or could because the superintendents had no control over them. This was because the superintendents had no backing from their senior staff. Headquarters had distanced itself from the prison and no one from there would even bother to make visits. So, if they could not understand the prisoners' and the prison's problems they could not offer any solutions and, therefore, they also became a part of the problem. It was apparent that no one wanted to even try and do anything because they were overawed by the enormity of the problem and had a defeatist attitude right from the word go. No efforts were made in trying to build up a team, and it is only a team that can work collectively, and collective effort was the need of the hour.

I knew that the staff used to resort to beating, abusing, corruption, unreasonableness and insensitivity. But this was from hearsay and it would have gone against me if I had accused them on that basis. It was only when situations exposed such actions that I would confront them with the reality and point out what was wrong and what should, or could, have been done. Sometimes the staff would tell me that if they had not resorted to beatings then the prisoners would have caught them by the throat. I told them that what they meant was that they did not have enough security. The solution lay in providing more security and not in beating.

In this way I would be tackling the staff, and their problems, on a one-to-one basis. That fostered confidence in them and they became willing to go by my suggestions. I realised that this one-to-one basis was sending better signals to the staff than any theoretical lecture would have done. Sometimes the staff would come up and tell me that all these prisoners were thieves and criminals and that they deserved only what they were getting. I had to be very patient and explain to them that they had no business to decide on matters that were not within their scope of duties. They were only supposed to be the custodians and bodyguards of the prisoners. Their job was only to look after the security and well-being of these prisoners under their charge. They should therefore set for themselves clear-cut parameters of work and not go beyond them in judging prisoners' characters or condemning their alleged guilt. They could not become the judge.

For the first eight months of Kiran's posting, she, the DIG (Jaidev Sarangi) and the four superintendents (K.R. Kishore, D.P. Diwedi, P.R. Meena and Tarseem Kumar) would lunch together. During the lunch sessions, they would discuss their morning's observations, highlighting specific problems, and chalk out strategies to resolve such problems. There was much to share, and many distances to close, and these luncheon meetings helped save a lot of time. The signals to all and sundry were very clear, i.e., that headquarters and staff at Tihar worked as a team. The lower staff's options to exploit the situation were thus successfully checked. What emerged out of this approach was that for the first time headquarters was not passing down insensitive and incomprehensible orders that were not practical and had, therefore, to be shown as carried out on paper only.

Many earlier IGs held a dual charge and dealing with prisons was too infra dig for them to bother about. They would therefore suggest to the superintendents that they should presume that the IGs were not there. They told them to carry on exactly as they would if they were somewhere else. This meant that there was no responsibility and no accountability attached to the post, but only authority. The prison had never had the benefit of an indulgent and participative leadership. These lunch sessions truly proved beneficial in several ways. For the first time the lobby consisting of the old warders and assistant warders was made ineffective. They were now being told what to do, and how to do it, and they now knew that there was an effective leadership in the prison.

The headquarters' team and the superintendents would now assess not only the performance but also the behaviour of the lower staff through petitions, actual observation and apparent situations. They were each given ample opportunities to prove their worth. Those found not to have changed their earlier ways were shifted outside the jails so that they had no direct contact with the prisoners and were given security work at the outer perimeter or no work at all. It was better without them! Nothing, however, was presumed. If they did prove their merit, well and good. If they did not, then they were made *persona non grata* inside the prison. This lowered their prestige in the eyes of the others, and their treatment became exemplary. Their duties were also shuffled around a lot so that their earlier monopolies were effectively broken. But this was possible only because of constant and vigilant observation and coordination. All such endeavour took its toll in the form of extra duties and much longer working hours, but the net result was reward enough.

Gradually even the warders began to be called to attend briefing sessions. And they showed themselves to be responsive and started to prove themselves to be responsible as well. If they had conducted yoga classes, or prayer meetings, or had organised games in their respective jails, then their names would be put up on the notice boards of the headquarters and their respective jails. Seeing their names displayed on the notice boards made the warders a little competitive amongst themselves and when they had achieved the satisfaction of having done a good job, the entire prison benefited.

Even during the new regime, when a number of reforms were apparently taking place and the mindset of the prison staff was being persuasively changed, the hangovers of the past still continued. In a letter to her parents in England, a British girl inmate reported how she had asked a woman warder for some help regarding her visitor rights. She was told that one got nothing for nothing and also that only if she granted sexual favours would her request be attended to. The girl's parents wrote to the IG(P) and, after enquiring into the matter, the offending warder, a woman homeguard, was immediately discharged. This, explained Kiran to her staff during the annual review, was what happened when those who were neither trained nor had any inclination towards the requirements of this service were given such responsibilities. It would be far more in keeping with the present jail culture if the prison staff persuaded their own womenfolk to opt for such services.

One can imagine, when even with such a benevolent leadership in Tihar old habits are taking time to die out, what must have been the condition when the earlier leadership had left the entire system to run by itself.

A foreign correspondent once rang up Kiran at home to ask her about the inordinately long periods of incarceration of foreign nationals booked under the NDPS Act and awaiting trial. She told him that it was not in her hands to decide the period for which they languished in jail, but, yes, she could do a lot about the quality of the time they spent there. Certain special privileges were granted to them by way of letting them stay together, giving them a slightly modified menu, permitting books in various languages to pursue foreign language courses, allowing them to play guitars and other facilities. This sort of treatment was being accorded because this group of inmates had their own distinct cultural identities (different from the Indian ethos) and, in this way, their trauma was reduced. Of course, she explained, the prison was a microcosm of the outside world and therefore it had to be reflective of the general and average lifestyle of India and so it would be absurd to expect 'star' treatment.

Yes, the jail is indeed a microcosm of the India that lives outside it. And outside the condition of a majority of women is pathetic. They have virtually no rights and are merely treated as barely tolerable property to be passed from father, to husband, to son. At any of these stages she has only to prove herself to be interfering or burdensome and her life becomes a veritable hell. Those unfortunate women who find their way to prison are, by and large, uneducated, submissive and apathetic to their accepted lot in life. In prison they do not have the foggiest notion of the technicalities of legal or prison rights, rules of remission parole or premature release. Lawyers are quick to take them on as clients and hence the latter leave matters in the former's hands. Intermittently, lawyers fleece them for money, but even then they languish for years in prison without even once seeing the inside of a court.

For the prison staff such women become grist for their libidinous mill. The apathy of the outside world is turned to cruelty here. The more mental torment suffered by the women, the more pliable they become in the jail staff's hands. Physical punishments are awarded not as corrective measures but more to satisfy sadistic desires that find an unobstructed vent in the confines of the prison walls. And rape becomes a veritable right.

In Tihar, even today, because of overcrowding, women convicts, undertrials, prostitutes and even hardened criminals are all kept together. The general barracks contain four times their sanctioned capacity and prisoners who have been here longer have managed to curry favour with the staff so as to rule the roost. Young undertrials, expecting to be here for only a few days, weeks or months become their prime targets. The latter are quickly enslaved and made to perform chores like sweeping and washing clothes and, through persistent pressure, converted to lesbianism.

Even when taken to hospitals the women inmates were not given any preferential treatment. There would be no segregation from male prisoners. Most of the time they would be examined by male doctors.

If there was a hell on earth for women, this was it.

The levels of corruption to which the jail staff members had reduced themselves and the degradation to which the inmates were driven have been elucidated by the words of an ex-superintendent of the jail:

The mental hospital at Shahdara [a locality in Delhi] had opened a branch inside Tihar to cater to the needs of the inmates. Most of the patients were women. In the evenings some unfortunate women inmates from this branch hospital were forced to come and stand at the outer gates of the prison and customers brought in from the roadside who would pay the jail staff for the privilege of fondling these women through the bars of the main gate. Just after the Emergency Sanjay Gandhi was lodged in this jail and his wife Maneka would often come to visit him here. It was she who discovered this obscenity and published it in Surya, *a magazine she then ran.*

Such conditions obviously created a mindset. Excessive urge for any form of stimulation was felt by a large number of inmates. This urge probably could be fulfilled only by drugs or bizarre sexual behaviour. Tolerance was at an all-time low and this abnormal situation could have only bred feelings of hatred and revenge towards individual or specific sections of society, and also it could have led to despair. Thinking became tunnelled and inflexible, leading to the hardening of hearts and corruption of minds. The prisoners certainly lost all ability to process their own emotions, resulting in constant outbreaks of fights, hysteria and depression.

The Tihar situation raises certain very disturbing questions:

- Should a prison serve as penitentiary or should it be a means of societal revenge?
- Should society sit in judgement over an individual while ignoring its own collective guilt?
- Should our complacency, deriving from a conditioned adherence to prevailing systems, override our human compulsions of interaction and understanding?

- Should we continue to accept the myth that only those people who are guilty of criminal offences should serve periods of imprisonment?
- Should we believe that an aberration of judgement is indicative of a hardened heart and a criminal mind?
- Should our quest for legality be exclusive of our sensitivities towards another's rights as a human being?

Answers to such questions cannot be derived merely academically. The human condition that gives rise to such questions has to be lived and experienced. This chapter, entitled 'Freedom from Fear', is an attempt to provide such an experience to the reader.

As one recaptures the dramatic moments of the post-May 1993 events, one is inexorably drawn towards the conclusion that despite the fact that changes came about almost spontaneously and instinctively, there is a certain discernible pattern to them.

The conditions prevailing in the past in Tihar Jail had promoted a very unhealthy mentality which was steadily criminalising the minds of its unfortunate inmates. There was an unhealthy absence of any constructive or creative activity. The environment was overcrowded and unhygienic. Medical aid was almost nonexistent. If at all there was any responsibility given, it went without any sense of accountability. Above all, and probably what was the root cause of such an appalling situation was that there appeared to be no one with any sensitivity to the abounding misery.

In an attempt to make Tihar a correctional institution most of the reforms that have taken place there have successively and successfully eliminated the criminalising traits in its inmates. Their need for, and access to, sensory stimulation has been almost completely eliminated. The majority of them are occupied in acquiring self-monitoring skills. Progressively they are developing decision-making abilities and are thus in a position to exercise accountable responsibility. Procurement of basic life skills has given a large number of them some hope for the future. And all this has helped them greatly in achieving better control over their emotions.

15

Jailhouse Shocks

The Tihar complex, India's maximum-security prison, is a sprawling complex of over 180 acres, divided into four independent jails. The entire area is encompassed by high imposing walls, with the armed constabulary of the Tamil Nadu Police Force patrolling the perimeter. Grim sentinels perched in high sentry boxes have ominous-looking automatic weapons trained at entry and exit points. Massive iron gates with iron bars and huge padlocks appear as seals to the fates of the over 8500 humans enclosed within. It is truly a sight to fill the mind with trepidation and fear; an awesome sight to compel the entrant to abandon all hope, and push him or her to despair.

Inside the prison walls, however, the atmosphere today belies all such fears. Strains of religious hymns and songs greet you as you enter the prisoners' barracks. All around are groups of persons sitting and studying in regular classes. Every barrack has its own library where you see the inmates engrossed in reading newspapers, magazines and books. Everyone, yes everyone, is occupied with something or the other, be it studying, or exercising, or practising yoga, or repairing television sets, or knitting, or sewing or performing a score of other activities. The inmates do not appear tense or worked up but more like any other member of society busy with his or her daily work-a-day life. They certainly have complaints and frustrations in plenty about the quantity of time spent as undertrails, but almost none of them about the quality of the time they are spending here.

Yet, Tihar has had a most unenviable track record of corruption in the administration, of the brutality of a concentration camp, of a well-functioning prisoner mafia, of unethical practices by the medical staff, of free availability of narcotic drugs, of sex abuse by prisoners and staff alike, of extortion, blackmail, and unhygienic conditions – of anything and everything that it takes to make a hellhole on earth.

The Deputy Superintendent of Jail 4, Sunil Gupta, who has worked in Tihar for over 12 years, spoke quite candidly about Tihar's past:

The atmosphere here bred criminality. Prisoners with lesser or petty crimes were indoctrinated by the more hardened ones.

The rank and file of a number of gangs were recruited here. As a matter of fact, the infamous Tyagi and Manjit gangs (gang leaders who had unleashed a reign of terror in the Meerut, Ghaziabad and Bulandshahar districts of Uttar Pradesh and who were involved in innumerable cases of extortion, blackmail, ransom kidnappings and murder) were formed here itself. There were no attempts made to stop this because of fear of these criminals and more so because of a directionless leadership. The jail was run more by the diktat of the hardened criminals rather than by us.

One Wilfred, a tall and very outgoing black American, who has spent about seven and a half years in jail as an undertrial, confirms Gupta's statement:

These guys, belonging to gangs, would go up to the medical officer. There'd be the deputy jailer and other prison staff there too and prisoners queued up to get their medicines. But these guys would tell them to get out and then they'd take whatever and however much medicines they wanted — mostly diazepams — and nobody would do or say anything.

Ex-superintendent of jails, Jagdish Prasad Naithani, looks back over the years and tries to explain the reasons behind such a situation:

There are always two classes of prisoners in jails, the haves and the have-nots. Some of the haves in Tihar were powerful criminals who still wielded influence outside. They generated a fear of money and muscle and even the staff were intimidated by them. Fear, and greed for easy money, made the staff blind to the ugly goings-on. Added to this was overcrowding and, therefore, there was a much increased contact between prisoners. That's why there were so many prison offences and without formal complaints. Tihar had been administered as an additional charge of the District Commissioner of Police till as late as 1979-80. The staff was by and large inducted from the ranks of the Punjab and Haryana Police. The jail itself had a skeleton prison cadre staff mostly in the form of wardens and their assistants. Internecine departmental rivalries and jealousies were rampant and this told on the quality of administration. Unlike other state prisons in the country the judiciary held a lot of influence over the jail's administration. Penalties incurred by the staff for infraction of rules and duties were inquired into by the lower courts, where cases lingered on endlessly. The prisoners were quick to encash on this and almost on a regular basis the jail staff was defending itself in court on flimsy and falsely levelled charges. The staff got their own back in the only possible way they could, which was to create as inhospitable and as inhuman a climate as they could get away with.

Anne, a Nigerian student of Delhi University, shudders at the memory of events when she was sent to prison some five years ago:

When I came here I wanted to die. The conditions were so bad. I thought some of the prisoners were mad and we were all thrown in together. We were given regular beatings. I don't know Hindi, so I could not explain what I was asked and then I got punishments.

I was embarrassed. I asked myself, what am I doing here?

Bhupinder Singh Jarial (of the prison's cadre) and the then Deputy Superintendent of Jail 3 maintains that a lack of motivation amongst senior officers has been largely responsible for the terrible state of affairs in the past:

The tragedy of the department has been that it has always remained a headless body. Prisons is a state subject and every state must have its own management cadre. No system can be run without the involvement of technical experts. Not just anyone can run the show. For that a particular type of mental attitude and behaviour has to be developed first.

Tihar was under the administration of the Punjab and Haryana Government till 30 October 1966 on which date the Delhi Administration took over. Yet, till 1981 the same hand-to-mouth policy continued with some officers from Punjab and Haryana and some from the Delhi Administration managing its affairs. In my tenure itself I have seen about 18 IGPs and an equal number of superintendents. That gives an average of not more than nine months per head. The right attitude towards the job at hand was lacking because these people came here on a one-step promotion; they merely marked time here.

The present DIG at Tihar headquarters, Jaidev Sarangi, from the Delhi and Andaman Civil Services (non-police) was the Superintendent of Jail 1 from 1987 to 1990. He throws light on the situation as it then existed:

The working of each jail was the total responsibility of the superintendent then. The IG and DIG never interacted with the jail as far as its administration was concerned. They never made visits to the prison to see what was going on. Yet, they had the budgetary strings in their hands. The rations for 8000 prisoners were all controlled by them. But what the prisoners were actually getting, its quality, its quantity, was never looked into.

Opportunities for corruption for the jail staff were in plenty. For instance, we are required by the jail manual to provide each prisoner with three blankets each. But on payment of gratification money the tougher and richer prisoners could easily get more blankets. But since the issue to each jail was fixed, it was the weaker and poorer sections who would suffer, with, at times, some of them having to do with no blankets at all. For greater amounts of gratification one could get quilts from outside. These quilts could prove a big security problem as they could be used to store anything from drugs to weapons with none being any the wiser. I had all quilts seized and removed. As for the blankets they were all collected, counted and distributed back to the prisoners with each getting his quota of three. Periodical checks would then be made and the offenders punished.

At that time there was no complaint or suggestion system in the jail. One was started, though unlike today, it was "fixed". The complainant was interviewed. Lots of the complaints pertained to extortion and corruption by the junior jail staff. Again, through gratification, a prisoner could get himself transferred to any prison of his choice. And he would have so many reasons for it. A suggestion was made to the superintendents of the other jails also that the distribution of prisoners in each jail should be according to the alphabetical order of the prisoner's name. This was agreed upon and incorporated.

These were some of the ways in which the lower staff had indulged in corruption. They did not want the system to be changed and so were obviously bitter. One of the deputy superintendents planned out his revenge. He was making a large number of prisoners sign a complaint against me, supposedly written by one of the prisoners himself. Getting wind of the plan we were alerted and managed to recover bits of paper, which, when joined together, revealed that it was a draft, in the deputy's handwriting, of the letter supposed to have been written by a prisoner.

I sent a photocopy of the torn and reassembled letter to the Lt. Governor's office informing him that he should expect to soon receive a complaint against me from the jail. Such a letter he did receive. A vigilance enquiry is still being pursued against the person.

Apparently, there have been people coming as officers to Tihar who have stood by their conscience and tried to do their job properly. But due to an unambitious and lacklustre leadership, the system had proved itself to be stronger.

As DIG at Tihar headquarters, Jaidev Sarangi has successfully managed to persuade the lower staff to go in for insurance policies for themselves. Initially, most of them were opposed to this scheme, known as the 'Sarangi scheme', wherein for a monthly premium of Rs. 4-5 the insured person's family was assured a sum of Rs. 1 lakh at the time of his death. However, after two sepoys' families received Rs. 1 lakh each, everybody now wants to get insured and, that too, for double the amount.

16

The Inherited Legacy : Tihar Jail

Tihar has a housing capacity of only 2500 people, and yet there are over 8500 prisoners herded into that space. "This has happened," says one superintendent, "mainly because of two reasons. One is the Narcotic Drugs and Psychotropic Substances (NDPS) Act. The offence is non-bailable and a very large number of arrests are made under the Act. The other is the Dowry Act. This, again, is a non-bailable offence and, under the Act, whole families, at times even children, are arrested and imprisoned here."

The NDPS Act of 1985 and its amendment of 1988 appear in direct contravention of all human rights' directives. A survey of the more than 1200 prisoners awaiting trial under this Act (and many have been 'waiting' here for more than five years) reveals that almost 90 per cent of them have been arrested for possession of extremely small quantities of dı ugs or for being very small-time drug peddlers. The arrest and imprisonment of these small-timers do not make any impression on the larger flow of drugs because these people are clearly replaceable; at least this is the impression. A startling fact is that there are no cases of criminal conspiracy, with either national or international ramifications, which came to notice.

Again, irrespective of the quantity found in one's possession, the case may only be tried at the level of the sessions court and not at the subdivisional court level. The sessions court, already choked with pending trials, is thus further burdened by NDPS cases, wherein the majority of arrests are for possession of two to ten grams of illegal substances.

Let us discuss some individual cases.

Sukha, aged 55, has been awaiting trial for an NDPS offence for four-and-a-half years. His version of events is as follows:

I used to polish shoes on the streets of Connaught Place for a living. Big "saabs" would get their shoes polished by me. I worked the whole day and would take about two rupees worth of "charas" in the evening. In my locality there are so many who drink liquor every day and beat their wives and children. No harm comes to them. They are not bad for society. But I am. What justice is there for people like me? Where are those people who sell kilograms and quintals of the stuff? All are enjoying themselves.

Raj Kumar (name changed) has been an undertrial for six-and-a-half years, charged under the NDPS Act. A very steely composure hides the smouldering rage within him. He narrates his story:

> *I was running a business in Delhi for some years. I was friendly with a girl whose sister, I discovered subsequently, was involved with some group which was dealing in smuggling drugs to India from the Middle East. In what I realise now to be a naïve attempt to dissuade her from this, I threatened her with exposure if she did not dissociate herself from the group.*
>
> *On 11 March 1988 some people came to my flat accompanied by this girl Rita. I thought that she had brought members of the gang she worked with, so I told them that I had already intimated the Intelligence Service about them. This I did so that they would shy away from killing me or beating me up. I was dragged and pushed into a car waiting outside and it was only when I found myself in a police station that I realised my abductors were policemen. There I was questioned about whom I had informed in the Intelligence Service. I couldn't lie my way through. The station house inspector, Hukam Singh (name changed) then went out with Rita and came back after an hour with a group of people, of whom a couple looked like Afghanis; there were also a couple of Indian men and an Indian woman. They talked out of my hearing range for almost an hour and a half after which they went away leaving a briefcase behind. Rita handed over the keys of the briefcase to Hukam Singh, who, on opening it, declared that I had been carrying heroin with me. And ten kilograms at that.*

Later in the night I was beaten up badly and when I couldn't take any more they made me sign some papers, some in Hindi and some in English.

The next day I was taken to the courts and there they produced before the magistrate what they claimed to be my confessional statement. It was stated in the court that Hukam Singh had received information that I would be carrying heroin with me and that my contact code would be "Black Rose". That was how I was apprehended in the vicinity of the police station.

I was supposed to be carrying heroin worth ten crores of rupees on my person and the police department was not even concerned about who my contact person was supposed to be? After being sent to prison the police had no more questions to ask me about where I had got ten crores worth of heroin from and whom I was going to supply it to? Did they think that was all the heroin there was in the market and that they had bust the whole racket by apprehending me? What hurts the most is not that the inspector, who is also the investigating officer, is obviously in the payroll of the Middle East-based gang but that even after six-and-a-half years of the progress of my trial no magistrate has even bothered to question him as to why I was not interrogated so that others of my so-called gang could be identified and apprehended.

A subinspector of police was jailed with us for some time. He told me that nothing could be done about my case because Inspector Hukam Singh was very influential in both the police as well as the judiciary circles. He is supposed to be holding an American green card and owns properties worth at least a couple of million dollars there. It all sounds plausible. I have written to various authorities about my case as well as what this subinspector told me. But to date no one has even responded to my complaints.

In December 1993 the President of India approved the setting up of ten special courts to expedite the NDPS Act cases and clear them by 12 December 1994. To date only arguments, debates and disagreements on expeditious trials are going on.

"Medical care was bad," recalls an Anglo-Indian woman prisoner who remains an undertrial after four-and-a-half years. "There would be prisoners suffering and who would be waiting for hours before the doctor came." She went on to add:

> *I remember even things like books were not allowed. Some of us had some books, a few very expensive ones also, and magazines, and they would help us while away some time. But one day the superintendent ordered a* talaashi *[search] and they were all taken away. We cried when we saw them rotting outside in the rain.*
>
> *There used to be a lot of fights — over stupid, petty things. You moved my wash, you stole my slippers, or you stepped on my blanket. The matrons were not allowed to talk to us and we were treated worse than animals.*
>
> *Convict prisoners would gang up on new undertrials and make them do all their work and inflict physical and sexual abuse on them. The staff never intervened, and so these convicts could establish a master-and-slave relationship.*

Joseph Obi, a Nigerian (arrested under the NDPS Act), educated in India and working as an engineer, reflects on the years he has spent as an undertrial:

> *I have seen very bad times here. The prisoners were beaten mercilessly. A youngster, sentenced to seven days on a passport case, was beaten to death. People would be thirsty and there*

would be no clean water. People were dying here, seriously, and no help came
I didn't see the face of my earlier superintendent. We would all be locked up in our cells whenever he made a round. And the IG, oh, he would make one round or sometimes maybe two in one whole year.

Obviously what Joseph Obi is recollecting here is the harrowing time the prisoners had during the summer of 1991. Tihar faced an acute water shortage then and an absolute non-availability of clean drinking water. Gastroenteritis and other water-borne diseases were rampant. There was no one to listen to the prisoners' plight. It was only when cases of prisoners' deaths started being reported to the authorities that the administration woke up.

"Of the approximately 8500 prisoners lodged in Tihar almost 90 per cent are undertrials," says the superintendent of Jail 4. "Sometimes the period spent in jail as undertrial is almost as much as, if not more than, the sentence would be if convicted. We have the case of an inmate (Ajay) who was arrested in 1983 for murder. And his trial still continues today."

The very angry Joseph Obi bursts out again: "The courts want to try me. Okay try me. But for how long? 1991, 1992, 1993, 1994? Years of my precious life – it may not be so to the judge or to the police, but it is to me. Try me, I tell the court. If you have a case against me, show the evidence and convict me. Otherwise acquit me, release me! What will anybody gain by keeping me under trial for so many years?"

Saroj, a 28-year-old Indian woman, who ran a teastall, has spent three years as undertrial under the NDPS Act.

She is also very angry but in her case it leads her to tears and she exclaims between sobs: "I have been here for three years. I go to court and am told to come back after six months. A new date is given, that's all. I say, if I have done wrong, then sentence me, if I have not then leave me. But why this way? I gave 4000 rupees to a lawyer to handle my case. I have not seen the man again. Even the Public Prosecutor asks for money. Today, I own only these clothes that cover my body."

Forty-four-year-old Margo Nita, from Holland, was arrested at the Delhi airport under the NDPS Act on her very first visit to India and has been an undertrial for four-and-a-half years. She expresses her bewilderment: "This was my first visit to India and I don't know anyone. I have lawyer, but he cheat me. He take 45,000 rupees from me and I see him no more. It seems the judges they play games — I am so totally confused. In Holland they would try me, and within three months if I am guilty they would sentence me to two years, otherwise I would be let off. I would have been out and with my children a long time ago."

Shakira, an Anglo-Indian kindergarten teacher, has also spent four-and-a-half years here: "My case has not come up for trial as yet. That's the worst with the judicial system, the cases just linger on and even if one is acquitted you find they have already served more than half the sentence for the crime, even while they are innocent. Look at my friend Maria's case. A Spanish tourist, she spent almost six years here. Only last week she was acquitted."

Michael, an ex-army Englishman charged with smuggling hashish into India, has spent over seven years as an undertrial. His feelings? "Frustration, yeah and anger. I am a very physical person, and an unbeliever. I don't believe in theory. I don't believe anything, without seeing it myself. This has ruined my life, it's ruined the existence I had. It's ruined the relationship between me and my co-accused who is in the ladies' ward. The judges keep seeming to be dodging. I've been heard by six different judges, but they seem to keep stalling."

These individuals and so many others are the 'victims' of the country's choked up judicial system. Overburdening of the judiciary has led to undertrials spending much, much more time than necessary in prison.

This was the legacy bequeathed to Kiran who was entrusted with the unenviable charge of running Tihar Jail as its new Inspector-General (Prisons) on 1 May 1993.

17

Into Stormy Waters

The diminutive but dauntless IG (P) immediately plunged into her charge at Tihar. To the complete amazement of both the jail staff and the prisoners, she made frequent rounds of observation, by day and by night, of the four jails. She saw for herself the conditions, heard the prisoners' tales of woe, talked to the staff, looked into the details of the jail's ponderous machinery – and was appalled.

Some of her observations (listed at random), displayed on the notice boards of the various jails, are as follows:

Round 2, Jail 4, 7 May 1993, Ward II:

4. Convicts/prisoners who have come from Jail 2 for treatment in this ward have complained that supplies of drugs and "smack" are through the warders of Jail 2. This supply is made through convicts who are addicts and drug peddlers. The dispensary of Jail 2 only supplies diazepam as an alternative for drug addicts.

7. One prisoner reported that drugs are supplied through a small hole connecting Jails 1 and 3.

8. One prisoner reported that some warders on night duty also supplied drugs to the prisoners.

9. After mulaqaats *(meetings with visitors) some prisoners, who are also addicts, take drugs into the jail in their mouth or in bread or in bananas or in soap or in toothpaste or in the heels of their shoes.*

Round 5, 13 May 1993:

3. IG(P) directed all jail superintendents to introduce the prayer and reward in every jail before lock-up and after lock-up. The prayer is to be "Aye Malik Tere Bande Ham" *(Lord, We Are Your People).*

Round 6, 14 May 1993:

6. Vocational training to all the Munda Khana *(juvenile ward) prisoners will be imparted forthwith. For this purpose Rs. 50,000 will be diverted from each jail's prisoners' welfare fund to Jail 2 immediately.*

Round 7 (night round), 16 May 1993:

4. There were a lot of complaints against Assistant Superintendent Ranjit Singh (of misbehaviour). The concerned superintendent to look into the matter. His assistant's misbehaviour with the prisoners is not to be tolerated.

Round 10, 20 May 1993:

4. Storing of newspapers and magazines is of no advantage to the jail. Let these be circulated in the wards.

The prison staff was called to attend a meeting. The situation was analysed. "It became apparent that only a small section of the jail machinery was functional. There seemed to be no prison policy and there appeared to be an absolute lack of direction. There were no goals and no strategies. All we could see were problems all around," recalls Kiran.

And given Tihar's dubious track record, each problem appeared more insurmountable than the other.

Tackling drug abuse became her first concern.

As Kiran herself explains: "My day and night observation rounds of the jails revealed that a nexus of staff, drug peddlers and prisoner addicts were holding Jail 4 to ransom. The dispensaries were pathetically short of alternative drugs for prisoner-addicts and they had no option but to continue with their habits and become totally dependent on, and subservient to, the drug mafia operating within the jail. Nothing was possible, nothing could be done for the prisoners, till this rampant evil was rooted out."

Exactly six months after she took up this challenge, Wilfred (the black American prisoner) could not conceal his amazement: "Here's this lady who comes and tells us that the drug scene in the prison is bad. So, what else is new, we wonder. And, she says, she's going to put an end to it. She must be joking, we think, how is she ever going to manage such a thing? And now – (with a clap of the hands) – pooff! she's done it."

One ward in Jail 4 was converted into a de-addiction centre. Gupta, the Deputy Superintendent of the jail, explains: "'Ashiana' is our drug de-addiction centre where prisoner-addicts are referred to by our jail doctors. 'Ashiana' is a voluntary organisation which has provided a staff of doctors, nurses and ward-boys and has converted this barracks into a regular hospital. The patients undergo a treatment course of 15 to 30 days after which efforts are directed towards their rehabilitation. Earlier, there was no need of this place because 'smack' was available quite freely with the connivance of the jail staff."

But was he not aware of this earlier and did he not make any attempts to check it?

"I was certainly aware of this earlier but there was nothing much we could do about it. We could only report the cases to our senior officers and ultimately the IG(P)'s office would bury the file. A lot depends upon the leader. Now it's different. Staff who were involved in this activity have been reprimanded and some have even been jailed. Today we have a clear-cut policy towards drugs in jail. A new awareness has come in and I can say with conviction that today our jails are totally free of 'smack'."

Now, over to Kiran to recount how she achieved it all:

The earlier situation in Tihar was shocking. As in Mizoram, here also the barriers of the prison were very porous. Those who were not drug addicts before coming to prison had become so while doing time here. Even those who were being supposedly treated for drug abuse had free access to drugs. All along, in my earlier posting in Delhi, I had insisted that our work in

"Navjyoti" was being jeopardised by the situation in the prison. But now I was at the helm of affairs and I decided to attack this problem with all I had. Now I had a chance to do what I had been requesting others to do in 1988.

I realised that the first step to be taken was to check the porosity of the barrier. My warders, some of whom were drug addicts themselves, were also actively engaged in peddling drugs in prison and making quite a packet. Security was at a discount. Because of this availability there was a lot of infighting among the prisoners and a staff-prisoner nexus had been formed. There was only one NGO-run centre for drug treatment but it was proving ineffective because all their work was being undone by the easy availability of the drugs. Mockery had been made of the system. I started work with the staff. We made checks on the drug smuggling into prison, trained the staff, sent a number of them for treatment at the "Navjyoti" clinics. I gave them a clear choice — either they go for treatment or I have them out of the force. Some volunteered, a few I had to axe.

We then shifted our efforts to the internal scene. The internal management system was made transparent. More centres for treatment were opened. Each jail has its own treatment centre where a new prisoner is taken directly on arrival. Immediately his physical condition is diagnosed and he is sent for treatment accordingly. We lay stress on homoeopathic treatment at the centres because at "Navjyoti" I had learnt that it was very effective, low cost and reduced dependence on allopathic drugs like proxyvon that itself created dependence. A number of NGOs came forward to offer help in treatment and counselling. So, at present we have "Navjyoti" working in Jail 1, internal work in Jail 2, "Sahara", an NGO, is working in Jail 3 and "Ashiana" continues its good work in Jail 4. Another group, "Aasra", supports the centre in Jail 4.

These efforts are showing results now. Many prisoners have now been able to become rehabilitated because they have been able to kick the habit that had been compelling them to recidivism. The new trend I noticed is that prisoners are coming to prison for treatment. By word of mouth of detoxified patients, new patients keep coming because now they know they can be detoxified because there is no accessibility to drugs in the jails any longer. Of course, attempts are still made by new inmates to smuggle in the stuff, but by and large supervision and surveillance are quite effective in checking them.

Out of the average of 300 prisoners coming in every day, 50 are drug addicts. The incidence of drug-related crimes being so high, it is most essential that this problem be dealt with effectively in the prisons. We still have far too little space in our treatment centres. We are, therefore, trying to institutionalise them. And, for that we have sent a proposal to the Ministry of Health, Government of India, for establishing treatment centres like "Navjyoti" in the prisons to be run by the superintendent of the jail. We have requested for funds, in the form of grants from government, so that the superintendent can employ a team of homoeopaths, vocational trainers, yoga instructors, psychiatrists and social workers. It would involve an amount of Rs. 10,000 to Rs. 12,000 per superintendent per month to enable him to do so. These funds would go to the prisoners' welfare fund and be at the disposal of the respective superintendents to provide a holistic infrastructure to deal with the drug problem in prisons. The proposal is under active consideration of the government and is also being considered by the UN Drug Control Programme. NGOs have their own limitations and the institutionalising of the programme would bring in much greater control in functioning by the jail staff itself. One large prison is on the verge of being declared a demonstration project to be steered by Dr. Harinder Sethi of Aasra (an NGO).

Yet another serious problem I noticed concerning the prisoners' health was their problem of smoking. Quarters in the jails are confined and smoking was creating bronchial and other respiratory tract problems even in non-smokers through passive smoking. But this was a problem in which very large numbers were involved and I kept my mind open to opportunities that might enable me to stop this. One day, on my rounds in the adolescent wards, I was standing behind a prisoner when he coughed and spat a little distance away. It landed in front of a boy sitting in his educational class. I pounced on the opportunity and declared to the lot sitting there that this was how a privilege given to inmates was being abused. Spitting into a class was sacrilege and if concessions like smoking were causing this then I had no option but to stop it henceforth. Smoking was immediately banned for the adolescents and strict instructions were issued that no visitor would bring beedis *for his or her ward. Just like liquor brings a lot of money to the government's coffers so also were* beedis *and cigarettes bringing in a lot of money to the prisoners' welfare funds in the jails. But my superintendent agreed with me that we would rather bear the financial loss but we would ban consumption of tobacco in the jails. Since we had approached them at the psychological level the youngsters realised that it was because of their misuse of privileges that this ban had been imposed and therefore they were quite silent about it. They were all young with flexible and receptive minds and they opted for showing obedience to the ban orders. This affected their mind control a lot and they soon realised they were better off with the ban. They reported that spitting in the barracks had come to a stop. They were now living in cleaner barracks* and a lot of their throat and chest problems had disappeared. That made us happy.

The problem now was with the more hardened and longer addicted adults! How should we set about effecting the ban for them? The opportunity presented itself one day. On one of our rounds in Jail 3 one of the prisoners attending classes pointed out to me that a particular prisoner was selling beedis in black, i.e., charging more than the normal rates. I asked him why he would be doing so when they were freely available in the jail canteen and he told me that sometimes the canteen would be closed for two days, or there would be a short supply. On being questioned, the concerned prisoner refuted the charge saying that the other had some personal enmity with him and that is why he was saying so. So I ordered a search of his belongings in his barracks and sure enough the search revealed a tin full of beedis. I took this opportunity to tell them that this privilege we had been giving them had been misused and that a criminal offence was being committed because of this. Blackmarketing would not be allowed to thrive in the prison and therefore I was going to impose a ban on smoking in all prisons. I drove on the initiative I had got and expressed my anger at them. Here I was, I told them, spending over one and a half crores of rupees on their health problems and at no cost would I let them undo all that I had been trying to do. I told them that here I was trying to cure them of TB and bronchial and other problems, and spending so much money on them, and they dared to take tonic from me and poison from the prisoners. No more would I permit this, I told them. If they wanted to continue taking the poison then let them pay for the cure. I certainly was not going to do it!

Immediately on imposing the ban market forces exerted themselves in the jails' townships. People started hoarding *whatever stocks were available and there was a flourishing black market. We were aware this would happen, and we were also aware that this would last only till such time as the stock started to dry up. Massive searches were conducted and violators punished. Stocks soon petered out and so that concern of ours was over with. The major concern, however, was the withdrawal symptoms that had begun to become apparent. Also, the convicts realised that the undertrials got a chance to smoke when they went to the courts but for them there was no such opportunity. This was putting them into depression. The response to this move was a mixed one, as was expressed through the petition box system. Some claimed that it was a good thing I had done but there were very vituperative and abusive responses also. I did not react to them. I was accused of having done the most stupid thing and that all my efforts at providing them better living conditions, and a more liberal atmosphere, had all come to nought.*

How much of a dependence they had developed on beedis *became apparent just 24 hours after this. The cooks said they could not work in the* langars *without their* beedis. *A large number of prisoners refused to eat because of stomach aches they had developed. I wondered if my superintendents would be able to manage the situation and whether I had not bitten off more than I could chew. But then I realised what an opium-like effect their smoking had on them and that knowing this and yet permitting it would, for me, be absolutely immoral. I, therefore, let the ban continue. My superintendents cooperated with me totally. They persuaded them, they counselled them and showed determination to continue along with me. This gave me heart. The superintendents had to do a lot of excess work and face a lot of hassles but they stood by me. Without their implicit support it would just not have been possible. We kept on at it. We gave them extra milk, fruits, medicines, anything to keep their minds off smoking. It required tremendous effort but then the results started becoming apparent. I was told that their habits had started improving and that they were saying that I was very strict and that they might as well learn to do without smoking.*

I recommenced my rounds in the jail. Groups started forming, some telling me I had done the right thing and some started pointing out that even the Jail Manual gave the prison in charge the prerogative of issuing two beedis *a day to each prisoner. I said this was impossible because the logistics were too cumbersome, and also that it was not possible to find out who smoked and who did not so that the sum total would again be a situation where there was excess smoking and blackmarketing. Some of the staff members who were heavy smokers themselves were not supportive of the ban and therefore we gave them external duties where they did not have to interact with the prisoners. The situation had come to a make or break stage. If we could hold our own for a little while longer, then we were through; and if we failed now, then it would never be possible to attempt such a thing ever again.*

Then came my most crucial test, like a bombshell. I entered the prison for one of our regular performance appraisal meetings. Normally, the prisoners would clap and thus show their approval of the way I was handling and managing things. That day there was no such clapping. I thought probably they had come to the conclusion that it was a silly thing to do and that it might be construed as hypocrisy, and that is why they had stopped the practice. My superintendent, Tarseem Kumar, had been telling me that he was facing a lot of problems here but that he was managing to cope. His problems soon became apparent. I lectured the prisoners on the reasons for the ban on smoking and tried to get the prisoners to agree with me. There was absolutely no response. So I told them it was getting late and that we would, as usual, all stand up and say our prayers. No one stood up! So I told them it was alright if they did not want to stand and that we would say our prayers sitting. There were about 1200 of them with the convicts on my right and the undertials in front of me. I managed to get a group of the undertrials to sing along with me and then I told them to go back to their barracks. With a little persuasion the undertrials went away but the convicts remained sullen and unmoved. I told them that I would listen to their complaints later and that they should go now. Some of them then spoke up and said that they would only leave if they were given beedis. *They claimed that I was doing injustice to them. They did not want eggs and milk or fruit but they wanted their* beedis, *which, they said, was like their beloved and that they could not live without them. "If you do not give it to us then we will all commit suicide." For the first time I started to sweat. The other three jails had effectively accepted the ban; if I gave these convicts any concessions then everything would be undone. I had to overcome the situation and so I plunged headlong into it. I told them that what was making them behave like this was because of the withdrawal symptoms. What they were undergoing was the* tootan *phase (a period of withdrawal where the body seems to be breaking). At that they all laughed and said, "Madam knows what is* 'tootan'". *I said yes, and that I would provide six more doctors so that they could get medical assistance in this difficult period. They would administer a homoeopathic drug called 'tobaccum', I told them, and that would reduce their desire for tobacco. They told me they had stooped to killing lizards and were drying them and eating them to kill their urge. We had a lot of discussion that day about what I should do and what I should not. So ultimately I told them that I would hold discussions with doctors and psychiatrists and only then tell them what had been decided. Till then, I told them, the ban continues. I was desperate to buy time because I was also apprehensive that the situation might go out of control. That would have undone all the good we had managed in the other areas. I was given suggestions by my staff that we should isolate the more vocal of the lot and that would have a restraining effect on the others. I did not agree with this because that would have meant that people would stop speaking out and that would undermine our attempts at bringing about transparency in the jail. Finally, I persuaded them to give me two days' time to make consultations with doctors and then I would let them know my decision. We managed to save the situation and the convicts went back to their barracks.*

That night I could not go to sleep as I kept wondering what could be happening in the prison. In the morning I consulted Dr. Harinder Sethi (a psychiatrist doing voluntary service with us) and told him the situation. I asked him if he would stand by me in maintaining that the ban was necessary on grounds of health if the prisoners filed an appeal against it in court? He asured me he would and so I asked him to send me his written opinion. The doctor had been working in the "Aasra" treatment centre and had often complained about the smoking habit of the prisoners and now he was more than willing to help me. Every day one of my superintendents, Tarseem Kumar, would ask me what I had decided in the hope that I would relent a little. Whatever I told him was sure to be spread among the prisoners and so I told him that I was consulting psychiatrists and doctors on the matter. This way I was able to borrow five days. On the sixth day I told them there was no change in policy. But by now matters had quite settled down. On the seventh day I visited the jail. I deliberately did not go to the convict section. Promptly a letter was sent to me through the petition box. It was signed by a number of convicts and they wanted to know if I was still annoyed with them and that they were truly apologetic about their behaviour and would I not forgive them? They knew that I had come to visit the jail but that I did not come to their section. They asked me to visit them and I wrote back that I would do so after a day. I knew then that we had succeeded! As per the Jail Manual the IG is given a lot of discretionary powers and I was only allowing them privileges that I thought were for their good and withdrawing those that were bad. Today there is a Bill pending in the Delhi Legislative Assembly to ban smoking in public places and so I am certainly not wrong in wanting to remove the smoking clause from the Manual. That would effectively put an end to this practice in the future too.

"There are many gangsters here who trade in hashish, smack and other drugs," observes the warden. "The move is to isolate these prisoners. Here they will not be allowed to avail of any prison benefits. No *mulaqaat* for these inmates – they will not be allowed any visitors, nor will they be permitted any food or eatables from outside. No canteen items, either – like biscuits, cigarettes, nail polish and such. Their rooms will have no ceiling fans. And, most important, they will be under constant vigilance."

The move had the desired effect on the violators. Knowing how serious the new regime was about the step, a number of prisoner-addicts requested the new IG to provide them medical treatment.

Exemplary punishment was meted out to a member of the staff, namely, warder Raj Singh, who was an addict himself and who peddled drugs in jail to support his addiction. He was dismissed from service and is now serving time in prison.

"If we had to convince the inmates of our positive intentions, then we had to first gain their trust and confidence," explains the Superintendent of Jail 2. "The opportunity came on 2 August, on the festival of *Raksha Bandhan*. This is a deeply emotive occasion between brothers and sisters (an occasion when sisters tie colourful *rakhis* on the wrists of their brothers as a token of the love that binds them together; brothers, in turn, are thus symbolically bound to love, honour and protect their sisters) and this was a good opportunity for us to contact the prisoners at the emotional level. We decided that, on *Raksha Bandhan* day, we would permit the prisoners' sisters to tie *rakhis* on their brothers' wrists within the prison doors. We of course planned our security arrangements in meticulous detail. We communicated this to the prisoners. Tears welled up in their eyes when they reassured us that they would do nothing that would force us to hang our heads in shame. How could they, they asked, when it was all being done for their sake? On 2 August, amidst very emotional scenes, brothers vowed to their sisters that they would give up their wrong ways. No effort on our part could have achieved as much as this occasion did. We get repeated requests from a number of inmates to be shown the video tapes and the albums again and again. This charges them up emotionally."

Similarly, all festive occasions of the various communities that make up the composite culture of India were celebrated. The inmates' response to, and participation in, the festivities during Guru Purv, Diwali, Christmas, and New Year were total and wholesome.

18

Reforms Take Form

There was an urgent need to interact with the prisoners, for it was they who would be the beneficiaries of any schemes launched. A very imaginative innovation was introduced in the form of the *petition box*. The usual practice of suggestion boxes proved ineffective because of the inherent flaws in the system. The keys to the earlier box would be with the jail staff who would intercept and destroy any complaints against them. In the new system the petition (or complaint and suggestion) box has been made mobile. A constable appointed by headquarters carries this box around the jail on his bicycle during the prisoners' free time. The keys to the box are with a gazetted officer at HQ who sorts out the petitions according to their nature. The main points are listed for the IG(P)'s perusal, after which, a pink acknowledgement card is sent to the petitioner. Expeditious inquiries, where necessary, are conducted and within a week the petitioner receives a green card which states the action taken, or conclusions drawn. If any such case requires more time, then such information also is communicated to the petitioner within a week.

"The petitions inform me of what exactly happens inside," says Kiran. "The complaints range from lack of amenities, quality of food, need for medical aid to harassment by jail staff and the use of corrupt practices. In fact, one head warder was shifted on the basis of one such complaint. The complainant pointed out how this warder was beating prisoners like animals. The petitioner's identity is kept confidential if he or she so requires or if the petition officer feels it necessary on grounds of security. This system has resulted in the diversion of petitions from the high courts to the jail administration. It has reduced the workload of the court, saved time on legal representations, and has vastly improved the quality of supervision."

Supplementing this system in Tihar is another, namely, that of the panchayat or forum.

"This forum," explains Deputy Superintendent Sunil Gupta, "comprises representatives from each barrack and we have a daily sitting with them. This is our main link through which we can implement new ideas and programmes. The 'panchayat' members suggest changes and schemes and we give them a good hearing. If found feasible, we try to incorporate them. Now since it is these members themselves who have suggested them it is not difficult at all to implement them in their respective barracks. And two juvenile wards, or *Munda Khanas,* named the 'Kambli Ward' and the 'Sachin Ward' [after the famous cricketers] were opened in July 1993."

"There are 1000 teenagers in these wards," further informs the Deputy Superintendent of the jail. "These are the potential criminals and if we can do something to make them appreciate the difference between right and wrong and to make them utilise their energies constructively, then that would be a big step in the right direction."

Kesar Kumar, an 18-year-old 12th class student, declares: "I have been running this library for my fellow prisoners, and I am happy that a lot of them visit this place frequently and spend considerable time here. Even the jail superintendent takes a book from here whenever he visits the ward. Earlier, of course. I couldn't have run a place like this because I would not have got any support or encouragement from anyone. We make our choice of books be known through the petition box or through the forum."

Bhupinder Singh, another 18-year-old, came to Tihar in June 1993 as an undertrial in a murder case. He says that he was terribly afraid of what he thought lay in store for him in jail: "Before coming here I had the impression that the jail would be a terrible place – like what I had seen in the movies, that we all would have to wear the same dress, and there would be beatings and the food would be terrible. But it's not like that at all. As a matter of fact, this is more like a school hostel, where all of us are of the same age group. There's a lot of friendship amongst us."

Deputy Superintendent Gupta describes the administration's efforts towards educating the prisoners: "Today, we have a clear-cut policy on education. Whoever is imprisoned here must go out literate or better educated than what he was. On entry, the prisoner is classified according to his literacy status. The illiterates are taught the alphabet and learn to read and write within a couple of weeks. The others are divided into groups and join their respectively graded classes. The teachers are selected from amongst the prisoners themselves and their dedication to their job must be seen to be believed. And as an incentive they receive up to Rs. 200 per month. For half the day the jail is like a school with classes and language courses going on everywhere."

Sardar Singh, 50 years old and an undertrial under the NDPS Act for the past few years, is almost stoic about his situation. He has quite accepted the fact that given the system with which the country has to live, such Acts will be misused. Nevertheless, he has not given up hope: "But, somehow, and at least in my case, we have got so involved in our activities here that we don't know when morning turns to night."

Sardar Singh, popularly known as Guruji, and addressed as such by the IG(P) herself, is overall in charge of the education cell of the juvenile wards. As he himself observes:

I started off as an adult educator in Jail 3, in 1989, but now I've been given charge of these wards. The inmates here were quite an indisciplined lot initially with just about 20 to 30 boys interested in studies. The rest would roam round the ward compound and mostly be arguing and fighting with each other. But now they've started sitting in organised groups and regular classes are being held. Those who do not have a class going on visit the library and are content to spend a lot of time there.

I feel this has been made possible by the fact that all the jail staff now appear to be very helpful. Whatever suggestions we make to them are heard and the required help is extended. This has resulted in this ward appearing almost like a residential school.

This much I can say today. Before they were involved in this school-like discipline, the boys were mostly thinking about their condition here, their homes and all sorts of related problems. This would make them morose, or hyperexcitable and that would affect both their physical as well as mental health.

I tell these students of mine, whatever be the circumstances you face at present, the humaneness in you must come out in the future. What's happened is the past, and you have no control over it. But the future is something you can prepare yourself for. That is what we are trying here.

The reaction regarding one of India's most publicised undertrials, Phoolan Devi, as expressed by Meena Lukre, Assistant Superintendent of the jail, is as follows:

Phoolan came to our jail after having spent 11 years in Gwalior. We put her in a separate cell and asked some of our more humane convicts to stay with her. They were the ones who would ensure that she had her medicines on time (she was suspected to be suffering from cancer, which was ruled out here) and generally got her responding to the humane environment. I persuaded her to take up some activity like sewing or knitting but she couldn't keep it up for long. But she took to learning. Today she can take dictation and enjoys reading the light books we give her. Now she maintains that had she been given this opportunity earlier, she would not have wasted these 11 years.

Those who have experienced the previous regimes and the earlier conditions are apprehensive about the possibility of this changed environment continuing. The main question bothering them is: "What will happen when the present IG is transferred? One wrong posting and everything would be undone." This is the common apprehension voiced by a large number of persons. But Sarita, charged with the murder of her husband, and with her trial yet to start, still cannot keep the amazement out of her voice:

I thought it would be terrible. I had visions of prisoners being beaten with sticks, being made to do all sorts of dirty jobs. We would not be able to move about. I was almost hysterical with fear. But when I came here I was amazed. This did not seem like a prison at all. There were classes going on, people were busy with different things and everyone had something to do. This was more of a women's hostel than anything else.

"What's changed now", explains Urmilla Rana, the matron of the women's ward, "is that now they can at least do something with their time. Earlier there was nothing for them except to be locked up in their cells or to be let out for sometime in the courtyard. Most of them would only talk about their cases and be crying all the time. They were irritable and angry and fights would break out over the smallest of things. Of course, punishments were frequent; that was the only way to keep them in check. That made some of them worse and they would take it out on the others. Now they have lots to do. Their day is spent in education classes, or sewing, or knitting, or in yoga classes.

The tension has been reduced very much and naturally this has led to a drastic reduction in fights and quarrels."

Children up to four years also 'spend time' with their mothers in jail. A recent count showed that there were 40 such children in the ladies' ward. "It used to be heart-rending," says Meena Lukre, herself a mother of two, "when a child would tell me, 'okay aunty, I have to go and get locked up.' The cell was their home, and going home meant being locked up."

"The mothers would not look after them; they would not bathe them or care for them. They would be moving about in rags. When the new IG(P) saw this she was moved," adds Meena.

Moved indeed, and moved to immediate action. The Social Welfare Department of the Delhi Administration was contacted and outings were organised for the children. They were taken to the Raj Ghat lawns and to the Delhi Zoo. The only humans they had ever seen were women, and so everybody was 'aunty' to them. The only animals they had seen were the two cats in the ward, Sheru and Chein Chein, and the birds that visited it. Thus, the peacock was to them a 'big bird' and the buffalo 'a very big cat'.

As Superintendent K.R. Kishore explains: "This [outing] has had a salutary effect on the mothers, who have started accepting their children and caring for them. Tension has certainly come down."

The jail superintendent further focusses on this aspect: "The majority of the Indian women prisoners are very poor and so special attention has been given to this aspect. A number of voluntary organisations were contacted and these prisoners got job works. As a result about 40 women prisoners have even opened bank accounts for themselves.

Every week a bank official comes and explains to them the interest they have earned as well as the current status of their accounts. This is done so that our credibility is maintained with them lest suspicion brew that their money is being misused".

"I need teachers, I need preachers, I need books, I need jobs..." appealed Kiran Bedi to the community. The response was overwhelming. Tihar HQ was flooded with proposals, projects, and applications from volunteers – individuals and groups alike.

The Indira Gandhi National Open University (IGNOU) announced the establishment of a regular study centre in Tihar for providing higher education to inmates and staff. IGNOU even agreed to modify its norms and consented to conduct the examinations in the jail premises itself. It offered to provide education, study material and audiovisual aids free of cost to prisoners as also help to set up an educational video library, again free of cost.

Postgraduate and graduate courses are offered along with programmes and diplomas in management, computers, rural development, nutrition and health care as also creative writing. Twenty-five people, including staff and prisoners, have already undertaken these courses.

Jail 4, which houses the juvenile wards, has been adopted by the Bharat Vikas Parishad. The Parishad funds the sports activities of the jail and a number of inter-barracks and interjail tournaments have been organised. All the advantages and benefits that accrue from a healthy sports atmosphere are in evidence today. It was with a view to encouraging sports and games that the juvenile wards were named after the almost legendary figures of cricket,

Sachin Tendulkar and Vinod Kambli, as the 'Sachin' and 'Kambli' wards.

An ingenious scheme, devised by certain inmates, to 'beat the system', was exposed. The details are, indeed, worth narrating. In June 1993 three doctors were discovered to be involved in certain irregularities and they were immediately transferred. The *modus operandi* was soon discovered. Undertrials who were to appear in court (on police requests for them to be taken into their custody for uncovering evidence in their cases) would, on payment to certain doctors, be provided medical certificates to avoid such custody. The police are allowed by law a period of 15 days from arrest for keeping a suspect in custody. This period was thus made to comfortably lapse.

This tie-up with the doctors even permitted a number of prisoners to continue perpetrating crimes even from within the jail. In April 1993, the police of the Bara Hindu Rao area came upon a group of abductors who used to demand ransom money. This group was headed by Anil and Amit Tyagi, both of whom were lodged in Tihar Jail at that time.

A young student of the Maharashtra Polytechnic Institute had been abducted and his parents were asked to meet Amit Tyagi on the date he would come to AIIMS (All India Institute of Medical Sciences) on a 'referral' for a medical check-up by the Tihar doctor. It was, at that stage, discovered that this same Amit Tyagi had extorted Rs. 180,000 in an earlier abduction case by virtue of the same 'referral' system.

This revelation proved to have effectively destroyed the doctor-prisoner nexus which was the root of many serious problems in the jail.

The prison atmosphere, however, was not yet free from fear. The gangsters and hardened criminals, about forty in all, were spread over all the prisons. There were deep-rooted animosities and hatred amongst them and whenever they got an opportunity they would fly at each other's throats. They still spread fear amongst a large number of the undertrials and could still manage to dictate terms. All the opportunities offered to the rest were offered to them too, but to no avail. They continued on their self-destructive path. They stood warned, and yet they stood unmoved.

It was this group which would put pressure on the other inmates to resist the changes being effected in the prison. The reformative attempts that were being made were adversely affecting the sway and clout they exercised. To date, they had been functioning undisturbed by their incarceration and it was conducive to their well-being to permit the old order to continue.

Hardly any one of these hardened criminals would have had eaten prison food. Each prisoner is permitted two *mulaqaats*, or meetings, per week. These visits had been so organised that almost every day each group would be getting home-cooked food brought by these visitors. Their visitors would come, enter false names and addresses in the *mulaqaat* register, and request permission to meet specific members of these groups. Earlier, of course, for the reasons explained, these visits would take place in the rooms of the administrative block and not in the regular visitors' room. During the new regime the old practice was stopped, but it still did not prove much of a deterrent because the identities of the visitors were still being concealed.

the prison a lot of good and I'm sure for the first time they must also be learning something.

The fact that the rest of the prisoners are so participative in the changing scenario of the jail indicates that this move has certainly acted as an effective deterrent to any possible and potential trouble-maker and rabble-rouser.

By and large there is always a tremendous positive response from the prisoners whenever the IG comes in contact with them. This is indicative of the trust they repose in her and the direction in which she is moving for the amelioration of their condition. Therefore, isn't she a little disturbed by the animosity which these isolated gangster-prisoners must be holding towards her?

"No," Kiran reflects, "there is no tangible animosity. I would say they have a sort of neutral stance. You see, even they realise that I am not doing this to them out of spite or to just make things easier for myself. They know that I have never ever arrested anyone wrongly. They are even very much aware of the fact that whenever I did make an arrest I followed the case to its conclusion. I never gave up on the persons but continued to pursue their rehabilitation and correction. For this I even interacted with their families and, where need be, I did my utmost to help them as best as I could."

She cites a specific instance: "I remember when I arrested Vinod Tyagi (notorious gang leader), he never pleaded innocence before me. All he told me was that his wife was having some health problems. So, we ensured that she got the right treatment. She was admitted to hospital and had a safe delivery. Even afterwards we kept ourselves informed of her condition. I have always felt that a person must be punished for the wrongs he does, but also, we must not lapse in our attempt to help make him a corrected and better human being. There is a man in the high-security wards who spent time with Vinod Tyagi then. Even he admits I have done no wrong to them."

She finally expresses her optimism: "I know these people will ultimately respond. Then I intend to gradually extend all the facilities to them also."

In a gesture honouring her intentions, these isolated gangster-prisoners were provided facilities to watch the 1994 Wimbledon Tennis and the World Cup football championships in their barracks.

Help was sought from voluntary agencies outside and an Ayurvedic-cum-homoeopathic clinic under the aegis of the Central Health Services Scheme was installed within the prison. Medical supplies through regular purchase and also through donations were ensured so that the health support system in the jail could be beefed up.

The statement of petitions and suggestions posted on all notice boards at the end of the year is indicative of the effect that this move has had. Complaints about medical benefits and facilities had gradually petered down from 231, in June 1993, to a paltry 27 in December 1994. And, simultaneously, the number of referrals to hospitals had also been drastically reduced.

The highlight of the medical care programme came on 26 January 1994. This day was celebrated by Tihar as Medical Care Day. Over 500 medical and paramedical staff visited the jail along with sophisticated medical equipment. Renowned specialists in various fields and in different schools of medicine spent the day at Tihar. Almost each and every one of the 8500 prisoners, including the children, were given thorough check-ups. Different coloured cards were handed over to the

his company's expertise in converting organic garbage into odourless, rich manure. The offer was grabbed and within days the project was launched. Excel provided the chemicals and knowhow and the inmates volunteered to run the project. This odourless, highly nutrient biofertiliser has been marketed by the prison to local nurseries for kitchen garden purposes. Thus, the 3000 kg (per day) of organic prison garbage would, on projections made on actuals, fetch the prisoners' welfare fund a sum of about Rs. 21 lakhs per annum. As a result, about Rs. 11 lakhs of expenditure would have been saved annually and on top of that a profit of about Rs. 10 lakhs would have accrued: in effect Rs. 21 lakhs in hand by the year-end.

19

The Scenario Changeth

For the purposes of security and supervision, Tihar has a force of 1500 officers and *jawans*. Their welfare, too, is part and parcel of jail administration.

"In the effort to bring about changes in the living conditions of prisoners," says Deputy Superintendent Jarial, "a lot has also been demanded of the jail staff. They certainly have put in a lot of extra effort and that too with a marked change in their attitude. Their welfare is therefore equally important. This job requires total

DELHI CM SEEKS KIRAN BEDI'S HELP

"I want Mrs. Kiran Bedi's help to bring about revolutionary changes in Delhi," the Chief Minister, Mr. Madan Lal Khurana, said today.

Speaking at a function organised in the Central Tihar Jail complex here, Mr. Khurana said Delhi's Inspector General of Prisons, Mrs. Kiran Bedi, has introduced a series of reforms in the jail. "We are also planning revolutionary changes in Delhi. For this I want Mrs. Kiran Bedi's help."

Mr. Khurana recalled that he had fought with Mrs. Bedi several times in the past. "But there was nothing personal in these fights. I am proud of her."

Several jail officials entreated Mr. Khurana, while he was leaving, not to transfer Mrs. Bedi from Tihar and added that if this were to happen the jail staff as well as the prisoners would stage a dharna at his residence.

Mrs. Bedi, who was listening to this conversation, interjected to say: "I am jailed".

(The Hindu, 29 December 1993)

20

Correction through Meditation

On 4 November 1993 the Vipassana Sadhana Sansthan established contact with the Tihar IG and offered its expertise in a particular science relating to meditation. The Sansthan had been founded by S.N. Goenka, an Indian Burmese. He had learnt the science of *Vipassana* from his teacher Sayagyi U Ba Khin, a Burmese meditation master. This is an age-old science which, it is claimed, was rediscovered by Lord Buddha more than 2500 years ago. "The technique", as disclosed by Ram Singh (retired Secretary in the Department of Home Affairs, Rajasthan),

hold nothing against them today except a sense of gratitude."

Young Bashir is a Kashmiri doing time under the NDPS Act. He claims that he was framed by an influential Kashmiri trader from whom he had sought payment of his dues. During his incarceration his child-daughter died and he was refused permission to attend her funeral. That had made him very bitter, he states. He claims he used to always remain worked up and tense and thus could not ever go to sleep before 1 a.m. or 2 a.m. Then during the fourth day of the meditation course, he was absolutely amazed to suddenly realise that for the past two days he had been invariably fast asleep by about 9 p.m. and would wake up much refreshed at 4 a.m. As he himself discloses:

My problem had always been not being able to achieve peace of mind or peace of heart. I had even written to my mother that she should forget that I ever existed. Even if I came out of prison I would still be no better off for my own house would also be a prison to me. One day I heard some prisoners talking about this thing called Vipassana. *The first thing that came to my mind was that this was some sort of Hindu indoctrination. Even though I am a Muslim I decided to give it a try. During the course I realised that it had nothing to do with religion nor could one's faith be a barrier to it. It was just a way to learn how to refine your conduct and your thinking. Today I think I have found myself. I am at peace with my mind and my heart. Am I in jail? I ask myself. I look around and my senses tell me yes, but my heart says no. Today I am free.*

Subhash, an inmate of Jail 4, has a more philosophic approach towards the changes that have taken place in him:

After Tihar was made a 'no smoking zone' — ingenious methods
to smuggle in *beedis.*

The mobile petition box.

A foreign national meditating during *Vipassana* course.

Release of Website kiranbedi.com by H.H. Dalai Lama

Interacting with recovering addicts at her Navjyoti Drug House
Treatment Centre.

Kiran in her street schools.

Street schools

With President Bill Clinton and his wife Hillary Clinton, in Washington, attending the National Prayer Breakfast Meeting (February 1995).

Inspector General Kiran with her forces (Chandigarh).

The quote on the plaque reads:

" ... you will not have
a united India, if you have not
a good all India service which
has the independence to speak
out its mind..."

Sardar Vallabhbhai J. Patel
10 October, 1949
Constituent Assembly

Kiran's role model — Sardar Patel: The architect of the civil services
at the Lal Bahadur Shastri National Academy (LBSNA), Mussoorie.

I have learnt that all those things which make life difficult for us do not lie outside of us. They are all within — be it anger, jealousy, lust, greed, revenge or such like. This is what we must discover and then wash away. The past four years I have spent here I would always be planning revenge on those because of whom I landed here. But now I realise that it was no one's fault. It was all because of my own feelings; had I not been like I was I would not have done what I did. I realise my feelings now. And it's as if the bitterness and the anger have been washed away. I am determined now to cleanse myself of all the evil within me. The way I feel today I cannot see myself committing any crime ever.

Amrik Singh jailed under TADA (Terrorist and Disruptive Activities Prevention Act) gives an analogy indicative of his reactions: "It posed a big problem, and put a man under great stress, when he had some jaggery and he was asked to describe its taste. What this course of *Vipassana* does to a person cannot truly be described. It must be experienced and only then would one come to know of its benefits and the complete transformation of personality it can bring about."

Even a large section of the administrative staff have undergone this meditation course. The results have brought about a marked change in their attitude towards the inmates. An atmosphere of humaneness has pervaded the prison campus, and the aura of fear seems to have disappeared. Even the staffers' families maintain that after their husbands completed these courses their domestic life has changed for the better.

At the end of one such course Kiran in her address to the inmates pointed out: "Our staff has also undergone this course. One of the superintendents of the four jails,

Tarseem Kumar, a few of the deputy superintendents, Subhash Sharma, V.P. Garg, M.S. Rittu and Sunil Gupta, as also wardens and assistant superintendents have undertaken this course. So this is not just an opportunity for you or for us separately. This is an opportunity which we can partake of together, collectively. This is an opportunity for all of us to become one big family and to learn and to get to know ourselves together."

On 4 April 1994, a remarkable occurrence took place in Jail 4 of Tihar, where over 1000 male prisoners and 60 women prisoners, separately, undertook the *Vipassana* course. Never had so many prisoners committed themselves voluntarily to the regimen of a course which forbade them to interact with each other for a period of eleven long days and in which they had to take a vow of silence. Such a phenomenon had never been witnessed in prisons. In monasteries, yes; in convents, yes; in ashrams, yes; but in prisons, never.

The head of the Vipassana Mission, Guru S.N. Goenka, conducted the programme himself. In a very patient, gentle and endearing tone, he addresses himself to the group of women *Vipassanis* on the third day of the course:

> *You are breathing. . .you are concentrating on your breath. . . as it goes over the area between your upper lip and your nostril. . .feel it, feel it. . . around the outside of your nostril. . .up, along the insides of the nose. . . . The breath comes out. . .feel it. . .feel it. . .constant awareness. . . be aware. . .feel it. . .now. Today, you are aware of the breath, . . .as it rubs against the skin. . .as it rubs. . .it rubs. . . . Do you feel it? . . . Do you feel the slight irritation? . . . Concentrate on it. . .concentrate. . .it will go*

. . . no? . . . Stop breathing for a couple of
seconds. . .breathe again . . . . Come back to that spot. . .it
will go. This happens with every breath. . .friction will create
irritation. . . . But today you are aware of it. Be aware.
Slowly, gradually, you will learn to transfer your concentration
and awareness to other functions of the body. They are all
happening, always, without fail, but you are not aware. Now,
you will be.
This is what Vipassana *is. It is not religion. It is only*
awareness, of yourself, of your mind; it only leads to better
conduct, better understanding, better behaviour.
You see, Vipassana *can be seen as surgery. It is surgery of*
the mind. It is a dharma, a code of conduct, right conduct,
moral conduct.

With rapt attention, the *Vipassanis* listen to this almost
hypnotic discourse. Guru Goenka asks them to state any
problems they may have.

Several voices were heard. One was that of a Sikh
prisoner. She was used to performing her *paath* daily and
now, because she was required to devote total
concentration to this course, she was unable to do so. This
aspect was troubling her a lot. The Guru replied: "My
child. You have been performing your *paath* for years every
day. It helps you in concentrating on the right moral code
that you should follow. It is like a form of meditation.
Without betraying your faith you are learning another
form. For this your full attention is required. You cannot
digress. After eleven days, start your prayers again. You will
be more involved; you will be able to understand what you
are doing much better. You will be doubly benefited by
your faith, and by your conduct."

A British girl, who is doing time under the NDPS Act, and who has been in Tihar for more than four years, has a more physical problem to contend with. She is uncertain whether she can continue with this course as she gets nauseous at times and feels she cannot cope with this physical discomfort.

The Guru responds: "But why are you afraid? What is happening to you is an operation. If a doctor severs a boil on your body, will not the pus flow out? You are undergoing a surgery of the mind. What is wrong within you is flowing out. It was like a pus in you. Let it flow out. Be happy that it is flowing out." The girl returns to her place of *sadhana* with tears besmearing her face. And yet her expression betokens a glimpse of salvation.

Tarseem Kumar, Superintendent of Jail 2, conducted a survey on *Vipassana* in his jail three weeks after the launch of the course. Two sets of interviews were arranged. One was with those prisoners who had undergone the course and the other was with their cellmates in order to verify the authenticity of the former's claims. The results speak volumes about the beneficial effect the course has had on the participants:

1. Ninety-six per cent now have control over their anger. Four per cent have not achieved total control, but the frequency has come down considerably.

2. Ninety per cent feel less stressful and have achieved a marked degree of peace of mind.

3. Ninety-six per cent can now concentrate on subjects of their choice.

4. All of them exhibit a sense of benevolence and compassion towards fellow inmates and staff.

5.   Ninety-eight per cent are in a better physical condition. They no longer suffer from repeated bouts of stomachache, headache and other such minor ailments.
6.   All of them have become more truthful.
7.   Sixty-six per cent have stopped thinking about the past and are focussing on the present.
8.   Eighty-six per cent have become more tolerant of others and so less selfish.
9.   All of them have found an improvement in self-discipline.
10. Eighty-eight per cent meditate twice a day; 6 per cent once a day; and 6 per cent irregularly.

Amongst members of the staff, the survey revealed the following factors:

1.   An increase in their sense of duty and devotion.
2.   Positive change in their behaviour pattern.
3.   Improved relationship with the prisoners.

A young white American male undertrial, not wishing to give his name, did not think much about what's happening in Tihar: "Look, there's nothing great happening here. We have our human rights. They have to be respected. We are not animals, man, so we have to be treated like human beings. As a matter of fact there's still so much more that should be given to us. So what she [IG (Prisons)] is doing is no big deal."

"Hey", chips in Wilfred, a 'seasoned' inmate, "this guy's been here only six months. He's just a weekender. I've been here for over eight years. Who respected our rights earlier? We were beaten, abused, given food you wouldn't give a stray dog. It's only now that we are being treated like human beings. Boy, it sure takes guts to change people's attitudes in such a short time. I think she's doing a great job here. But I wonder what will happen here when she is posted out. Will the old days come back with a vengeance?"

21

Dignity Restored

The media's favourite, and the most popularised prisoner of Tihar Jail, Charles Sobhraj, who has spent around 10 years as an undertrial on various charges, including those pinned on him as a result of his successful escape from jail in 1986 (he was subsequently apprehended and brought back), is very moved by the events taking place there after Kiran Bedi took over:

> *It's very, very difficult to bring about changes within the Indian system. It's only someone with a lot of guts who can try to do it. What's happening here is very important and I*

think it should be shared with others. Not just in India but abroad also.

I feel what is happening here is that an element of the prisoners' dignity is being restored to them. When I first came here I was shocked to see the submissiveness of the prisoners. Specially the poorer ones. They would be perpetually cowering with fear. Now some nobility at least has been restored to them, some dignity. It is this which has made them lay their trust in the prison administration.

The IG reached out to the prisoners and established a relationship of mutual trust with them. She looks for positive things to do. Not: stop this, don't do this. But, do this, try that. She seems to believe that there is good in everyone and she is willing to give everybody a chance.

So, this way, she's trying the behaviourism method. If you have to change a system then you have to first change the minds of the people. The mind, the spirit and the system were all British here. For them (the British) it was all right as they were a colonial power. But even after independence no changes have been made at all. The Mulla Commission reforms have been left sleeping. Nobody wanted to do anything.

Earlier there was no balance of power. Everything was in the hands of the jail staff. You could get an extra blanket for a hundred rupees; a television in your cell for five hundred. You could get anything, for a price. But now they are all provided as prisoner privileges. So there was a lot of resentment by the lower staff. Their minds had to be conditioned first. The prisoners came later.

It's this humaneness that has made these changes possible. The prisoners have gradually become humanised and are free from fear now.

Look, each jail has an alarm siren installed in its deodis. *The wailing of these sirens was a regular feature every three or four days. Fights amongst the prisoners constituted the main reason. Since May 1993 these sirens have not wailed, not once. Get what I mean?*

The siren rang the loudest one day in September 1990. Prisoners were igniting LPG (liquefied petroleum gas) cylinders wrapped in blankets and placed against the security walls to blast holes in them. Thousands of male prisoners were trying to scale the walls of the women's barracks or break open the barracks' gates. The riot was quelled only when the Tamil Nadu special police force opened fire, in which ten prisoners were killed. The reason for the riot was the claim by the prisoners that one of them had died because of gross medical neglect, in spite of their long-drawn-out repeated appeals for medicare.

However, the situation has changed dramatically since then. The prisoners of Tihar appear to have laid implicit trust and faith in the jail staff's attempts to make their lives more comfortable and to give them a new sense of direction. Kiran was sensitive to this aspect and so repeatedly reminded her staff:

We must never forget our gratitude to the 8500 prisoners who have given us their hearts and who are the main dramatis personae in enabling us to achieve our goals. The cooperation, the discipline, the obedience which these inmates have extended to us, let us not ever forget. What we have done was merely our duty.

The greatest change I perceive that has come about in this system is that you have transformed yourselves from security guards to time managers. You have taken on the responsibility of managing the lives of 8500 people by scheduling and directing their time towards constructive and satisfying goals. None bears a greater responsibility than you.

The staff apparently appreciates the efforts of a benevolent leadership, and the rapidity with which reforms took place in Tihar was a direct result of their cooperation and new sense of duty. In May 1993 Kiran inherited 127 vigilance cases, including a lot of suspensions and departmental enquiries. When she left the total number of cases was 31 with minimum suspensions. Each case was taken on its merits and those who deserved punishment for infringement and breaking of rules for selfish reasons are to date spending time in prison. The others have been absolved.

The message given to the staff was very clear: "Each case of infringement will be taken on individual merit. Anyone trying to perpetrate a fraud on this jail will not be suspended at all but will be immediately booked under the Prisons Act. The magisterial enquiry will be completed within a month and, if found guilty, the person will be dismissed from service immediately. No suspensions whatsoever. We will not permit such persons to continue to draw 80 per cent of their salaries and do a side business as well. That was a system practised in the past. We consider it wrong and we shall not follow it. We do not have the money to pay such people without their having to do their duty."

"Just look at the enormity of the situation we faced," says a very pertinent Kiran. "Prisons had no training pattern whatsoever. The jail came up in 1958 and would you believe it, since then, there has been no training manual, no school, no training centre, nothing. No training concept, no training wing, not even any training material. I am shocked. It is only now in recent times that two such regional institutes have come up. One in Chandigarh and one in Vellore."

"But how could I send my staff there for training? I was already so understaffed here," she queries. "Still we were sending those we could."

And yet efforts had to be made in this direction because training was central to the whole concept of running a prison as a correctional centre. So, an assistant superintendent's crash training course was commenced.

"As a first reaction to this course I was completely taken aback," confesses Kiran. "My men did not know even the basic judgements on which their conduct should be based. They did not have even an inkling of the rules. But then, wasn't it to be expected?"

These men had been taken into the service and immediately put on the job. The same pressures must have existed then as they do now, namely, a shortage of staff. Kiran Bedi puts events in perspective:

> So, there was no law training. No correctional training. No knowledge whatsoever of the Prison Act. The only time a person read the Prison Manual was when there was an inquiry instituted against him.
>
> There was no way I could compromise on this. A modicum of training just had to be imparted to them, otherwise our effort would have been an absolute non-starter.
>
> So, we commenced a two weeks' course. One hour each day. The staff get about two to two-and-a-half hours' free time in the afternoons during the prisoners' lock-up duration. That's when they can go home and spend some time with their families. It is from this time that I took an hour. I knew it was hard on them, but then what could I do?

Initially there was a lot of disgruntlement because of their scepticism. What could we tell them about prison training, they thought. We were no experts in the field. But soon they realised how little they knew about the situation they were in. They realised that they were acting only as security men, whereas their true role was that of time managers and correctional staff.

The feedback I got was a desire for more of this training. And they did not want it condensed into a two-week course. They wanted it to be more expansive, more detailed and more spread over. So then we chalked out a longer course. The two-week course is now spread over four months, of an hour-long lecture per day.

We have a Jail Manual, but even that does not specify what an assistant superintendent's duties are. Today they are engaged in a plethora of duties which they do only because they feel someone has to do them. Nothing in the rule book binds them to it, or suggests what they can and should do.

They are now doing medical duties, canteen duties, and also handling education of the convict section. They are involved in welfare measures like running a legal section, and the hospital section, and in PRO duties. What in effect they are doing is learning their duties on the job. Obviously there is no streamlining. So, that's what we had to do. We had to list out their duties, regularise them, and document them for posterity.

Yes, that's how we worked on a new, purposeful and more effective Jail Manual so that our successors will not have to go through all that we did to bring about a touch of humaneness to the prison.

A system of *participatory management* has been evolved in Tihar and the inmates are more than willing participants in it. The Superintendent of Jail 2, Tarseem Kumar, elaborates upon this programme: "We have worked out a system of panchayats to aid us in our effort towards improving the quality of time the prisoners spend here. We have a cultural panchayat, a mess panchayat, an education panchayat and the prisoners do not find it at all uncomfortable to follow as this system is very indigenous to our country. A large portion of the problems, which are mostly minor administrative problems, are resolved and sorted out at these panchayats by the prisoners themselves. This has taken a big load off us."

Jail 3 has its own academic council which looks after the various educational, vocational and cultural activities. This council regularly makes project reports and offers suggestions which are then studied carefully by the administrative staff and are later, by and large, implemented.

A series of seminars have been held with the prisoners as the main participants. The topics range from 'Why crime ?' to 'Why *Vipassana* ?'

"It is from these seminars," explains the superintendent, "that a number of suggestions come to us. This is the workshop where new programmes are forged and because the changes pertain to the participants and because the suggestions also come from them, the new changes are very readily accepted by all."

The factory in Jail 2 has reached a level of self-sufficiency because of such participation and interaction.

"We were short of looms in our factory," says Superintendent Tarseem Kumar, "and we were contemplating buying some from Ludhiana. But the prisoners suggested that they would make the looms themselves. Now five such looms have already been completed and another five are being made. This has increased our output tremendously. We have started making *khaes*, cotton shawls, cotton dusters, uniform cloth, etc., in this factory. In the carpentry section we have decided to switch over from making bigger items to smaller ones which we have realised are more popular with our customers – items like *chakla belans* [rolling pins], peg tables, children's chairs, small round tables and so on."

He goes on to list some of the other activities and plans: "In the tailoring section we have undertaken job works for the Khadi Gram Udyog and this has proved most beneficial. In the chemicals factory, we have now started making our own sulphurated soaps which were a long-felt requirement of the prisoners. Our plan now is to open a factory showroom outside the jail premises which would greatly facilitate the sale of our products."

All the profits, of course, are channelled into the prisoners' welfare fund.

Another inmate, Satendra Kumar, writes in the monthly magazine *Nav Chetna*, now being published by Central Jail No. 4:

A Legal Aid Programme was introduced in Central Jail No. 4, Tihar, in the month of July 1993. The aim of the programme is to ensure that all prisoners who are unable to engage an advocate, who has been visiting this jail and with the help of undertrial prisoners Satendra Kumar and Prit Pal Singh, has been drafting, typing and despatching the applications and other petitions for the prisoners to different courts, can do so.

A large number of prisoners have been benefited by the Legal Aid Cell which is provided by the Delhi Legal Aid and Advice

Board. Many prisoners have been granted bail by the courts through the petitions filed by this cell. Also, many prisoners were able to file their appeals in the Delhi High Court through this cell. As a result of the petitions filed by the Legal Aid Cell to eliminate delay in trials the honourable Delhi High Court has directed the Delhi Administration to constitute ten more special courts so that the trial of the NDPS Act cases could be conducted speedily. A number of these cases have been transferred from the court of Shri Kuldeep Singh, Additional Sessions Judge (ASI) Delhi, and now the dates given by the courts are shorter than given earlier. The Legal Aid Cell advocate used to visit this jail three times a week earlier. But now the visiting days have been increased for educating the prisoners about legal matters connected with their cases. With the cooperation of the jail administration the legal service has shown signs of considerable improvement.

Superintendent of Jail 3, D.P. Diwedi, requested its inmates to donate their labour under a *Shram Daan* scheme. The inmates did not hesitate and their beaming superintendent says: "In a week's time the complete prison bore a new look, with the entire premises cleaned up and all the buildings whitewashed. We had been contemplating over requesting the PWD to assist us in this task but our own prisoners suggested that they would do it themselves. And a more professional job we could not have seen."

All the superintendents commonly expressed the need to incorporate such discipline as part and parcel of their duties. No amount of rules and regulations in jail manuals, they maintained, would be able to help them if they did not put their hearts into what they were doing. Only that would put life into the system and make it a permanent achievement of Tihar.

With the present changes and reforms taking place in Tihar, one is quite convinced that the inmates' conditions would, as they already are, be considerably ameliorated. However, how could the ultimate goal, of making the prison system a part of the crime prevention package, be achieved?

Kiran Bedi ponders over this question and then replies:

> *The biggest tragedy I perceive is that there is no coordination in the administrative system. Each department is, in principle, linked with the other. Yet it works in complete isolation. One is not even aware of the workings of the other. We have never looked at criminal justice in a holistic way. The police does not understand why we are doing something in the prison. We have a lot of things to tell them, but they have no time for us. If they would coordinate with the prison authorities, and develop a sensitivity in the police force – after all we are both trying to bring the crime rate down – if we are to sustain our efforts then there should be certain inputs into their training. To sustain this it is absolutely necessary to develop a crime prevention package. We must have a coordinating system and develop coordinating skills. But this coordination can come only from a political leadership – the Home Minister or the Home Secretary. They should develop coordination skills and not be just seeking explanations, not just seeking reports and reprimanding but be looking at broader issues and grappling with them. What I'm suggesting is not something idealistic. It's a management exercise that can very well be understood and learned. With this coordination would come interaction among the concerned departments – the police, the judiciary, and the prison.*

How do we prevent recidivism? First we need to know what's causing it. There must be a feedback to the prison. The police can monitor this. They can have month-to-month reports on the activities of released criminals. Only they can tell us what measures they are taking to prevent recidivism and what their crime prevention plan is.

The end-product is the public. Voluntary agencies must take on the task of overseeing the ex-prisoners' rehabilitation into society. NGOs (non-government organisations) can do a lot here.

At present we have a situation where we are told "don't touch me, I'm judiciary" or "I'm police". But each, in turn, feels free to criticise the other. So the coordination can only come at the political level, that is, at the ministry level. The ministry would point out then – "You gentleman/lady, you are not being able to fit into this programme. So, it is better we put you somewhere else where your particular attitude would be better suited."

In the West and, some of the Asia Pacific regions, they are working on these lines. They have a range of after-care officers. We are far behind in this. But now at least we are aware of the problems we face and that's as good a start as any for doing something about it.

We banned smoking for the prisoners because it is a stimulation dependence just as any other drug. It may appear harmless to the smoker. But I, as manager of their health, cannot be deceived by that. As drugs have a bad effect, so does smoking tobacco. Innumerable bronchial and lung problems are caused by it. If you're handling your own life and paying for its upkeep, it's okay with me. But when it is my responsibility to keep the prisoner healthy, when it is my responsibility to pay for his physical upkeep, and to pay from resources which as it is fall short of the more beneficial targets at higher priorities, then I have to make my own choices. Just look at the overcrowding in the jails. Where there is space meant for 20 prisoners we have 80. You can imagine what the incidence of passive smoking must be. Till I left we were treating several prisoners for bronchial problems, and for TB. Where does the money come from for their medical treatment? From the prison budget. So, whether you like us for it or not, we just do not have the funds or the inclination to push your habit.

22

The 'Leading' Role

The rapidity and incisiveness with which changes have been brought about in Tihar have left everyone almost breathless, especially the prison staff itself. To a person, they had been willing or unwilling partners in the corruption and decadence that were rife in Tihar in the earlier years. To them it is almost as if a whirlwind of change had swept them off their feet. This incredible transformation cannot be attributed to anything other than the one single factor of charismatic leadership. Such leadership was essential for a place like Tihar, and it was very fortunate that it did get this leadership when it did.

At this stage, therefore, one is tempted to digress a bit, i.e., in order to enumerate those qualities which are essential for exhibiting such leadership.

The foremost is, naturally, an overpowering urge to make realistic commitments and fulfil them within a given time-frame. Next comes the willingness to shoulder responsibility, without flinching, for actions taken on the courage of convictions.

The other qualities include the ability to create an open and honest environment wherein provisions are made for everyone's physical, emotional and spiritual well-being and the capacity to repose confidence and trust in the staff which inspires them to keep themselves informed of latest developments and also instils in them the trait of honestly admitting their own mistakes. This ensures loyalty and cohesion among all team members. Such a situation ensures a change in the mindset from merely obeying orders to acting on one's own initiative.

The courage to stand up for what is right, irrespective of what others may think, encourages confidence in the staff. The ability to act as a shock absorber between the staff and the powers-that-be, irrespective of the toll it takes in terms of stress and other psychological factors, ensures deep-rooted loyalty.

The proclivity and ability to take decisions promptly and to ensure follow-up action forthwith are needed. The aptitude for articulating concepts, strategies and tactics concisely and forcefully is important.

Enthusiasm for the accomplishment of the task at hand appears to be the driving force behind a sustainable leadership. It is this trait which ensures performance to the best of one's ability and inspires almost contagiously.

Taking the initiative appears as much the hallmark of the leader as is his or her ability to inspire subordinates to develop this quality. Close contact with good leadership will almost invariably inspire similar qualities and it is this which ensures the continued performance of a task even in the leader's absence.

Integrity, of course, is an essential characteristic which is non-negotiable. Truth occupies a predominant position and its pursuit should encourage candid and uninhibited communication.

The leader must be able to make sound judgements. This ability, of course, is the product of technical and tactical proficiency. It is this ability which enables the team to keep its goals in sight and work smoothly.

An unfailing sense of justice is imperative. This quality ensures caution in dealing with all kinds of cases and provides a correct perspective of the entire scenario. Also, it underpins one's ability to command with impartiality and consistency.

Finally, the essence of leadership appears to be in the display of a supreme degree of unselfishness. A leader never ever takes advantage of situations for personal pleasure, gain or safety at the cost of his subordinates or the institution in which he or she serves. A totally uncompromising commitment to one's profession takes precedence over all other factors.

By and large, public attention is focussed on a crime after it has been committed and on the criminal only as long as the trial takes place. (In India, because of the inordinate delay in prosecution and the extremely long periods of incarceration in prison pending trial, the role of the authorities is more often than not limited to arrest and imprisonment.) It is in this context that the 'criminal' has been isolated from society and therefore he or she does not pose any further threat to it. But that is not as it should be. It is here that fresh-thinking innovative leadership should make its presence felt. Imprisonment should be viewed as only a deterrent and a periodic sanction and the offender must ultimately return to the same society of which he or she is a part. It, therefore, becomes imperative that during the time spent in prison the leadership must ensure that the offender is suitably corrected so that his or her reinduction into society proves successful. Imprisonment, therefore, cannot be treated as meaning a mere locking up of the 'criminal' and throwing the key away. This awareness has pervaded prison managements worldwide and has compelled them into desiring to become progressive, receptive to change and to work under public scrutiny.

23

Lessons from Tihar

The story of Tihar leads us inevitably to certain conclusions. The way events have taken shape has been on an almost day-to-day, problem-solving basis. An inhouse search for the various factors which individually or collectively made the running of the ponderous machinery of Tihar difficult, and at times even impossible, was carried out and these factors were identified. Corrective action was then taken, which over a period of time took such a form that it could be systematised and almost incorporated into a manual of statutes of human rights, correctional staff duties and prisoners' privileges and quality of time spent in prison. Considering the large numbers of prisoners and staff who had to be dealt with almost simultaneously, the immensity of the task becomes evident and the quantum of effort put in is extremely laudable. The whole exercise has apparently been based on the concern that all corrective measures in the prisons have been taken with the idea of integrating them completely with the general needs and aspirations of the total community of which 'prisons' form only a part.

What makes the 'Tihar story' unique is the fact that its approach to the prison problems here has been novel. As mentioned at the outset, correctional reforms in prisons have become a reality which currently engages the attention of the governments of almost all countries. Regular international conferences take place and several committees have been formed in different countries to look into the plight of prison management. In the case of Tihar too, the same concerns have governed the reform movement with the difference that instead of first getting involved in the time-consuming activity of forming committees and subcommittees with their ensuing recommendations, the bull here has been taken by the horns. Only after the efficacy of each and every correctional activity had been tested out was it recorded and documented and that too not merely as a recommendation but as a directive to the staff.

Two very major issues emerge from the foregoing approach. The first pertains to the highlighting of certain general principles which must inform our outlook towards, and understanding of, the prison situation, not just in our own country but abroad as well. The second issue pertains to the fact that no reform or correctional activity is possible unless and until a sensitivity to the human condition is developed. This basic understanding lies at the root of all reform measures. In whatever condition, and in whatever place we may discover the human being, his or her rights ensuing from this virtue must be recognised and appreciated. The 'working material' is human; any system not permeated by humaneness will not, and cannot, be expected to work.

The essence of the prison concept is the time spent there, in isolation from society, of which one was earlier a part. Proper channelisation and utilisation of this time are therefore essentially what any prison administrative or correctional staff should be concerned with. It is the quality of time spent in jail which can offer opportunities to prisoners to at least have options of converting themselves to a non-criminal life and way of thinking. For the innumerable number of prisoners who spend time without ever being convicted (and their number is absolutely disproportional to the ones who are) mismanagement of this time can criminalise them. It is, therefore, imperative that nothing be permitted which can directly or through induction corrupt and criminalise this major population of prison inmates.

Substance abuse, or drug abuse, has been discovered to be convincingly instrumental in leading individuals down the criminal path. It can do so by removing self-restraining inhibitions, by creating aberrations in thinking and functional skills, or by compelling the individual to take to crime to maintain the habit. In the new order of prison reforms such abuse, if permitted to exist because of an inability to control it, would at the outset itself undo any correctional attempts on the part of the management. The environment in a prison is a controlled one which, therefore, with sensitivity and sincerity of effort, could become conducive to an anti-substance abuse programme. This feat has been very effectively and tellingly achieved in Tihar.

A major portion of the prisoners, at least in Indian jails, come from the economically deprived sections of society. These people normally do not possess skills and, therefore, are unable to make a place for themselves in society. These are the persons who are the most prone to acquiring negative and criminal attitudes if the time spent by them in prison is not managed properly. Imparting of education and self-improvement skills to them should, therefore, stand out as a high-priority effort in prison administration. When there is so much human resource material in a controlled environment, then efforts made towards counselling and directing of their energies towards constructive and creative directions should invariably prove fruitful.

Catering to creature comforts and acquiring of material skills alone would not be sufficient. Efforts, therefore, must be directed towards the prisoners' moral development too. Moral conduct rises above religious beliefs and customs and, therefore, does not influence religious belief nor is so influenced by it. Religious beliefs and customs of various segments of the prison population must be respected not only because they constitute a basic right of the individual but also because such respect is psychologically uplifting. Good human conduct would only help in the better tolerance of, and interaction between, different religious sects.

Community participation in as many reform programmes as possible should not only be encouraged but also insisted upon. Communities could participate in programmes relating to prevention of drug abuse, prisoners' education, religious or moral discourses, imparting of technical skills, or providing job work, yoga training, medical assistance, or legal assistance. A whole vista of possibilities could be explored in this context. There already exists a healthy infrastructure of community groups, voluntary agencies and non-government organisations which can be approached and which are already working on various such programmes. These agencies would prove invaluable in any such correctional programme. The community itself would be most helpful in the successful translation of any rehabilitation programme into reality.

Organised gangs within prisons can prove a great deterrent to any reform programme by acting as pressure groups. It will always be in the interests of these groups to continue a system of destabilisation in the prisons. Isolation of hardened criminals from the rest of the prison population has proved effective in Tihar. Its long-term effects are still to be seen. The ultimate success of such a correctional system would, of course, depend on the extension of such programmes to these groups. However, the fact remains that though these pressure groups are always everywhere in a minority, yet they exercise the maximum disruptive influence.

One of the main reasons for such influence – and what has been seen to be the biggest problem in Tihar – is overcrowding. Interdepartmental coordination and cooperation can go a long way in checking the influx of prisoners to jail. Constructing new prisons and thus increasing the capacity is an obvious solution, which can prove to be a little misleading. Given the system that currently prevails it would not appear far-fetched to see even the new prisons becoming overcrowded if certain changes are not made in the entire system. This leads to the consideration of the *role of prisons in society*. We must come to the educated conclusion that only such people should be sent to prison who indulge in violence or activities dangerous to the well-being of society. There are innumerable deterrents which already exist in society and its institutions and more can be reasonably created wherein a person does not necessarily have to go to prison for any and all offences. It is only when these deterrents fail that imprisonment should be considered. Only in the case of such offences where it is felt that any other punishment would diminish the seriousness of the offence or crime committed should imprisonment be resorted to. For instance: where a life of crime has been deliberately chosen by the offender as his or her mode of existence and livelihood; or, where a person shows continued insensitivity to the other deterrents imposed upon him or her.

It is for society to reflect upon these issues and to devise a system wherein prison management is not isolated and where it can work in coordination with society and its other institutions which, in essence, have a common goal.

However, given the present system, the story of Tihar stands out as an outstanding example of what can be achieved by a sensitive, humane and benevolent leadership.

24

They Stoop to Conquer

"**O**ff with her head," said the Department of Home Affairs one fine May morning and promptly Kiran found herself occupying the office of the Deputy Commissioner of Police, Vigilance Branch, at Delhi Police Headquarters. This, of course, was to be a very temporary position because her new office as Additional Commissioner of Police, Planning and Implementation, was yet to be physically made because this charge had never been an independent one to date. Probably because of the effectiveness with which Kiran had brought reforms in the almost hopeless Tihar Jail, the Commissioner of Police, Delhi, Nikhil Kumar, entrusted her with the task of "planning for the Delhi Police to be the Police of the 21st century". She would be required to draw up a Master Plan whereby the duties of the Delhi Police could be placed in their proper perspective and its administrative and operational infrastructure could be matched. Better late than never, one should rightly think, although it apparently took the single-minded and determined efforts of a single officer in the field of prison reforms to bring about this new turn in reforming the Delhi Police.

However much such a change in the force may be required and however much it may be justified that the force gets just such an officer whose talents are suited for this purpose to a 'T', the manner in which the entire affair was handled leaves a very bitter taste in the mouth. And, therefore, one attempts to draw certain conclusions.

Kiran's posting as IG (Prisons) had, at the outset, been apparently a 'dump' posting because from September 1992 to April 1993 the Home Ministry had been quite seized of the problem of having a police officer of the Delhi cadre whiling away nine months in Delhi without any assignment. Tihar Central Jail appeared to be the ideal place to 'dump' this officer. To the acute discomfiture of her seniors, Kiran's work created a high profile for her even in this 'punishment' posting. Yet, again, she dared to stand up to the powers-that-be and instead of snivelling and grovelling as was expected of her by them, she impudently flung the Magsaysay Award and the Nehru Fellowship at them. Not content with just this she made her work in Tihar so transparent that the outside world was apprised of the tidal wave of correctional reforms that were taking place there. And the work was impressive enough to catch the people's imagination not only in India but also abroad.

The Government of the United States of America was impressed enough for the Congressional Committee of the US Senate to invite her for a Prayer Breakfast with President Bill Clinton and Mrs. Hillary Clinton. The United Nations Organisation was impressed enough with her achievements to invite her to Copenhagen, Denmark, to attend the United Nations World Summit for Social Development (6-12 March 1995). The British Foreign Office was impressed enough to have the British High Commission invite her to visit their prisons.

Kiran's superiors, however, were not impressed! When the world was watching the dramatic way in which Tihar was metamorphosing from a hellhole of a prison into an ashram, her superiors were watching the increased wattage of the spotlight that was focussing on her. All the effort that was being put into the overhauling of the rusted Tihar machinery and in making directional changes in the focus of such effort were perfunctorily summed up as being so much effort to merely hog publicity.

Tihar, on an average, contains about a hundred and fifty to two hundred foreign inmates at any given time. A short time before Kiran became the IG (Prisons) in May 1993 there had been a newspaper report emanating from the USA that highlighted the miserable plight of these prisoners. Indian groups working on issues of human rights, like the PUDR and the PUCL (People's Union for Democratic Rights and People's Union for Civil Liberties) took up this issue and a hullabaloo was raised about it.

The various foreign embassies and high commissions had also taken up the cause of the prisoners from their countries with the Government of India. This persistent foreign concern was part of the legacy of Tihar inherited by its new IG. A short while later, though, when effective changes had commenced to take place, these very inmates mentioned these changes through word of mouth. This catapulted the foreign press and media to seek to record for their viewers the changing scenario and probably bring some relief to the unfortunate families of the prisoners.

Kiran had all along believed in accessible and transparent functioning. She had also all along in her career encouraged participatory management, from both within the staff and the community at large. The media was a part of the same community. In the case of the prison, it had a special role of working as a bridge between the closed walls and the apprehensive society. Tihar had been and is always in the news – so what kind of news are they going to get now? Steal or manage, or see for themselves? Kiran decided on the last option. She had the power under the prison rules to allow visitors duly conducted. Instead of 'briefings', whoever expressed genuine concern for the prisoners was allowed inside with cameras. They could come in, talk to prisoners, see the progress, discuss matters with officials and write on their own. Their own reporting enabled objectivity with conviction. Such reporting also put in perspective matters such as (a) delayed trials, (b) overcrowding, (c) misuse of TADA, (d) the agony behind dowry offences, (e) women prisoners and (f) neglect of prison staff. On the positive side the media could project what participative community support could do to turn a jail around and make it an ashram.

During her tenure Kiran had some noteworthy visitors from a cross-section of society, namely: Khushwant Singh, Amrita Pritam, Rajmohan Gandhi, Dr. Lee Brown, an American official concerned with drug policy in the USA, Mrs. Frank Wisner, wife of the American Ambassador to

India, V.N. Narayanan (editor, *The Hindustan Times*), Anup Jalota (composer and singer), Naseeruddin Shah (actor), Manoj Prabhakar (cricketer), and Dr. Charles W. Colson of the Prison Fellowship.

Among the Central Government dignitaries the visitors included Salman Khurshid (Minister of State for External Affairs), Sita Ram Kesri (Welfare Minister), Arjun Singh (former Minister for Human Resource Development) and Mukul Wasnik (Deputy Minister for Sports).

The Delhi State officials included the LG (P.K. Dave), the CM (M.L. Khurana), the Health Minister (Dr. Harsh Vardhan) and Minister of Education (Sahib Singh Verma).

Members of the Human Rights Commission, such as Fatima Bibi, also visited Tihar.

Spiritual leaders (and intellectuals) belonging to groups such as ISKCON, Brahmakumaris, OSHO, Jain Samaj, Gandhi Bhawan, Ramakrishna Mission and Chinmaya Mission visited Tihar. Apart from the aforementioned luminaries, a vast spectrum of visitors also came to help Tihar actually move towards becoming an ashram. For instance: counsellors, linguists and storytellers, writers, doctors (both generalists and specialists), practising allopathy, homoeopathy, Ayurveda, naturopathy and others, psychiatrists, Gandhians, theologians, evangelists, social workers, members from the prison fellowships, computer experts, social science researchers, teachers (educational, moral and spiritual), priests, artists (from the theatre and also musicians), sportspersons, crèche workers, legal aid advocates, librarians, bankers, vocational training specialists, horticulturists and donors.

His Holiness the Dalai Lama expressed his desire to visit Tihar and bless the prisoners personally.

Since the visits of the aforementioned luminaries and other categories had great information value for the people outside, even when the media was not directly present in the prison, they got due coverage. However, a few of them had brought along their own media entourage as well. The fact of the matter was that the media was no longer buying news but seeing and reporting directly. This strengthened the information base for the prison and brought in more and more community support for the reforms taking place. There has not been a single instance of sensational news which had a destructive effect on reforms in Tihar. In fact, what people got through the news was 'Tihar as it is'.

Such news obviously would transcend the boundaries of the country. Foreign media naturally would also have an interest not only for the reason that many foreign nationals were housed in Tihar but also because of the human interest angle. After all, prisons exist all over the world and some problems are similar. They started to show keenness in special culture-based reform programmes which were unique to Tihar and the Indian ethos, such as *Vipassana* meditation, spiritual discourses, yoga, community support to total literacy, the petition box system, drug abuse treatment, keeping of small children with their mothers, and how the prison could accept being a no-smoking zone.

Kiran saw no reason for depriving the media persons of letting them know and see Tihar as it was. While this did prove a big boon for Indian human rights handling, it also got her invitations from abroad to enable interaction amongst prison systems suffering from the Tihar kind of challenges.

But this was not how her seniors thought! Permitting any media into Tihar Jail began to be construed as a compromise on security. Her acceptance of invitations abroad began to be construed as manipulation of foreign trips. Denial of banned items to politically favoured prisoners was construed as a deliberate bias towards the Delhi State Government. Also, her inability, because of circumstances beyond her control, to keep an appointment sought by herself with the Chief Minister was construed as her not wanting to work for the Delhi State Government. This was, indeed, a volte face of the extreme kind. What could have triggered off this snowball effect? In this context, several factors stand out for detailed consideration.

As stated earlier, Kiran had received a personal invitation from the Congressional Committee of the Senate of the United States of America to be their guest at a National Prayer Breakfast in the first week of January 1994. She requested clearance from the Home Ministry and, meanwhile, made her bookings. A day after her intended departure, she received a denial of permission from the ministry. The invitation, however, was repeated for the year 1995 and the press was quick to ask her whether she thought she would again be denied permission. Her candid reply was that that probably is what would happen. However, she got an okay the second time and was able to attend the breakfast meet.

This invitation was soon followed by another from the United Nations to attend a World Summit for Social Development in Copenhagen, Denmark, in March 1995. She was requested to exchange her views there on the situation of prisoners in this context. Now this was very much a part of the work that she was to take up under the Nehru Fellowship granted to her and she was already building up her academic framework for it. Very naturally, therefore, she was very keen to avail of this opportunity.

The Ministry for Home Affairs (Government of Delhi), however, did not quite view it in this same way and a denial was very much on the cards. Kiran, therefore, sought an appointment with Rajesh Pilot, Minister of State for Home Affairs, Government of India. The same day and time that she was with Rajesh Pilot she had an appointment with the Chief Minister of Delhi, Madan Lal Khurana, a meeting she herself had solicited. The meeting with Rajesh Pilot, however, got extended and she was left with no option but to tender her regrets to the CM's office. Kiran says that she went to see Rajesh Pilot so as to bring to his notice how rare and valuable invitations are made to fall by the wayside because of inadequate interest taken by the bureaucracy. Rajesh Pilot effectively intervened and directed the file to be sent up to S.B. Chavan (the Union Home Minister) for further orders. Till then it had not gone to him. S.B. Chavan, on Kiran's file, approved both the pending invitations – one for the UN Summit and the other for British prisons. The approval of the Central Government came as a shock to Kiran herself! But for bureaucrats in the Delhi Government this approval became a cause for revenge against Kiran! They managed to turn the CM against her by convincing him that there was an obvious effort to affront him. This apparently convinced the CM and he went public with his resentment by stating that "if that is how she feels why does she want to work for the Delhi State Government?"

During her absence from Tihar the Bharatiya Kisan Union leader, Mahendra Singh Tikait, was sent as a political prisoner there for a few days. Harsharan Singh Balli, the Delhi Minister for Industries and Prison, requested the jail staff to permit Tikait to smoke his *hookah* (a kind of pipe) in prison and thereby allow the tobacco required for it. As mentioned earlier in this book, one of the biggest challenges that Kiran and her jail staff had faced in Tihar was the imposition of the ban on smoking and all tobacco products. They were certainly not going to allow all that effort to come to nought merely for appeasing the whims of any one individual. The request, therefore, was quite naturally turned down by the DIG (Prisons) Sarangi.

This refusal of a 'simple request' quite peeved the concerned minister. So much so that he declared to the press that where his friend was being denied the 'humble *hookah*', her 'friend' Charles Sobhraj was being permitted foreign pipes and foreign tobacco. This, of course, was out of sheer peevishness and utterly baseless because Sobhraj is known to be a non-smoker. In another book on Tihar, written in the early nineties, Kumkum Chaddha of *The Hindustan Times* has also mentioned this fact of Sobhraj abstaining from tobacco. As a matter of fact, one of the Sikh prisoners was quite irked about the minister (who is also a Sikh) insisting on permitting the *hookah* for Tikait and declared that why did he not insist on a *hookah* in the gurdwara? This faux pas was meant to be covered up by another claim that Sobhraj was permitted the use of a typewriter that went against the Delhi Jail Manual. Wilson John, of *The Hindustan Times*, even quoted the relevant section from the Manual that stipulated that a typewriter was amongst one of the items that were treated as prohibited property. However, he stopped short in his quote of the rider that states that the abovelisted items (in the section) are prohibited only till such time as they are not provided to the prisoners with the *permission of the jail superintendent*. As a matter of fact, typewriting is one of the functional skills that are taught to the inmates of Tihar and typewriters are provided freely to them. Here is the relevant excerpt from the Jail Manual:

Prohibited Articles

33. The articles specified or included in any of the descriptions contained in the list annexed to this rule shall be deemed to be prohibited articles, within the meaning of section 42 and clause (12) of section 45 of the Prisons Act, 1894, unless any such article shall be —

(a) introduced into any jail,

(b) removed from any jail,

(c) supplied to any prisoner outside the limit of any jail, or

(d) received, possessed or transferred by any prisoner

with the permission of the Supdt. or other officer empowered by him in this behalf.

List of prohibited articles:

(1) Spirituous liquors of every description, ganja, bhang, opium, smack and other intoxicants.

(2) All explosive, intoxicating or poisonous substances and chemicals, whether fluid or solid, or whatever description, etc.

Charles Sobhraj had been first permitted a typewriter way back in 1978 by the then Assistant Sessions Judge, T.S. Oberoi, who was the trial judge in his YMCA passport case. Other prisoners had also been given this facility as is evinced by the fact that Dr. N.S. Jain was permitted one in 1977 and so was Sunil Batra in 1979. As to Charles Sobhraj being served meat rations (230 gm), this was done on the express orders of the then Additional Sessions Judge, H.L. Malhotra, in 1990. All these orders were given much before Kiran came to Tihar. But one's selective reading of the rules to suit one's story constitutes one way of selling sensationalism on the part of some news reporters. This matter has been taken to the Press Council by Kiran's lawyer P.S. Sharda.

In quick succession, yet another report of *The Hindustan Times* mentioned that Charles Sobhraj's lawyer, Debashish Mazumdar, after a meeting with him in jail, was caught trying to smuggle out the electronic typewriter that his client had been permitted to use in his cell. The matter was given an apparent slant that made it appear as if evidence against the IG (Prisons) was being removed. This ruse appears quite in keeping with the canard of disinformation that was being projected about her. What actually took place was that during his meeting with his lawyer in the Tamil Nadu Special Police guardroom, under the supervision of a TSP subinspector, Charles Sobhraj had sought recorded permission from the SI to permit his lawyer to take out his electronic typewriter for repairs. An entry to this effect was made in the 'legal interview register' maintained at the high-security prison and he was then permitted to hand over the typewriter. If information of this incident was given to the *Hindustan Times* reporter, obviously, the relevant facts of the case were conveniently withheld and the story was thus filed with only insufficient information.

What comes out to be more amusing is the fact of Charles Sobhraj being repeatedly called Kiran's 'friend'. This apparently emanates from the fact that he had stated to a reporter that having given up a life of crime he was going to turn to writing and that he was already working, among other things, on Kiran's Bedi's jail reforms in Tihar over the past two years. When Kiran was asked about this, she said that being an intelligent human being who had spent quite some time in prison Charles was in quite the right situation to be working on such a project if he had so decided. This view was given a different slant and made to appear as if Kiran had authorised her biography by him. Naturally, in the eyes of her detractors, he became a 'friend' who had to be given any and all facilities to aid and abet her 'narcissism'. Much, therefore, was made of the typewriter issue to the extent that Kiran was now suddenly seen to be compromising security to achieve much shallower ends.

Even more interesting was the claim that she had not enforced the Jail Manual stipulation, of making jail escapees wear red caps, on Charles Sobhraj. He had been there much before Kiran became IG (P) and his escape and recapture also took place much before her time. He has never been made to wear a red cap and yet no jail official has ever been charged with favouring him on this count. The Punjab Prison Manual that governs the Tihar Jail since its creation in the 1950s was slightly amended only as late as 1988 to become the Delhi Prison Manual. As mentioned earlier, till 1988 the Manual also stipulated that "all women prisoners were to be transferred to the women's prison in Lahore (now in Pakistan)". Obviously, the Delhi Jail Manual has to be completely rewritten and updated to relate realistically to the present-day Indian reality as against that of British colonial times. And, as it exists, it is to be followed more in the spirit than in the letter.

Anil Baijal, Home Secretary in the Delhi Administration (since asked to relinquish his post) stated to the press (*Hindustan Times*, 21 April 1995) that a confirmed report had been sought from the IG (Prisons) about her alleged favoured treatment to Charles Sobhraj and that a reply was being awaited by his office. Kiran, for her part, claims that she learnt of this only from the newspapers. The journalists came to know of it much before she herself did. The moment she got this letter she promptly wrote to the Lt. Governor of Delhi and also faxed a message to the Department of Home Affairs (NCT, Delhi) pointing out that the concerned officials should at least read the rules and regulations themselves before charging anyone with breaking them. One cannot fault her for this 'request' because the Department of Home Affairs has a complete legal secretariat that could have given them proper advice. This would certainly have saved them from jumping the gun which only gave the impression that they were only too keen to pin something on her.

Finally, came the leaked news in the *Indian Express* dated 21 April 1995, which rocked Tihar and many others, of Kiran being asked to be shifted:

SHIFT OUT KIRAN BEDI, DAVE TELLS MINISTRY

Lt. Governor P.K. Dave has asked the Union Home Ministry to transfer the high-profile Tihar Jail Inspector-General, Ms Kiran Bedi, on the ground of manipulating foreign tours and taking "populist measures".

In a letter to Union Home Secretary K. Padmanabhaiah, the Lt. Governor said that Ms Bedi, in her desire to get publicity, was taking measures that could compromise the security requirements of the prison. Around 8000 prisoners are currently lodged in the jail.

In the two-page letter written late last month, Mr Dave had cited instances where people were allowed inside the prison without screening. One occasion was on Rakshabandhan *day. Another example was the visit of the United States Embassy officials to the prison.*

Mr Dave also referred to the alleged filming of the prison by foreign media and the general "populist stance" taken by Ms Bedi.

The senior Home Ministry officials chose to keep silent about the contents of the letter, but they confirmed that the written intimation had been sent to the Ministry requesting the transfer of the first woman Indian Police Service officer.

The letter talks about the Tihar jail chief manipulating trips to various foreign countries such as Denmark and United Kingdom. While the Denmark trip was sponsored by the Delhi-based United Nations office, the UK trip was organised by the British High Commission.

However, in both the cases, there was no formal letter to the Government of India and Ms Bedi was approached directly. Normally, the sponsoring agency sends an invitation to the Union Government, which decides whether to send the particular officer or not.

Ms Bedi was also invited by the US President Bill Clinton for breakfast on February 2, but this time the trip was cleared by the breakfast committee and the Union Home Ministry.

The letter also speaks of her populist stance towards jail inmates, who are allowed to approach the National Human Rights Commission directly. The special facilities accorded to Charles Sobhraj and the high-profile criminal's project of writing a biography for Ms Bedi has also not gone done [sic] well with the Ministry of Home Affairs.

This is the second time in Ms Bedi's career that the State Administration has gone against her. Prior to her posting in Tihar Jail, Ms Bedi was moved out of the post of DIG, Mizoram, after she openly criticised the State Administration over the admission issue. She wanted her daughter to be admitted through the State quota into Capital's Lady Hardinge Medical College.

(Indian Express, 21 April 1995)

To this Kiran replied by writing a letter to the LG:

Central Jail, Tihar
D.O. No. PA/IG (P)/95/179
Dated 21 April 1995

Hon'ble Lt. Governor Mr. Dave,

This is to invite your attention to a news item in Indian Express *today (21 April 1995) under the heading "Shift out Kiran Bedi, Dave tells ministry" (page 1).*
2. Could your office please confirm the news item? You will appreciate that this will enable me apprise you, if you so desire, on various issues of Prison Management and myself which find mention in the news report.
3. In all fairness, this would be in the spirit of natural justice.

With regards,

Yours sincerely,

(Dr. KIRAN BEDI)

Kiran has not received any reply to this date.
Kiran then wrote another letter to the Secretariat, which was as follows:

No. 42/PA-ADDL.CP/P&I
dated New Delhi, 26 May 95

To

The Joint Secretary (Home)
National Capital Territory of Delhi,
DELHI.

Sir,

I was working as Inspector-General (Prisons) from 1 May
1993 to 5 May 1995. I stood "relieved" on 5 May 1995 (AN)
vide your order No. F. 5/3/95-Home (P) Estt., Govt. of Delhi
dated 3 May 1995. I thereafter handed over charge on same
day afternoon.

The news report of 21 April 1995, Indian Express, *page 1*
under caption "Shift out Kiran Bedi, Dave tells ministry'
reveals the allegations on the basis of which Central Govt.
appears to have been approached for my transfer out of the
Tihar Jail posting. This was subsequently elaborated and
apparently clarified in a news item of Punjab Kesri *of*
22 April 1995 page 5. In all fairness, I requested for
confirmation of these news items as well as time from the
Hon'ble Lt. Governor vide my letter No. PA/IG(P)/95/179,
dated 21 April 1995 so as to explain matters in reference to
the allegations made which had now become apparently 'too'
public. I also wrote to the Hon'ble Prisons Minister (Ref. news
item in Punjab Kesri*). I have not so far been favoured with*
the reply from either the Hon'ble Lt. Governor or Hon'ble
Minister for Jails.

I only wish to reiterate that as an officer of Indian Police
Service, I can have no objections to a transfer.... However, in

my case the manner of my transfer has tended to become one of my "public trial" which regretfully became extremely punitive in nature. I submit that as a service officer I owe it to myself and my family to protect my reputation and save myself from the adverse effects it would have on my family and our social position. I submit that in the present case I was given no opportunity to explain my conduct to my superiors prior to or after the mind was made up. It would appear, therefore, that the decision for my transfer was made without consideration of my explanation and of my conduct but on a prima facie impression of my work given by some other individuals. I hope you will be kind enough to devise measures to redeem adverse effects which I have suffered as a consequence of the above events.

Yours faithfully,

KIRAN BEDI
Addl. Commissioner of Police
Planning & Implementation
26 May 1995

Till date Kiran has not received a reply to this letter either.

The Home Department went further in stating that "new practices in the management of the jail (were being followed) which do not seem to be strictly in accordance with the provisions of the Jail Manual/Prisons Act". These practices, it claimed, were "journalists being allowed to take interviews and photographs of inmates; preparation of television features in jail and allowing up to four hundred visitors at a time on *Raksha Bandhan* without search". As the press had easy access to the jail activities, there was plenty of footage in the national and international media. Interestingly, however, the Delhi Administration officials claimed that they came to know about all these so-called 'irregularities' only through a book written by a jail superintendent and published in early 1995. Anyway, when they claim that the changes taking place in Tihar "do not seem to be strictly in accordance with the provisions" (operative words being 'seem' and 'strictly') it is quite obvious that this is merely a case of myopic versus broader vision.

Given Kiran's nature, she was not the one who was going to take all these charges and insinuations lying down. She took up each charge and shot back her rejoinders with pinpoint precision. She told the press that all these ministers and bureaucrats who were finding so much fault with her work had never themselves bothered to visit the prison for personally assessing the problems in Tihar Jail. All they had ever been bothered about was to interfere in the jail functioning by seeking favours for their 'friends' who found themselves in prison. The Chief Minister of Delhi, M.L. Khurana, chose to view her rejoinders as a breach of the civil service officers' code of conduct and asked for an enquiry to be made into her mode of functioning as head of Tihar for her acts of omission and commission.

As far as the government and the administration were concerned, matters could not be left lying as they were because such a state of affairs would have meant that Kiran had ridden roughshod over them once again. Leave Tihar she must, they decided. But then the immediate problem arose: where could they send her? She had already done her stint of out-of-state postings and had been long due for a posting with the Delhi Police. Maybe that would be too close for comfort. Repeated efforts, therefore, were made to ask her to seek leave to follow her academic pursuits in furtherance of the Nehru Fellowship that had been granted to her. Her compliance would have served them in two ways. One, they could beat their chests and claim that they had effectively subdued and tamed the spirits of this 'maverick' officer and, two, as far as postings were concerned, they would not have to retrench any of their long established officers in the Delhi Police service. Over and above all this, it would have effectively left her in 'limbo', which would have suited them very much. But they were quite mistaken if they thought she was going to be glad to grab this dangled temptation. She told them she would take her sabbatical as and only when she was ready for it and when she needed it.

The powers-that-be were left with no option but to transfer her from Tihar. On 5 May 1995, with almost a full year left of her tenure as IG (Prisons) (which could be the case) Kiran was served her transfer orders. She was told to relinquish charge of Tihar and report to the Commissioner of Police, Delhi, to take over as Additional Commissioner of Police, Training, Planning and Implementation.

In 1988, under pressure of the Delhi lawyers' lobby, Kiran had been hastily transferred from DCP (North) to Commandant (CRPF) (see Chapter 9). The haste and confusion were apparent when even before she could take up her new assignment she was yet again transferred to the Narcotics Control Bureau (NCB). The same situation was repeated at this juncture. She gave up her charge at Tihar and even before she could take up her new assignment, she was transferred yet again to take up the duties of Additional Commissioner of Police, Planning and Policy, minus training, a department, as mentioned earlier, that had never been an independent one.

The eminent writer and journalist Khushwant Singh summed it all in a nutshell when he described Kiran's transfer from Tihar as "a victory for a handful of small-minded envious people over a gutsy woman who has won laurels for herself and her country."

In the excitement of the chase where Kiran was being pursued by the hounds of politics and bureaucracy, the hunters slipped up very drastically on two major points: First, the Mulla Committee Report is a major work that records the abysmal depths to which the Indian prison system had sunk to and recommends the ways and means of altering this hellish scenario into one where human diginity could be restored to the unfortunate who found themselves within prison walls. The Central Government had accepted the Report in principle and expressed its desire to have its recommendations incorporated in the present prison system. The Mulla Committee Report, thus, should rightfully serve as a guidance manual and override all outdated prison manuals that merely helped to serve British interests in pre-independence India. The major features of the Report are that prison authorities should ensure that human rights of prisoners are not violated. It discloses a much larger vision in maintaining that prisons must interact with the press because it is only in this way that the work going on within them can be made authentically transparent to the world outside and society at large can keep in touch with those who have been isolated from it. Secondly, various apex court judgements have directed the Tihar Prison administration to implement humane methods of prison management and integrate the prisoners with the society outside.

Here, it would be relevant to quote from the report of the All-India Committee on Jail Reforms (1980-83) under the chairmanship of Justice (retd.) Anand Narain Mulla (Chapter III, Section 3.45.1):

> *Since time immemorial crime has been a social problem and social problems cannot be tackled merely through legislation or pronouncement of laudable objectives. Unless a large section of the society believes in the reformative and rehabilitative approaches, a progressive and modern system of prisons cannot become a reality. Public opinion has to be built up in such a way that people accept that rehabilitation of wrong-doers in society itself. This can be achieved through the education of people regarding the all-pervading implications of crime as a social and economic problem. People must be informed about the progressive and modern methods of dealing with the wrong-doers.... We, therefore, recommend that a regular plan aiming at creating a favourable rehabilitation culture in the society should be drawn up and implemented by the prison administration.*

The press obviously has a very realistic role to play in any such educative venture and that is why the print and electronic media were permitted to cover the developments in Tihar so extensively.

An overview of all the charges levelled against Kiran as IG (Prisons) merely indicates how assiduously she had pursued these very humanitarian recommendations. Also, a very interesting feature of her work methodology emerges. It strives to achieve goals and targets in keeping with those drawn up through considered opinion and purposeful deliberations condensed to policies and recommendations. In her case the methodology is derived not through abstract considerations but rather through the management of day-to-day problems on a day-to-day basis. It is only her clarity and range of vision that direct all her efforts towards the right ends.

Her achievements at Tihar, in just one year, were precisely those recommended for American prisons after a year of deliberation and analysis by an American Correctional Reforms Committee. And, interestingly, the time period is the same. While she was working on it through 1993-1994, the American Committee was simultaneously deliberating over the problems facing it for the same duration. Similarly, that was exactly what she was doing without being aware of any existing recommendations which were already incorporated in the Mulla Committee Report. Unfortunately, this humanistic and progressive Report had almost been thrust into oblivion because the two essential qualities required for its implementation had been grossly lacking in the system: namely, commitment and effort. So, when these qualities dared to raise their heads the system immediately closed ranks and launched into a head-on assault.

For the time being, the politicians and bureaucrats may have apparently won. The vibrant hope, however, remains that this episode represents but a small battle and the larger war still continues.

Police officers from foreign countries visiting India have already started questioning the ethics of a service that, instead of supporting its own member for furthering the principles that are ideally the service's *raison d'être*, they have merely derived apparent pleasure out of any discomfiture that may have been caused. They have started even doubting the bona fides of their intentions as against the worldwide concern to radically alter the functioning and goals of the law-enforcing authorities.

25

Tihar after Kiran

Apprehensions that the correctional reforms that were taking place in Tihar and the openness that the jail was being subjected to would last only till such time that the dynamic and innovative incumbent to the post of its Inspector-General remained there have all but proven to be true even in the short space of time since Kiran's transfer. The inmates had, at the outset, expressed these very doubts when they had claimed that they had only one fear: that of having the old system come back with a vengeance. Today, the earlier regime has already started rearing its ugly head.

A case in point relates to the biscuit tycoon Rajan Pillai. Regarding the tragic death of Rajan Pillai in judicial custody, Kiran expresses her feelings rather strongly:

I am agonised. Agonised over the manner in which people have been taken for a ride yet again. An announcement of a magisterial enquiry into the circumstances of Rajan Pillai's death on 7 July 1995 in jail is really no big deal. It is mandatory under the rules. So what is the announcement all about? What the medical causes are can be commented upon only by experts in the profession; I can certainly tell you from my managerial experience at Tihar that this jail has been a victim of apathetic governance. Tragedies of these kinds totally expose the system once in a while, and the administration only waits for some other sensational event to overshadow the present one, with public memory being short.

Tihar jail has all along been grossly inadequate as far as health services are concerned. Time and again all the 'provisioners' not providers — for the latter is a very respectable term for those who do exercise responsibility — never cared to respond. They have been treating this prison, crammed with thousands of hapless deviants, with apathy. The poor die a quiet death. It's only cases like those of the high-profile Rajan Pillai which expose the cheapness with which life is treated in there. To underscore my earlier point: an enquiry is mandatory. It is not required to be 'ordered'. So what's special? It could be special if an enquiry had been ordered to look into the following fundamental questions:

(1)   Since when have the doctors' vacancies not been filled?
(2)   And pray why?
(3)   Who all are the persons whose responsibility it was to do so?

(4) *Even if directions had been given, whose responsibility was it to ensure that these are fulfilled?*

(5) *Isn't regular review of coordination called for of organisational functioning where the direct functioning is reviewed?*

At least during my tenure, nothing of this kind happened. One lone IG has the following top 'provisioners' for all matters, starting with the Lt. Governor, Chief Minister, Minister for Jail, Health Minister, Chief Secretary, Home Secretary, Health Secretary and Director of Health Services (all from the Delhi State Government). Why did not any one of them ensure that Tihar had the minimum required basics for saving human life? And should the enquiry not take up the issue of their quality and capability of 'provisioning'? What is their role in problem solving? Aren't they in these positions for just that — and if they did not do so, then what are the penalties for them? Can they only be judges, but not judged ?

Our administration groans under feudal ways. Its methods are a product of the feudal era. Have we an independent, constitutional agency which can look into its non-performance and affix due criminal liability? We do.

After the Rajan Pillai incident I got to talk to some officials in Tihar Jail. They told me that the CM and the Minister for Prisons came to the cell in which Rajan Pillai had been lodged. They brought the press along to ensure coverage of the fact that the CM had visited Tihar. However, they kept the press persons in such a place where they could not have access to the inner precincts. After the visit the CM raised some basic queries such as (not in the presence of the press):

(1) *What time did the incident happen?*

(2) *What was done after that?*

(3) When did the doctor/s arrive?

(4) Why couldn't the doctor/s arrive sooner?

(5) Why were there insufficient doctors?

(6) How is Tihar going to defend itself in this matter?

After that the CM gave a short press briefing and left. The Minister of Prisons who was well aware of the shortage of doctors, when asked by the CM as to why the vacancies had not been filled, looked the other way. I am told that the Home Secretary, whose direct responsibility it is to supervise the work, had not visited the jail till then (up to 10 July 1995).

I strongly feel that, in all fairness, the enquiry needs to go beyond Tihar as well. Within Tihar, it should find out the quality of response of jail officials. Outside Tihar, it should ascertain whether the 'provisioners' did what they were supposed to do and then fix responsibility for non-performance on specific individuals. The enquiry should be held by a group of independent eminent citizens and not by a subordinate of the Delhi Administration.

Deaths of this kind will reoccur (which may not hit the headlines), the reason being that four independent Central jails, situated within one huge complex, are without proper round-the-clock medical facilities. The minimum they should get without delay is at least four qualified doctors available within the premises all the 24 hours.

Along with doctors, Tihar Jail (and all others) need to be provided with life-saving devices and medicines and also with adequately equipped hospitals. What could be worse than to say that while tuberculosis cases are high in Tihar it does not even have a TB specialist!

The enquiry should go into 'non-performance' of 'provisioners' — and who will allow themselves to be judged?

This is not possible in feudal bodies with Democratic (sic)
Gowns!

Members belonging to voluntary agencies, who were the
backbone of the community participative reforms, are
already almost at their wit's end wondering how to
continue with their work with the inmates that they had
been committed to and had set time limits on. Prison
headquarters maintain that such members have not been
restricted from doing their work. However, the warders of
the different jails that these volunteers visit insist that all
permissions for them to enter the jail have been withdrawn
in practice. They further insist that if there is any
interaction that they want with the inmates then it should
be only in the visitors' galleries. These volunteers report
that they are made to wait for, at times, even more than
two hours before the warders decide that they can enter
for a brief period. These volunteers have started forming
the distinct impression that things are being made very
difficult for them so that they may be dissuaded on their
own and the warders may claim that the good work
stopped because of lack of interest on the volunteers' part
and not because of any express orders from them (i.e., the
warders).

A group that interacts with the women inmates was
obviously pained to report that the latter had already been
told by their assistant warder, who is directly in charge of
them, that their days of breathing fresh air were now over
and that they would have to breathe the air that would be
allowed only by her. The same warder had earlier, when
Kiran was at the helm of affairs, shown deep concern for
the condition of the unfortunate women inmates and

claimed that nothing better could have happened for these unfortunates than the taking over of the charge of the jail by Kiran Bedi. The hypocrisy of such staff members is a painful awareness of the plight of the inmates in the re-emergence of the old and sordid realities of the jail.

The price of a bundle of *beedis* has already fallen to Rs. 50 from Rs. 150. Obviously, access to them has become easier. The inmates are no longer allowed to visit the supermarket which had been put up for them and which was run by both the jail staff and the inmates. Money accruing from the sales went partly to the prisoners who ran the supermarket. Items are now purchased and given to the inmates by the staff at exorbitant rates and the poorer lot are now denied this facility. Money now exchanges hands even for *mulaqaats*. Patients sent out on referrals are taken around in the police van and only allowed into the hospitals when the requisite money has been handed over. One diabetic prisoner complained that although the outside medical report showed that his blood sugar count had soared to as high as 385 the jail hospital report mentioned it to be only 125, which is very normal. The inmate is poor and claims that such manipulation has been done because he does not have any money to give to the doctor-warder nexus that has already started functioning quite effectively.

One researcher who somehow still manages to be patient enough to go into the jail after long hours of waiting reports that she has been an eyewitness to a number of beatings inflicted by long-term prisoners on inmates who had not even spent a day in prison as yet. This, she says, is being done in the presence of the jail staff. When she approached them on one such occasion she was told that the inmates knew what they were doing and that they had their own system of sorting out such things. She was quite shocked to see such blatant irresponsibility on the part of the staff on whom the well-being of the inmates depended. Obviously, the old mindset has very smoothly slipped back into place where the only onus that the jail authorities at the lower level are willing to bear is that of beatings and punishments. They have started reiterating their old statements that all inmates who come to Tihar Jail are criminals and their time there should be made as uncomfortable as possible.

The prison garbage dump has started stinking once again. Prisoners who had been so willing to work on the 'garbage-into-manure' project that had started earning considerable amounts of money for the prisoners' welfare fund have now stopped doing so. They explain to the volunteers and social activists that they know that the money so earned would now no longer be used for their benefit and would only fatten the jail staff's purses. The result is that garbage has started accumulating in the same way as in the past and the stench of decaying organic matter has already started pervading the jail campus.

Of course, claims continue to be made that the correctional reforms continue to proceed as they had been and that nothing had been done to check them. However, these are but mere claims without any substantiation as there is no more any transparency. By a secret order the Delhi Government has already prohibited access of the media to the prison. Organisations that had helped build up the education system in the jail and which had been so well accepted and liked by the inmates are now being told that the classes would be disturbed if they entered the prison. Even so, whenever they do manage to gain entry they claim that signals are passed to the staff within and the scenario soon becomes stage-managed. Jail factories have slowed down almost to a stop because of lack of raw material and absence of supervision.

Saroj Vashisht is a very versatile and active social worker who has been interacting with the inmates of the prison for almost two years now. She has organised cultural activity groups, poetry classes and teaching classes besides introducing a number of other measures. She maintains that as soon as the controversy about Kiran's activities in the jail started being reported in the newspapers, the inmates, by and large, had considered it to be a foregone conclusion that her transfer was imminent. A short time thereafter transfer orders were served to her. While the majority of the inmates almost felt bereaved, a small group of prison staff distributed sweets to all and sundry in the knowledge that their days of power and pelf in the confines of the prison walls had returned. Saroj states that by and large the inmates are very disturbed about the fact that Kiran did not come to bid them farewell. "It was a careful decision. I did not want to see men cry. Also this would have been the first time that I would have interacted with them and not been able to give any answers to their questions. Over and above, I was not going to give any opportunities to authorities to lay anything on me," clarifies Kiran. Her decision was a very judicious one if one is to go by what some of the prisoners had to say. They claimed that the situation in the jail was so volatile that the 1990 scenario could well have been repeated. They obviously referred to the riots that had taken place then.

One of the prisoners who has spent almost four years in jail and is, more or less, the jail's inhouse poet claims that the Chakkar Dharam Sabhas, i.e., the evening congregation of prisoners for spiritual discourses and announcements that were so popular with the inmates just a short while ago, have completely stopped and there is a marked segregation of Hindus, Muslims, Sikhs and Christians. Corruption, he says, is at the moment in its infancy and without fail will soon bloom into its youth. He also says that smoking is now back and an indicator of the easier access to tobacco is the sharp drop in prices of *beedis* and cigarettes.

A Kenyan, convicted of murder and who has completed his fourteen-year term, reminds Saroj of the times before Kiran was posted to Tihar. He had spent five years in a Kerala jail and been then shifted to Tihar because his life had been at risk at the hands of a gang of smugglers. When he entered prison he was given duties in the jail *langar* (kitchen) and soon told to pay the superintendent Rs. 500 and the deputy superintendent Rs. 300 per week. He did not know how to manage it and was therefore stripped naked, tied to a tree and beaten to near death. After that he was explained that all he had to do was sell the rations coming to the *langar* to the prisoners and pay the officers from the money earned. To save his skin he had to resort to such corrupt practices. He says that he is seeing the same system now coming back and very soon it will be like the old days again in Tihar. If anyone, he says, could come to the foreign prisoners' wards they could see for themselves that a regular superbazaar in drugs was functioning there.

"When I first entered the women's cells after Kiran's transfer," says Saroj, "I was met with a stunned silence. There is no better way I can describe it. No one was willing to speak anything and when overly cajoled and persuaded they would just mutter that it was alright." One of the women prisoners who relates to her very well told her that foreign prisoners were now again being asked to get the ward authorities foreign goods through their visitors or else they would be given no privileges and life would be made difficult for them.

The word around the jail is that Ram Rajya has gone and Ravan Rajya has returned. One adolescent even went to the extent of telling her the next time he went to court for his trial he would make good his escape and would shoot the man who had transferred her. When reminded that would bring to nought all the effort put in over the past two years, he apologised. He said he would pray in prison that the concerned person met with a car accident and died or at least be demoted.

One can quite rightly claim that Tihar has come round full circle and that soon all the earlier names it had earned for itself would be given back to it. Kiran had renamed Tihar Jail as Tihar Ashram, meaning a place of REFORM. After her transfer inmates renamed it as Tihar *Anaath Ashram,* meaning an orphanage...

26

Kiran After Tihar

Kiran reported back to the Delhi Police. The transfer order put her in-charge of training and policy implementation. Overnight training was withdrawn and she was left with policy implementation. Nobody explained why the order was changed. In policy implementation, there was nothing spelled out. It was now for Kiran to decide what she wanted to do. Sit around or be on her own for which she had done prior homework. Kiran had secured the prestigious Jawaharlal Nehru Scholarship while she was working in Tihar. It appears Kiran had a sixth sense guiding her when she had applied for the Nehru Fellowship. On being asked, she said:

When I applied for the Nehru Fellowship, Tihar Jail reforms were at their peak and everything was going smoothly. But, I had a feeling that it would get hurt as these were too good to last in our envious system. Therefore, it was necessary to document the transformation for posterity. It might also be self-respecting to leave on my own terms in case a situation arose. I had something telling me that I may have to take this decision at any time, sooner or later. In fact, I did consider leaving while it was smooth, and discussed it with my colleague Sarangi. After discussions, I decided to postpone writing the Fellowship in order to complete the tasks in hand, such as: computerisation, cable network, health plans consolidation, NGO participation, institutionalisation, linkage with universities, etc. I thought if we as a team gave Tihar one more year, we may take it where we wanted it to be. But my gut feeling was right. Envy struck and I had to leave Tihar. Back in Delhi Police I saw nothing really waiting for me. I felt free. I decided to go for the writing of my Fellowship.

Kiran applied for study leave and got into a non-sparing frame of mind with habitual optimism. She took to writing and finally published a book three years later entitled *It's Always Possible* with a CD Rom, another first in many ways.

27

'It's Always Possible'

Inherited from her tennis days, anticipation and preparation were Kiran's habits by training. She had all along preserved her prison worknotes with meticulous care. This was certainly not the first time. Her home library is a systematic documentation of records, which she keeps with great care. She acquired this habit from her father, who would keep a regular record of her tennis clippings for Kiran to see on her return from matches all over the country.

Now Kiran was back home again on study leave. Overnight her mother converted the living room of their home into a study, inclusive of a bed, to enable her daughter to work through odd hours. Then, Kiran got on to categorise, analyse and review all the material she had carefully preserved. Interestingly, many released prisoners, Indians and foreigners, started to call on her at her residence. They talked to her freely. Kiran has all the tape recordings. A new dimension emerged. Clarifications were now available. She could quiz them on issues she had not probed earlier. They too were more forthcoming since both she and they were no more 'imprisoned'. One of the freed inmates, a British national, assisted her in transcribing the tape recordings. Another freed inmate, a woman, drew the sketches to depict the inner scenes, as she had seen, of the state of affairs inside the prison before the changes came about. Thousands of prisoners' letters to Kiran were categorised and analysed to understand the progression in their thoughts. Besides the written documentation, Kiran had also preserved a lot of audio-visual and print material. This she decided to put in a CD-ROM to complement the book. It was an experiment of its kind, unique but expensive. Her organization, which was born with the Ramon Magsaysay Award, decided to fund the CD-ROM with the objective of spreading the prison reforms.

During this 'writing leave' Kiran travelled extensively within India and abroad. She visited prisons in Australia, Austria, Denmark, Germany Italy, Japan, Philippines, Slovakia, Sri Lanka, UK and the US. Within India, she visited prisons of UP, Bihar, Madhya Pradesh, Kerala, Tamil Nadu, Karnataka and West Bengal. At all these places she was facilitated to interact with the inmates — men, women and adolescents. She could see the facilities and the programmes initiated in the prisons she had visited. She held interactive sessions with officials, floor managers and prison inmates. To her surprise, the corrective programmes carried out at Tihar prison had reached them through media reports or the internet and they were no strangers to what Kiran had to share. Just before Kiran was asked to leave Tihar, a short documentary called 'Miracle of Tihar' had been produced. This came to good use as she met with prison officials.

Kiran developed a personal style of writing. She was known to write all day long, and for as many days as the thoughts flowed. She would travel out to break mental saturation and come back to writing when her mind was fresh again. But visits to various prisons helped her see and compare what had happened in Tihar and what were the conditions in other prisons. This is what she said on this:

My book travelled with me in a way. It strengthened my resolve to say it all, for it was bound to be of help. Prisons, I felt, were in need of new ideas and attitudes. What was somewhat universal, and what was managed to be changed, was also a universal challenge. The visits educated me that most of all what needed to be 'corrected' was the mindset of the prison policy-makers and prison managers, and what we had collectively attempted inside Tihar, with some degree of success. It was my belief that this book would also be a salute to this collective effort of prison staff, prisoners and the supporting community from outside. I thought we could offer a correctional model which had worked! The book called it — the 3 Cs Model, i.e. corrective collective, and community-based, drawn as a ship sailing smoothly towards its destination.

The book opens with her first day in the prison. The chapter entitled 'Do You Pray' narrates her first day's experience inside the prison. It's a moving account of a woman police officer who is, at the core, a rehabilitator, a crime-preventer and a reformer, establishing a strong bond of communication between her and the inmates in the very first meeting she had with them. From this opening account, she makes the reader travel with her into all that existed inside the prison — be it the living conditions, health hazards, debauching of adolescents and children, harassing of women, control by gangsters, the cancer of corruption and addiction, and the insecure staff, etc. This portion of the book is interspersed with sketches of the state of affairs as it existed and seen by an inmate. This part is an authoritative documentation of 'what existed'.

The second part of the book is a narration of what was done with what existed. It is entitled 'What Evolved'. It illustrates the 'how' of the growth of a prison to an 'ashram' — a reformatory. This part clearly brings forth the restorative process of prison management. It is a narration of the concerted and collective effort of the prison staff, the prisoners and the community. No wonder Kiran calls it a 3 Cs Model — the three Cs meaning it was corrective, collective and community-based prison management. In fact, Kiran has most modestly chosen to place herself in the background, and given all the credit for the change to the prison staff for their acceptance of change, and facilitating it with enthusiasm and sincerity. Gratitude towards many individuals, and organised members of the community is writ large with the 'how' of their contributions which made the difference. The text vividly explains the manner in which prisoners became a responsible society within the prison walls, conducting all the positive activities for themselves in an organised way, realising all for their benefit, now and later.

The concluding part of the book is the 'Emergence' Kiran draws very interesting graphs and charts which are a visual summary of t'1e emergence. It's a visual depiction of how Tihar moved on from a vulture culture to a 3C model, designed as a 'noble ship' in which all were sailing together in preparation towards restoration and integration. It is this which says — 'It's Always Possible'.

His Holiness the Dalai Lama wrote the foreward of the book. It was released in Delhi by Natwar Singh, the Former Minister of State for External Affair on 25 September 1998, followed by similar releases in various Indian cities, namely, Mumbai, Calcutta, Chennai, Trivandrum, Chandigarh and Amritsar. The book also did well in cities/towns in the United States and Britain. In the USA, book purchases were made in Atlanta, New York, Washington, Houston, Kansas, Salt Lake City and Baton Rouge. In UK, there was a special release of the book in London by Lalit Man Singh the then Indian High Commissioner and later the Foreign Secretary, Government of India.

The book has been translated and published in Marathi and Hindi. It has also been published in Australia and Bangladesh. The book has been reviewed in the prime journals of UK and USA. 'It's Always Possible' is presently being translated into Italian to be published in Italy. It is on its way to be a course book in the University of Milan. From a story of prison reforms, it has emerged as a book on 'management of situations' and what makes one succeed against all odds. Most of all, it is a whole new concept of reformation of offenders, crime prevention and participative governance beyond prisons.

28

On a Mission with a Missionary

From policing to prisons, to book-writing and then to assisting the Lieutenant-Governor of Delhi in city management was a long haul. Her posting as Special Secretary to the Lieutenant-Governor, Tejendra Khanna, an outstanding civil servant, came by an ironic quirk of destiny. Kiran had been removed from Tihar Jail by P.K. Dave, Khanna's immediate predecessor. Interestingly, she was being appointed to work in the same office in a special capacity. The waiting room in which she once sat to call on the person who had removed her was converted into her office which was adjacent to the office of the Lieutenant Governor. This is what Kiran had to say on her prestigious appointment:

After the first draft of my book (It's Always Possible) was with the editor, I decided to report back to Delhi Police. But again I was kept waiting. Meanwhile, the Union Territory of Delhi got a new Lieutenant-Governor, Tejendra Khanna. Mr. Khanna, as I had seen and read about, was an open, honest person and a thorough professional. I sought an appointment with him to pay a courtesy call. The Delhi Police Commissioner reports to the Lieutenant Governor, Delhi. Mr. Khanna discussed matters of policing in the capital with me and my concepts of crime prevention. He listened to me with respect. Ironically again, I was before the incumbent whose predecessor had not even given me an opportunity to be heard before being removed from Tihar with the accompanying news splashed, despite my written requests, and here the present Lieutenant Governor was keen to 'hear' what I had to say.

I went away from the LG's office, thinking I would get some place in the Delhi Police soon, whatever it might be. But instead, a few days later, I got a call from the LG's office that the LG wanted to see me. I was pleasantly surprised. I went. The Lieutenant Governor came straight to the point and asked, "Would you like to work with me?" I said, "Thank you, Sir but what for?" He said, "Together we work for the city and redress the people's grievances". I said, "Sir, it's a great opportunity, but I would prefer to return to mainstream policing at this point in my career." He said, "It's fine, but do think about it and get back to me." I went back and waited for Police Headquarters orders on my posting. Nothing came. I got another message from the Lieutenant-Governor's office to consider the offer he had made, and to see him if the offer was acceptable. Meanwhile, information had leaked that the Lieutenant-Governor was keen to appoint me as his Special Secretary, as he had already appointed another recently retired senior police officer from the Central Bureau of Investigation Shantanu Sen as his Special Secretary for assisting him in law and investigation matters. Sen had a very successful tenure with the CBI. I went to see the Lieutenant-Governor not for the posting, but to ask if I could know why was I still on hold. Mr. Khanna was straightforward and said, "Kiran, I don't think the present top brass in Delhi Police would want you to be a part of the police setup. Why not work from here. Consider it and we begin rightaway." I said "Sir, in that case, could it be a temporary arrangement, I may return after we set up the redressal and response systems." He said yes. I thanked him and left.

The Lieutenant-Governor had created two posts in his office for two Special Secretaries as advisors. It was for the first time that the two prestigious posts as advisors to the LG had gone to two police officers. There was a great surprise, and even anguish, in certain circles that Kiran was going to work with one of the finest civil servants India had produced. Being at the LG's office, for many, was a very sensitive and a prestigious appointment — for Kiran it was finally being back to work, but this time with a 'missionary'.

The news of Kiran's appointment spread through the media. It was confirmed by Khanna himself through various public interactions that he used to have. He was always for voluntary observance of laws with emphasis on a participative-transparent-accountable administration. He was a people-friendly, sensitive and ethical civil servant. He hoped to mould his administration to be the same way. LG's public confidence soared and so did the people's expectations. Complainants wanting redressal of their grievances started to flock the LG's office, which hitherto was not for general public in such numbers at all and certainly not for people coming without appointment. The complaints received were forwarded to the concerned departments for action as deemed fit. In very few matters reports were called. There was only one personal computer, which was almost idle. Khanna had declared that his office shall not be a post office, but a resolver of problems with the best of technology. This set the mission statement and the work methodology at the LG's office.

On all days, throughout the day, Kiran's office started to receive complaints and complaints. They ranged from garbage not being cleared for years to existing and ongoing unauthorized constructions made in collusion with enforcement agencies; public parks being occupied; non-attendance of staff; callous misbehaviour; files missing for years and on various other matters coming under Delhi Police. The seat became a huge mirror screen of all that was going wrong with the city management. While those who met the LG personally were by appointment, which too was a large number daily and in once-a-week public hearings, you could just walk in to meet Kiran Bedi and not leave till she heard you out. Since the post in which she worked was new, it had no backup infrastructure to deliver. These were matters of details, but critical to match the performance with the expectations generated. With prior concurrence of the LG, Kiran drew upon some personal staff who had worked with her earlier when she was with the Delhi Police, and who she knew would understand the LG's mission statement without any loss of time. She put together a team of serving and retired officers assisted by a band of young student computer operators. She created office space with all the infra-structure necessary, such as 12 computers, telephones lines, fax machine, photo copiers, etc. to meet the growing demands of the increasing number of visitors. She called on Sheshagiri, then Chairman of the National Informatics Centre (NIC) and sought help for computerisation of redressal system at LG's office. Kiran and her team of officers with NIC computer staff designed programmes to meet the needs of the hour. Within weeks, a fully computerised system was functional. A round-the-clock telephone control room for grievance redressal system was made public, with telephone number of LG's control room regularly publicised. All this was documented, computerized and analysed along with the correction time taken to redress the people's problems. A mobile team to cross-check the reports received was put in place to reduce hoodwinking. A daily personal public hearing time was declared and adhered to. This enabled planning of the rest of the day for follow-ups, implementation, coordination, analysis, reviews and meetings. Every grievance received whether by wireless/post/fax/telephone/in person was computerised and the complainant received an official acknowledgement with a computer reference number with endorsements to whom he will need to communicate with for follow-up. There used to be a monthly audit of all units receiving the mail, and a review date with Kiran of each unit was planned in advance and circulated to all for information. At the end of each month a computer graphic of each unit performance was circulated for all to see their work, comparatively. It was a transparent record for performers and non-performers. The doers got LG's appreciation while the non-doers got an advice. Neither of this had ever happened before in such a sustained, methodical and regular manner. This system was appreciated, admired, replicated — and envied!

It was a grievance redressal system, perhaps for the first time in the history of an Indian governor's office where the governor became a people's governor.

As a part of systemisation, the LG initiated a people's participation scheme called the Citizen Warden Scheme. The LG appointed citizen wardens from eminent citizens who had the motivation to work for their neighbourhoods as office bearers of resident associations. They included members of Rotary and Lions Clubs, retired members of the armed forces, civilian forces and others. They all received an identity card signed by the Secretary to the LG, with an appointment letter and the charter of duties. Thereafter, they reported their achievements on a monthly basis to the LG's Citizen Warden Desk headed by Inspector Sarabpal Singh. Kiran personally supervised this. She used to regularly call their meetings, arrange coordination sittings with their area officers, and even got them visited by LG's Citizen Warden Desk. A newsletter of Citizen Warden Desk was also published to share achievements and ideas with all citizen wardens and government departments. From citizen wardens, the LG moved on to appoint Citizen Traffic Wardens. All those who opted for duties in road safety were given traffic violation record slips and a colourfully designed traffic jacket to assist law enforcement in checking traffic offences. In fact, the LG made the citizens his eyes and ears.

This kind of participation was seen in some quarters as an open challenge to the elected representatives. Many felt threatened and insecure. Some declared open opposition to this while others supported it. But the citizens welcomed it, as it was something they had always wanted. It was a democratic, responsive and participative governance. It earned wide acceptance and respect amongst the residents and common citizens, with a lurking question as to how long would the system last? The answer was obvious, as long as the LG lasts? And Kiran? As long as the LG is there!

This is exactly what happened — and fairly soon in about a year and a half. With a change at the Centre in 1998 (as LG is a Central Government appointee), Khanna was relieved of his charge. Soon after that a press statement was issued that the LG's house did not need a watchdog while also admitting that a lot had been achieved. There were no answers in the media or otherwise as to what would happen to the Citizen Warden Scheme, despite a large number of letters the citizen wardens wrote. They finally gave up.

Priorities and method of governance changed. Raj Niwas was no more open to masses. A staffer at Raj Niwas remarked, "now again not even a bird will be able to flap its wings leave alone enter without appointment."

Kiran was moved back to Delhi Police. This time she got her order to be Joint Commissioner (Training) but with not even a toehold in Police Headquarters — from where all other Joint Commissioners of Police worked and coordinated. She was to work as Joint Commissioner Police (Training) in two tenures with a break in between of the 41 days she spent as Inspector General of Police, Chandigarh. The Police Training College from where she carried out her responsbilities of steering and supervising the training was at the far end, rural part of the south-west Delhi. The institution was begging to be equipped, starved of funds, isolated and largely unattended, but inhabited by the next generation of Delhi Police. Kiran saw in them the future of her force and the security of her country.

29

Chandigarh — 41 Days

The one city which Kiran loved was Chandigarh. She knew this place, inch by inch, through her cycling when she was a post-graduate student there. "Every time it rained, I would pick up my bicycle, and go cycling in Chandigarh. One way the wind would be favourable and I had to struggle the other way. I enjoyed it then. It built my stamina for tennis championships."

Chandigarh Police Chief's position was overdue for a change. Kiran requested for a posting to Chandigarh. She got it. She had put in ten months as Joint Commissioner Police Training. In her farewell address to the trainees at the Police Training College, she said she was going to Chandigarh to to raise her challenge and test herself on what it was to be the head of a police force? How would she lead the force and provide the professionalism which was expected from the police services? How would she deal with the pressures which come with that leadership and would she herself live up to her own convictions?

These thoughts were prophetic!

Kiran was tested many times over on all these counts in just 41 days she spent as Inspector-General of Police, Chandigarh, the shortest posting of her career but the most eventful and traumatic.

Kiran's colleagues recall her first two weeks in office:

The collapsed systems of policing became functional. All diverted manpower towards personal staffing in the garb of keeping security came back. Mrs. Bedi herself returned her escort vehicle and the staff. Traffic Police cleaned up its act and became visible. The traffic cranes were back on the roads. Drivers became alert, and went looking for parking lots. Pollution check centres had long queues. Cyclists went into the cycle lanes. Youngsters driving two-wheelers abandoned their vehicles out of fear of getting caught. Markets appeared orderly, for the shopkeepers and vendors vacated the footpaths on which they had displayed their goods for the use of pedestrians for whom they were meant. Police stations got their diverted men back. Hundreds of home guards were recalled to duty. Vacancies in these were ordered to be filled up. Women police were sent back to police stations. Police Control Room staff returned the calls to check if they had been attended to. The staff earlier on twelve-hour shift now did eight-hourly duty. Absenteeism was now a thing of the past.

The IGP herself was in any police station at 9 a.m. sharp. Hence all of us were out, checking our things for ourselves before

*she detected our lapses. We were on the road, correcting,
directing and helping the people. The police stations got the
resources — human, material and financial — which were
earlier completely missing. It was amazing how soon changes
came about. The police force began to feel responsible to patrol
the villages and slum areas around Chandigarh to prevent
night crime. Women NGOs were invited to be present in the police
stations, if they so wanted to assist in responding to women
complainants. Meetings with school and college principals were
held to check the eve-teasing menace. It was amazing to see how
Mrs. Bedi found the resources to address all the issues. Special
Branch personnel, who would earlier idle around, went for a
few hours daily to colleges at odd timings in plain clothes, thus
putting eve-teasers on the run. Welfare of families of the police
personnel was an equal priority. Computer centres for police
officers' children and creches for children of policewomen were
established. Get-togethers were organised, where all ranks met.
The focus of attention was women and children. The drunken
men in the police force came to realise they had no options but
to behave. Families felt emboldened now, for they knew they had
a guardian amongst them.*

So did the public. Beat officers were calling on their
area homes to check if anyone had anything to report. From
a reactive to proactive and preventive policing, the path
ahead was set.

But someone was really upset, the Home Secretary —
a woman who, prior to Kiran's arrival, was in fact the
de facto IG of Chandigarh, even when there was a de jure
one present. The Home Secretary was transferring, posting,
suspending, calling explanations and warning all ranks of
the police force totally bypassing the responsibility and
authority of the then Inspector General Ram Pal Singh.
This is testified by the documents that follow.

CHANDIGARH ADMINISTRATION
HOME DEPARTMENT
ORDER

The following Police officials posted at Police Post, Sector-22, Chandigarh are hereby transferred and sent to the Police Lines, Sector-26, Chandigarh, forthwith:

S. No.	Name, Rank & No.
1.	ASI Gurmeet Singh, 499/CHG
2.	C. Sawarn Singh, 115/CP
3.	C. Prema Nand, 247/CP
4.	C. Kashmir Singh, 3690/CP
5.	C. Raj Kumar, 1361/CP
6.	C. Balbir Singh, 2683/CP
7.	C. Satish Kumar, 2884/CP

ANURADHA GUPTA, IAS
HOME SECRETARY,
CHANDIGARH ADMINISTRATION

Endst. No. 16435-HIII (I)-98/   Dated:

A copy is forwarded to the Inspector General of Police. U.T., Chadigarh for information and necessary action.

He is requested to arrange to post alternative personnel in place of the above said officials transferred from Police Post, Sector-22 to Police Lines.

Joint Secretary Home,
for Home Secretary,
Chandigarh Administration.

Endst. No. 16435-HIII (I)-98/25561   Dated: 18-12-98

A copy is forwarded to the following for immediate compliance to:

1. ASI Gurmeet Singh, 499/CHG
2. C. Sawarn Singh, 115/CP
3. C. Prema Nand, 247/CP
4. C. Kashmir Singh, 3690/CP
5. C. Raj Kumar, 1361/CP
6. C. Balbir Singh, 2683/CP
7. C. Satish Kumar, 2884/CP

Gurmel Singh

Joint Secretary Home,
for Home Secretary,
Chandigarh Administration.

* Evidential document of the Home Secretary bypassing the authority of the IG by issuing transfer orders.

The Home Secretary was signing suspension orders of the non-gazetted officers which was a clear usurpation of the IGP's functions, as the following documents testify.

No. 16435-HIII (I)-98/25589   Dated 17-12-1998

CHANDIGARH ADMINISTRATION
HOME DEPARTMENT
ORDER

1. Whereas disciplinary procedings against Sub Inspector Ved Parkash and Assistant Sub Inspector Azad Singh, Police Post Sector 22, Chandigarh are contomplated.
2. Now, therefore, in exercise of the powers conferred by Rule 16.18 of the Punjab Police Rules, 1934 as made

applicable to the Union Territory, Chandigarh Police Officials, the said Sub Inspector Ved Parkash and Assistant Sub Inspector Azad Singh are hereby placed under suspension with immediate effect.

3. It is further ordered that during the period that this order shall remain in force, the headquarters of Sub Inspector Ved Parkash and Assistant Sub Inspector Azad Singh shall be at Chandigarh and they will not leave the headquarter without obtaining prior permissin of the Competent AuthoritY. S.I. Ved Parkash and A.S.I. Azad Singh will be entitled to subsistence allowance as per rules.

(ANURADHUA GUPTA)
HOME SECRETARY.
CHANDIGARH ADMINISTRATION.

To

    1) S.I. Ved Parkash,
       PP, Sector 22, Chandigarh.
    2) A.S.I. Azad Singh,
       pp Sector 22, Chandigarh.

Endst. No. 16435-HIII (1)-98/   Dated:

A copy is forwarded for information and necessary action to the Inspector General of Police, U.T. Chandigarh.

Joint Secretary Home
for Home Secretary,
Chandigarh Administration

---

* Evidential document of the Home Secretary's suspension orders.

No. 4970-HIII (1)-99/8676
CHANDIGARH ADMINISTRATION
HOME DEPARTMENT
ORDER

1. Whereas disciplinary procedings against Sub Inspector, P.K. Dhawan, Sub Inspector Baihar Singh and MMHC Yash Pal, U.T. Chandigarh Police, are contemplated.

2. Now, therefore, in exercise of the powers conferred by Rule 16.18 of the Punjab Police Rules, 1934 as made applicable to the Union Territory, Chandigarh, the said Inspector P.K. Dhawan, Sub Inspector Balhar Singh and MMHC Yash Pal, U.T. Chandigarh Police, are hereby placed under suspension with immediate effect.

3. It is further ordered that during the period that this order shall remain in force, the Headquarter of the said Inspector P.K. Dhawan, Sub Inspector Balhar Singh and MMHC Yash Pal, U.T. Chandigarh Police shall be at Chandigarh and they shall not leave the Headquarter without obtaining prior permission of the Competent Authority. The said Inspector P.K. Dhawan, Sub Inspector Balhar Singh and MMHC Yash Pal, U.T. Chandigarh Police, shall be entitled to subsistence allowance as per rules.

(ANURADHUA GUPTA)
HOME SECRETARY.
CHANDIGARH ADMINISTRATION.

Chandigarh, dated,
the 6th May, 1999

To

1) Inspector P.K. Dhawan,
   U.T. Chandigarh Police

2) Sub Inspector Balhar Singh,
   U.T. Chandigarh Police

3) MMHC Yash Pal, 699/C.P.
   U.T. Chandigarh Police,

Endst. No. 4970-HIII (1)-99/   Dated:

A copy is forwarded for information and necessary action
to the Inspector General of Police, U.T. Chandigarh.

Joint Secretary Home,
for Home Secretary,
Chandigarh Administration.

---

* Evidential document of the Home Secretary's suspension orders.

And yet another was the transfer of ranks which
function, by the declared and written policy guidelines of
the Home Secretary herself, was to be exercised by the IG
Police.

CHANDIGARH ADMINISTRATION
HOME DEPARTMENT
ORDER

Inspector Jaswant Singh, S.H.O. North in hereby transferred and
sent to the Police Lines forthwith.

ANURADHA GUPTA,
HOME SECRETARY,
CHANDIGARH ADMINISTRATION

Endnt. No. 16440-HIII (1)-98/25584   Dated: 17-12-98

A copy in forwarded for information and necessary action to the:

1) Inspector General of Police, U.T. Chandigarh.
2) Senior Superiendent of Police, U.T. Chandigarh.

3) Shri Jaswant Singh, Inspector presently posted as S.H.O. North, U.T. Chandigarh.

> Joint Secretary Home
> for Home Secretary,
> Chanidgarh Administration

* Evidential document of the Home Secretary's transfer orders.

The Home Secretary issued the orders and, on second thought, she cancelled them at her whim, informing the IG Police when the whole process was over. The following document would testify that.

From   The Home Secretary,
                    Chandigarh Administration

To   The Inspector General of Police,
                    Union Territory, Chandigarh,

                    Memo. No. 74-HIII(1)-99/1004
                    Dated, Chandigarh the 18/1/97

Subject   Inquiry into the case of beating up of
                    S.H.O., P.S. North.

After considering the matter it has been decided to revert back Sh. Jaswant Singh as S.H.O. (North) from Police Line, who was transferred to the Police Lines by this Administration order issued by Endst. No. 16400-HIII(1)-98/25584 dated 17.12.1998.

You are, therefore, requested to inform the S.S.P. concern to take furhter action in the matter accordingly.

> *Carmel Surjit*
> Joint Secretary Home,
> for Home Secretary,
> Chandigarh Administration

* Evidential document of the cancellation of her order by the Home

As the order establishes, the worst was that all these orders and many others of these kind stood implemented. This was the state of affairs prior to Kiran's joining as the Inspector General of Chandigarh Police. The former IGP Ram Pal Singh had given up after his protests made no difference! He said that "no one listened to me, hence I had no choice but to let her do what she wanted." The Home Secretary tried to do the same with Kiran. She ordered the suspension of gazetted and non-gazetted police officers, and leaked the information to the press even before Kiran was informed. The Home Secretary was on an extended tenure, giving the impression that she was indispensable, particularly in view of the impending elections already announced as she was also the Chief Electoral Officer. Various police officers and others complained that she was despotic in her behaviour and brooked no questioning. She obviously had the establishment on her side, while Kiran was new in her job and was still to build bridges and yet to know the officials and her senior colleagues outside her department. In the first few weeks, her priority, unlike that of many others was, putting her house in order before she got on the social circuit.

But insecurity and vested interests struck fatally. The Home Secretary attacked Kiran where it hurt most. She ordered the suspension of two Deputy Superintendents of Police and one Inspector besides some other staff. Orders went to them directly yet again with the media being informed. As IG of the Chandigarh Police Force, Kiran learnt of the suspension through the sobbing officers and the newspapers.. The basis of the suspension was an enquiry instituted by the Home Secretary on 16 February 1999 during the tenure of Kiran's predecessor. (It may be recalled that Kiran had joined Chandigarh Police on 5 April 1999).

The genesis of the enquiry was a newspaper report of missing files of two terrorist acts which happened in 1983 and 1984. It may be recalled that by this time terrorism was at its peak in Punjab, including Chandigarh. On the basis of news reports, the District Senior Suprintendent of Police CSR Reddy had already ordered an enquiry and asked the City Superitendent of Police Baldev Singh to conduct the enquiry and submit his report. He went ahead and recovered the files. But, without waiting for the enquiry to be completed and without consulting the IGP, the Home Secretary ordered an enquiry of her own. This enquiry was completed without the following inputs:

(a) The statement of the then SSP CSR Reddy who was at the the helm of affairs and was in the know of the matter. He had been there for a number of years and had had various opportunities to conduct police inspections.

(b) The statement and conclusion drawn by the SP who had conducted the enquiry, nearly completed it and even recovered the files from the same police station.

(c) The statements of various other important functionaries, including the IGP, who were in a position to know what could have happened.

Kiran was not informed of any such pending enquiry at the time of her taking charge of the city police. But once she was informed of the *fait accompli,* she set about and analysed all this herself. She pleaded. When that did not help, she sought an appointment to meet the Administrator, Chandigarh, to plead further. She gave him a written note enlisting the verfied reasons why she thought the suspension of officers was inappropriate. This is what she is known to have presented before the final judge.

- *That material witnesses, including the SP/City who had conducted the enquiry and other officers related with it and in the know of vital facts, were not examined in the enquiry.*
- *That no inspection of the police station after 1985 recorded the files to be missing and that the officers under enquiry who were proposed to be suspended had no malafide intentions to tamper with or destroy the records since they were in charge of the same areas in subsequent years.*
- *That the report of the expert was not from a government source — it was from a private expert who had (to the best of her knowledge) been compulsarily 'retired' from his service.*
- *That the special report was a contemporaneous record and was not commented upon by the enquiry report when seen by the EO.*
- *That the cases being untraced, the case files were expected to be destroyed after five years. These ought to have been considered destroyed in 1995.*
- *That there appeared to be no malafide intention as both files under enquiry were untraced, and missing or tampering of the files benefited or harmed nobody.*
- *That the enquiry report was incomplete and any conclusion drawn from there would lead to a miscarriage of justice.*

Kiran pleaded that the record of the officers under suspension had been examined. They were highly decorated and having decades of distinguished service on their record. The officers were worthy to professionally hold sensistive charges for a long period of time.

But all this was of no avail.

Her predecessor was not wrong. He had also made protests and no one was listening. Kiran did the same...and this time people listened. The media was full of versions, both Kiran's and the Home Secretary's. The indispensability syndrome of the Home Secretary was exposed. People for the first time started to offer evidence of the Home Secretary malfunctioning as the *de facto* IG of Chandigarh, and her interference in the Chandigarh Police affairs even in small matters. She had earlier denied any interference! She did not have any defence for this, except to make counter allegations against Kiran.

Kiran defended her police force and men, and resisted their suspension. She clearly said: "I was an IG of the City Police to lead my force, to deliver quality service to the people, not to preside over their exploitation. I was not to be an onlooker but a change agent for the betterment of the police service." But it appeared there were entrenched interests in the system which did not want this to happen. They wanted the police to remain subservient and unprofessional to carry on their diktats and be available to be lashed at when it suited them. According to Kiran, she "was not there to be a witness. I was now duty-bound to check the decline in the morale of the police force otherwise how do I expect them to work and take initiatives which the city expected of them."

But very few knew that while Kiran was striving to set right the policing system, she was all along a wounded soldier. Kiran was fighting a losing battle for the life of her mother. After a cerebral stroke, her mother was lying in coma at the Post Graduate Institute (a prime medical institute with a hospital in Chandigarh). Kiran's mother had travelled with Kiran to be with her in her new posting. She

was very fond of Kiran; both shared an intensely loving
mother-daughter relationship — almost an ideal one. Kiran
had never seen her mother sick, and here she was in deep
coma. Kiran, her sisters and her father thought it might be
worth trying to bring her back home to Delhi. Maybe, it
would work, for she will be home again. Such a miracle had
happened for Kiran in the case of her father when he was
posted in Aizwal (Mizoram) and a near-fatal surgery had
forced the airlifting of Kiran's father to Delhi. Kiran sent a
written request to the Government of India seeking a shift
out of Chandigarh on the ground of her mother's
condition. To take on the system in Chandigarh head-on
and see it through required undivided attention which,
under the prevailing circumstances, Kiran was in no position
to give.

Kiran's request was granted by the Union Ministry of
Home Affairs, and she handed over the charge. The first
order her successor passed was to suspend the officers
whom Kiran had declined to suspend.

Kiran meanwhile had come to Delhi to arrange a mobile
intensive-care unit fitted in an ambulance which could
bring her mother home. The Escorts Heart Institute had
arranged for it, and the family, with the unconscious
mother, sped back with the siren clearing the way to Delhi,
straight to the hospital praying for the miracle to happen
again. But Kiran's mother never regained consciousness and
gave in three days later. She had remained in coma for 41
days.

Kiran went back to Chandigarh to say the closing prayers
in the *mandir* and the *gurudwara* where non-stop prayers
and reading of the holy books for the recovery of her
mother had been started by hundreds of policemen and

their families from the day of her mother's hospitalisation. Kiran's mother was hospitalised for 41 days. The prayers had been recited 41 times. Kiran had been with Chandigarh Police for 41 days and she was posted back to training after these 41 days.

30

Humane Policing

After doing her graduation and waiting for admission in the university for post-graduation there was a three-month waiting period. Kiran, instead of resting it out, cycled down to a good school and offered to teach nursery rhymes to the tiny tots in nursery class. She played and sang the rhymes with them. Even before the announcement of the result of her Masters degree, Kiran was offered a lecturer's job in a women's college by virtue of her being a topper in Punjab University. She taught Political Science to graduate classes became a student after the classes.

Kiran was young and short haired — rather unusual in the city then. Twenty-eight years later, she became a trainer, for men and women in the Delhi Police force. She not only planned and supervised their training, but most of all this time meditated with them, adding a new dimension to police training. Kiran had come a long long way, nearing 30 years into the service.

Kiran conducts her training assignment in the Police Training College for Delhi Police. It is the first time when a senior police officer of the rank of Joint Commissioner (equivalent to Inspector-General) started to directly supervise training. The Police Training College is over 45 km. drive from her house. She commutes daily, using the commuting time to read and clear office work. Monitoring the quality of training, taking feedback from the students and coordinating with the staff are her priorities after reaching the college.

But soon after she took charge of training, it took her no time to call on the Police Commissioner V.N. Singh and the Union Home Minister L.K. Advani to apprise them of the serious inadequacies in the training of the force. One of the glaring ones was absence of computers and other basics needed for a modern training institution. Yet students were being trained in computers through drawings on the blackboards and even being declared passed. A small store of outdated books was what constituted the library. There was a serious shortage of law teachers due to which one class of over 250 students was being taken by a law instructor with the help of a microphone and a loudspeaker. The response of the Home Minister was spontaneous. He said, "Bring me proposals and tell me what is required." Kiran came back excited. She informed the Police Commissioner. She and her team of officers got down to work out their proposals.

A few days later she took along single-page proposals for a computer laboratory, firing and driving simulators and a multi-media, audio-visual distance learning equipment. The Home Minister took these notes and gave appropriate instructions. The results were instant. In the revised estimates for the Home Ministry, Delhi Police got additional funds to meet these costs. Kiran, present in the meeting, requested for the assistance of the Home Ministry to procure the equipment. They willingly offered to do so. This was a breakthrough for this removed all the obstacles in their procurement. Committed officials from the Police Training College teamed up with officials of the Home Ministry and achieved the unachievable in a record time. Within the same budget period, all the equipment was procured and made operational. The multi-media equipment comprising cameras, projectors, visualisers, screens and speakers, made possible simultaneous interactive learning, even through a single teacher, in 16 classrooms at the same time.

Kiran modernised the training college and made it possible to provide state-of-the-art professional skills to the police personnel. Also to be provided was what she did not tell the Home Minister and the Police Commissioner, but something which could be done by local initiatives but had been unattended, such as trainees' welfare, a canteen, a well-stocked grocery store, a bank, a milk booth with other health foods available, adequate regular water supply, proper bus transport system for the faculty and a provision for making telephone calls.

On the quality of training, a lot of learning of police practical work was prioritized with the focus on hands-on training and putting theory into practice. Additionally courses were provided on gender sensitisation, white-collar crimes, cyber crimes, giving evidence in courts, adventures in attitudes and various other topics of relevance.

The staff at the training college was not necessarily a motivated one, as most of them were of the view that a training posting implied being put aside! They had to be drawn in so that they could teach and motivate at the same time.

How could this be done, when most of them had grievances against the personnel policies of the Delhi Police. Kiran was back to her Tihar dilemma, where she had to make the inmates realise that each one of them was responsible for his/her own perceptions. If, by their own thinking, they thought training was a punishment then they were punishing themselves as well as their performance. It's always one's own decision how one treats oneself. The influence of the peer group was very high on these police officers. Each of them was highly dependent on social acceptance.

Kiran introduced the Vipassana meditation programme as an exercise in learning to police themselves and teach themselves before they police and teach others. But they were a harder lot. In this case, Kiran decided to volunteer to sit on the ten-day Vipassana meditation course herself which motivated the training faculty to do the course with her. A major breakthrough was achieved. Some colleagues heavily addicted to certain habits, including alcohol, declared publicly to give up these habits — which was a major confession for a senior to say in the presence of colleagues, juniors and trainees.

When the leaders lead, followers do not follow, they join in. Trainees wanted to learn what their teachers had experienced. History of sorts was created in the annals of policing when over 1100 police officers and trainees sat through the course. They were led by none other than the Principal of the Police Training College himself, Sunil Garg, a few faculty members, sub-inspector trainees and constable recruits who also were under training. The Police Training College was converted into a 'gurukul', a centre of learning and spiritual upliftment. A rare kind for a police force anywhere!

A survey conducted on the immediate results, achieved are very interesting. A question posed therein was: How many marks do you give yourself out of ten, before you did the course and after? Here are some of the replies: 3 out of 10 before, 7 out of 10 after, 2 out of 10 before, 8 out of 10 after, 5 out of 10 before, 9 out of 10 after, 0 out of 10 before, 7 out of 10 after. These were all anonymous replies. In fact, there wasn't a single trainee who had not reported self- improvement in his self-assessment on the difference the course had made to him.

But another, and most important, daily management practice which was put in place at the Police Training College was the feedback system. This meant something like the mobile petition box in Tihar. Here it was called the feedback box, placed in all the classes for students to interact and give a feedback on the quality of training. These were locked boxes with the key with Kiran, and opened daily for mail straight to her. She would read them and place them before the daily staff lunch meeting to correct matters. In the year 1999, she received feedback letters on many important issues, and all of them were attended and responded to the same day with the decision announced in the evening roll-call by the day officer who was incharge of the day's roll-call.

The practice of daily coordination meeting over lunch was a facilitator as well as a threat. Students loved it, but individuals in the staff felt threatened, and some who belonged to the hierarchical mindsets felt it to be a breach of rank structure. Rank structure mostly suffocates communication, unless efforts are made to facilitate it, and this was one of the many efforts so made.

On balance it was this feedback system which kept the students stress-free as they knew they could communicate and convey to the seniormost of their needs. Police training became interactive amongst trainees and trainers. There were free discusssions and also free flow of ideas, problems and challenges. There were open discussions on the visible clash of law as it is written and the dichotomy in its application.

Issues were resolved on legal and moral grounds and the answers became evident. But it was agonising at times to see the kind of insecurities the trainees suffered from their seniors, influential and organised groups and individuals, the politicians, the courts, etc. once they were posted in the field. Similarly, the fear of being punished even for bona fide errors was seen to be gnawing them for which Kiran and her PTC team really had no answers as these depended upon management styles of individuals in the field, which was beyond the control of the training institute. Another matter which seemed to be unanswered were the personnel policies. There was one consistent reply to all these and that was "you do your best wherever you are; remember you do not have control over others; you are to do what is right, wherever you are; you ought to neither ask for postings nor seek them; you will just get them, be trained to move on; for standing for truth, there will be a price, just as for telling lies, there will be penalties; hence choose which one you want to pay." Kiran would advise them by saying, "get detached from the insecurities and rewards of postings and work with courage of conviction, and concentrate on doing your best in whichever post you are. After all you will still be in the city of Delhi."

But interestingly the revelations of these officers after having been posted in the police stations are already revealing. One woman officer said, "I was posted in the police station as a duty officer. A complainant reported that he had been robbed at knife point by a group of pickpockets while on a bus." She said she went up to her station house officer and said: "Sir, a case of robbery is made out and I would need to register a case of robbery." The SHO said nothing doing, and advised her to treat it as a scuffle in a bus which led to a loss of a few hundred rupees and some scratches on his body. The case was minimised and the criminals got away. When this officer declined to oblige, she was shifted to patrolling and picket duties. Now for many months she has not been put on duty as a duty officer. She says she doesn't mind but this is what is happening.

Another instance quoted by another officer was that he was being compelled to make out a case against a builder so that the local police station might extract something out of him. When this young officer (till recently a trainee) refused to oblige he was threatened with punishment. (Fortunately this has remained a threat only so far). Yet another instance was when a parent came to report that his 13-year old daughter had been taken away by a neighbour's son. Instead of registering a case of kidnapping, a missing report was lodged. There were many more instances to reveal that the freshly trained officers were still resisting to be a part of the system. Moral training had put many of them at the crossroads. But for how long?

Time alone will tell this, but one area where impatience was brewing were the training centres of Delhi Police which were not under Kiran's supervision. Training in Delhi Police had so far been disjointed. There were reports that the trainees in these centres had started to petition that they should get the state-of-the-art and interactive training like it was being given in the Police Training College. Why must they be left out. Police Commissioner Ajai Raj Sharma sought the assessment of his college R.K. Sharma and directed him to visit these centres. The reports confirmed the grievances of the trainees. An order integrating the training centres followed. Kiran now supervises two other centres of training in Delhi Police which brings all induction and promotional courses under her supervision as Joint Commissioner of Police (Training). This decision was long overdue but was perhaps not taken earlier because there was no compelling reason, no grievance and no comparison.

Within hours of assuming the additional responsibility, Kiran took some major steps. She pulled out 51 recruit trainees from a training centre which had sub-human living conditions and lodged them at the Police Training College for further training, making available all the resources. With 151 women constables on promotional course to become head constables, she took the decision to shift the focus from theory to practical training when most of them complained they had no knowledge of actual police working despite the three months of training that they had already undergone. In small batches, all of them got attached to police stations to observe and study the practical side of policing under a guide deputed for them. The practical training included computer training in the nearest computer training centre.

But the most important step Kiran took, which perhaps was all she could do, was to free them from their 'imprisonment.' Women constables were staying at the centre and were permitted to go home only on week ends — that too as a special favour. Kiran told them to go back to their children after police station training. These women constables had left behind their children without reliable care, and were a distressed lot. Without their asking, Kiran gave them what they needed most to ensure that they put in their best to learn. For Kiran, each one of them is an investment for the future, near and far.

Delhi Police today is on a new road — not a bylane but a highway — and the credit goes to the present Delhi Police Commissioner Ajai Raj Sharma who dared to make training a priority. For the first time training stands unified by the following order:

ORDER

The modern day policing demands high professional skills and proper training plays a very vital role in preparing the police forces to meet the present and the future challenges. It has been observed that there is no uniformity in training of Constable Recruits which was being partly done by P.T.C., and partly by DAP IV Bn., and at R.T.C. Wazirabad without adequate facilities and supervision. This anomaly needs to be removed forthwith.

Henceforth, all training being conducted at DAP IV Bn. at Wazirabad (RTC) and at DAP VI Bn. is brought under the supervision and control of the Principal/ P.T.C., Jharoda Kalan under the overall supervision of Joint C.P. (Training). An Addl. DCP level officer will be posted under them as Vice-Principal/R.T.C. who will directly supervise the training in R.T.C. Wazirabad and the training of Women Constables presently in DAP VI Bn. Campus under the overall supervision. He will supervise at both the places i.e., Wazirabad and 6th Bn. DAP but sit in Wazirabad, while the Adjutant will sit at the 6th Bn. Training site. The Police Training College will now be expected to integrate training quality in content, delivery and supervision in its three institutions i.e. Jharoda Kalan, Wazirabad and the Women Recruits Barracks is DAP VI Bn. campus.

(AJAI RAJ SHARMA)
COMMISSIONER OF POLICE:
DELHI

No. 19211-95/Admn. (II)/PHQ, dated New Delhi, the 17.7/2000

Copy for information to:

(i) Secy. to the Lt. Governor for information of L.G., Delhi.
(ii) Pr. Secy. (Home), GNCT of Delhi.
(iii) Jt. Secy/U.T., Min. of Home Affairs, New Delhi.

Copy for information and necessary action to:

(i) All Spl. CsP, Delhi.
(ii) All Joint CsP, Delhi.
(iii) All Addl. CsP, Delhi.
(iv) All District & Unit DCsP, Delhi/New Delhi.
(v) S.O. to C.P., Delhi.
(vi) All ACsP. Insprs. (PHQ).
(vii) Inspr./Estt./PHQ for gazette notification.

This places a huge responsibility on Kiran and her team, and yet another challenge.

For her, training stands for addressing the body, mind and spirit of policing. It is not a mere vocation but an invocation to be fulfilled by humane spirit!

It now depends who takes over from Kiran, and when.

31

Beyond Herself

Crime prevention was always the priority for Kiran wherever she was posted. Her entire track record is replete with preventive measures taken to save situations from happening. Her approach has all along been to anticipate, prevent, understand, treat and cure. Her energies have been channelised towards proactive prevention rather than reactions. Her first community project in crime prevention began in her early days of district policing where she used her police powers in a benign way to get an erstwhile criminal tribe of bootleggers to abandon their ways of earning a livelihood by brewing illicit liquor and take up acceptable and non-criminal ways of living. She succeeded (for details see Chapter 8 Novel Methods, Novel Results). Six years later, in her next district police charge when she saw a strong nexus between drug abuse and crime, she went about setting up six drug abuse treatment centres in six police station premises, which was something absolutely unheard of. In a situation where a police officer does not want to handle even a drug addict lest something may happen to him, Kiran went about housing over a hundred addicts for treatment in her police stations. There are no words to admire the courage and conviction behind this endeavour.

Her work became a pioneering movement forcing the community and the government to sit up and respond. She travelled around the country giving slide presentations, explaining the consequences of drug addiction and the preventive lessons to be drawn for schools, universities, parents, police and the community at large. As she was about to be transferred, people of her district insisted that she incorporate the good work. She then instituted a foundation called 'Navjyoti' meaning 'new light'. The then Police Commissioner, Ved Marwah, also Kiran's favourite senior, blessed the organisation. Since then the foundation has treated over 12,000 addicts and reached out to many more thousands through its community programmes in Delhi, around it and far away. The centre has grown into a training-cum-treatment centre. It provides holistic treatment based on alternative medicines such as homeopathy, yoga, meditation, therapeutic community, counselling, etc. It now has a family support group called *the capable group* comprising the families of recovering addicts. Wives, mothers, fathers, husbands and adolescent children are organised for self-help. This is perhaps the first such group of its kind.

Navjyoti today is also the most recognised treatment centre in India that has been awarded national and international awards.

Kiran's Navjyoti went on expanding its community service. It entered in an extensive way in education of the street/slum children by establishing schools, vocational training for women inmates, slum women, rural poor, adolescents, disabled, health-care and counselling centres. The organisation with a professional staff of over 350 reaches out to at least 10,000 under-privileged men, women and children each day through its 50 projects, some funded and some through raised resources on daily basis. Kiran supervises the work of the foundation as its General Secretary.

The Ramon Magsaysay Award in 1994 gave birth to another organisation called the India Vision Foundation. This foundation's primary focus is the education of prisoners' children and prison reforms. Today, the organisation provides education with residential schooling and home visits to over 150 children of prisoners. It also supports and collaborates with Navjyoti in running slum schools, also called *gali schools,* vocational training in prisons and organising disability camps in rural areas. The Tihar prison got its bread unit and a poly green house through a corpus fund support from India Vision Foundation.

Kiran's voluntary work awaits her. She attends to this work in the time that is left to her from her official work. Basically, it's always going beyond herself. Yesterday, today and tomorrow, and certainly after she has had enough of her own profession. This work is waiting for her to go national and then international. Perhaps to live beyond and after her. Kiran's daughter Saina, a student of Psychology and an emerging entrepreneur is preparing to take over where her mother will leave. She is known to be even more strong-willed and determined. Like mother, like daughter — the sky shall be the limit.

APPENDIX 1

The Ramon Magsaysay Award

THE CITATION

No social relationship in Asia is more fraught with ambiguity than that between the police and the people. Called upon to maintain order and public safety, and to manage the region's paralyzing traffic, the police provides essential civilizing services. Yet, nearly everywhere its reputation is tarnished by incompetence and abuses, large and small. For too many people, the police is not a positive good, only a necessary evil. Kiran Bedi, India's highest ranking female police officer and currently Delhi's inspector general of prisons, believes the police can do bitter.

Taught by her unconventional parents to compete and "to think equally," Bedi excelled both at school and at tennis, the family passion. She sailed through college and a masters degrees and, in 1972, at the age twenty-two, won the women's lawn tennis championship of Asia. That same year she entered the police academy and, in 1974, became the first woman to enter the elite Indian Police Service. Assigned to the capital city, Bedi rose rapidly in the ranks, winning national accalim — and a presidential award — in 1978 by single-handedly driving off a band of club- and sword-wielding demonstrators with her police baton.

As deputy commissioner of police in Delhi's West and North Districts, Bedi posted constables in blue-and-white "beat boxes" where citizens could consult them daily. She redirected former bootleggers to honest livelihooods by arranging friendly loans and assistance. Women's peace committees, set up at her initiative, promoted neighbourhood harmony. As community participation rose, crimes fell. Observing the link between drug addiction and chornic criminality, Bedi set up community-supported detoxification clinics, a model she later developed for wider application as Deputy Director of the Narcotics Control Bureau.

As New Delhi's traffic chief, her meticulous planning and ruthlessly impartial enforcement of the rules kept the capital's motley caravanserai of vehicles moving at the 1982 Asian Games — although she admits she made some enemies in the process.

In 1993 Bedi became Inspector General of prisons (Delhi) and took charge of Tihar, India's largest prison complex. In this brutally overcrowded purgatory dwelled more than 8000 prisoners, 90 per cent of whom were unconvicted and merely awaiting trial. Bedi rapidly transformed Tihar. Today its inmates follow a positive regimen of work, study and play. Illiterate prisoners learn to read and write. Others earn higher degrees from cooperating colleges. In prison workshops, prisoners keep their skills tuned and earn wages to save in Tihar's new bank. Through their *panchayats* (elected councils) inmates share responsibility for community discipline and for organizing games and entertainment. In yoga classes they learn meditation techniques to still anger and improve concentration. Complaints placed in the mobile petition box go directly to the top and are taken seriously. Tihar is a different world today. In it Bedi's charges are being imbued with positive attitudes and practical skills for life beyond the walls.

In all of Bedi's innovations there is a pattern: each one seeks to break down adversarial relations between the police and the community, and each one seeks to replace the hard hand of punishment with the healing hand of rehabilitation.

The discipline, confidence, and competitive spirit of Bedi's youth remain with her at age forty-five. She is impatient and inclined to buck the system. "It is tough to go against the wave," she says, "but at least you reach where nobody else can."

In electing Kiran Bedi to receive the 1994 Ramon Magsaysay Award for Government Service, the Board of Trustees recognizes her building confidence in India's police through dynamic leadership and effective innovations in crime control, drug rehabilitation, and humane prison reform.

THE ACCEPTANCE SPEECH

Mr. President, Mrs. Magsaysay, trustees, ladies and gentlemen:

Twenty-two years ago when I decided to join the elite Indian Police Service, I saw in it great potential for the "Power to Do", the "Power to Get Things Done", and the "Power to Correct." I do firmly believe that police in any country can be the geatest protector of human rights and the rule of law — as it could as well be the greatest violator of both.

The Ramon Magsaysay Award has done a couple of magical things in my case, as it does in others:

(i) *It has recognized the "Power to Prevent".*
Crime prevention is usually given a lower priority and underestimated as an area of policing. What gets priority and headlines is detections and seizures, and not prevention of delinquency and breach of peace, which had all the potential of violent crime.

(ii) *The Power of Policing with People:*
"Policing is for People", therefore, people must be made partners in policing. Once that is done in a variety of ways, it provides transparency and accountability to the whole system. Resources which cannot alone come from police could come from participative policing.

(iii) *The Power of the Team:*
Leaders in police or government, if they want results, need to form teams, and allow them initiatives,

delegation, support, non-interference and training with total emphasis on professional integrity. While personal example is crucial, sharing of achievements will lead to more results. This will lead to not only " Keeping Security" but "Creating Security".

The Award has propelled me to consolidate and expand my work. For this I have registered a Trust, called India Vision, that I am breathing life into at this moment. I will carry forward projects in the fields of Prison Reform, Drug Abuse Prevention, Empowerment of Women, Mental Disability and Sports Promotion. I seek your greater support in these projects.

I accept the Ramon Magsaysay Award with total gratitude to the Foundation and the Philippines, on behalf of my team comprising Police-Prison-People and my family from India.

Just before leaving for ceremony, I received a call from my Prison Headquarters (from my DIG, Mr. Sarangi) that at this very time all my 9100 prisoners are having special celebrations within the prison premises.

Thank you,

31 August 1994   **Kiran Bedi**
Manila

APPENDIX 2

Kiran's Biodata

Ms. KIRAN BEDI nee PESHAWARIA
A PROFILE
(Website : www.kiranbedi.com)

Born   :   Amritsar - 1949

PERSONAL INFORMATION

Parents :   Prakash and Prem Peshawaria
Sisters   :   In all four

1. Shashi (settled in Canada)
2. Kiran
3. Reeta a Tennis champion and a well known author of books on Behavioural Therapy.
4. Anu (a Lawn & National Tennis champion three times and Wimbeldon player)
   Married - One Daughter, Saina Bedi
   Husband - Shri Brij Bedi, a Textile Engineer in Amritsar.

Academic	School - Sacred Heart School , Amritsar
	Graduation English (Hons.) Government College for Women, Amritsar
	Masters in Political Science from Punjab University, Chandigarh (Topped the University)
	Law Degree - Delhi University, New Delhi
	Ph.D - I.I.T., Delhi (Department of Social Sciences)
	on 'Drug Abuse and Domestic Violence'
	Awarded Jawaharlal Nehru Fellowship to write about the work done at Tihar Jail during her tenure as IG (Prisons)
Sports	Has been a National Junior Tennis Champion
	Has been a National Senior Tennis Champion
	Has been an Asian Tennis Champion. and represented India abroad.
Decoration	

- Received Police Medal for Gallantry by the President of India.
- Received Asia - Region Award for work done in the field of Drug Abuse Prevention by International Organization of Good Templars (IOGT), a Norway based organisation.
- Awarded the Ramon Magsaysay Award for Government Service, 1994, by the Ramon Magsaysay Foundation, Philippines. (This is first such award to a Police Officer in Asia. It is perhaps the first time a Police Officer in the world is awarded with a 'PEACE' Award).
- Received Joseph Beuys Foundation Award (Swiss Award) for Holistic and Innovative Management.
- Received International Award from Association of Christian Colleges and Universities: International Ecumenical Forum (ACCU-IEF) for promotion of quality of life through the

campaign against alcohol, drugs, AIDS and tobacco in September 1998.

- Conferred the Pride of India Award 1999 by American Federation of Muslims from India (AFMI) of the US and Canada for commitment towards human welfare, women's rights, outstanding services and for upholding secular values in October 1999.
- Awarded the first ever IIT - Delhi Alumni Association 1999 - 2000 Award for outstanding contribution to national development.

Important Invitations:

- To represent India in American, European and Asian International Forums on the subject of Drug Abuse, Drug Trafficking Prevention and Prison Reforms.
- To address International Police Chiefs Conference (1992), USA.
- To attend National Prayer Breakfast with the President of USA in 1995.
- To visit British Prisons on the invitation of British Foreign Office (1995).
- To attend United Nations World Social Summit in Denmark (1995).
- To attend United Nations Women Conference at BEIJING (1995).
- To attend United Nations Conference on Drug Abuse at New York (1998).
- Invited by the Mauritius Government to train Law Enforcement Agencies on Prevention of Domestic Violence (1998).
- Attended SAARC Workshop on Anti Narcotics, Planning & Development at Islamabad, Pakistan (1998).
- Invited to address Prison Governors Association, Annual Conference at Buxton, U.K. March 2000.

- Authored a book called 'It's Always Possible' on the transformation of one of the largest prisons in the world. It is accompanied by with a CD ROM with the same title produced by India Vision Foundation.
- Another biography entitled "The Kindly Baton" authored by a psychologist and a research scholar, Mrs. Meenakshi Saxena, has been published by Books India International.
- Placed in the 5th position amongst "Ten Most Admired Indians" as per an exclusive opinion poll amongst a list of 100 eminent Indians conducted jointly by *The Week* and marketing research and opinion polling agency TNS Mode and published in *The Week* in its issue dated 10 September 2000.

Career   Joined Indian Police Service in 1972 (the first woman in India to do so). Held various assignments, notable amongst them being with the District Police, Delhi Traffic Police during the Ninth Asian Games in Delhi and Special Traffic in Goa during Commonwealth Heads of Governments meet, Narcotics Control Bureau and as Deputy Inspector General (Range) Mizoram. Inspector General of Prisons, of Tihar Jails, Delhi. Special Secretary to the Lt. Governor of Delhi and as Joint Commissioner with Delhi Police. Also as Inspector General of Police, Chandigarh. Presently posted as Joint Commissioner of Police (Training), Delhi Police.

Special Interests

Community Work
Founded two organisations:
a) Navjyoti Regd. (1987)
b) India Vision Foundation Regd. (1994)
Navjyoti provides :
Cost-free residential therapeutic community based treatment and interventions for alcohol and drug dependents (treated by now, over 12,000 drug dependents).

- Creches, primary and *gali* schools for slum children
- Vocational and literacy centres for women and adolescents
- Creche training programmes for women in the prison

Navjyoti was awarded the UN-based Serge Sotiroff Memorial Award 1999 on International nominations for its pioneering work in the field of drug abuse prevention and treatment. This award was received on 26th June, 1999, the International Day against Drug Abuse.

Navjyoti has also received the Delhi Government sponsored State Award for its work in the field of education and rehabilitation of destitute children.

INDIA VISION FOUNDATION provides :

- Schooling for prisoners' children
- Gali schools for slum children
- Rural projects for village community
- Disability projects in backward areas.

Index